Sherman's Ghosts

Sherman's Ghosts

Soldiers, Civilians, and
the American Way of War

Matthew Carr

THE NEW PRESS

NEW YORK
LONDON

No part of this book may be reproduced, in any form,
without written permission from the publisher.

Requests for permission to reproduce selections from this book should be mailed to:
Permissions Department, The New Press, 120 Wall Street, 31st floor,
New York, NY 10005.

Published in the United States by The New Press, New York, 2015
Distributed by Perseus Distribution

ISBN 978-1-59558-955-2 (hardcover)
ISBN 978-1-62097-078-2 (e-book)
CIP data available.

The New Press publishes books that promote and enrich public discussion and
understanding of the issues vital to our democracy and to a more equitable world.
These books are made possible by the enthusiasm of our readers; the support of a
committed group of donors, large and small; the collaboration of our many partners
in the independent media and the not-for-profit sector; booksellers, who often
hand-sell New Press books; librarians; and above all by our authors.

www.thenewpress.com

Composition by Westchester Book Composition
This book was set in Adobe Caslon Pro

Printed in the United States of America

2 4 6 8 10 9 7 5 3 1

For Graham Usher, 1958–2013

To realize what war is, one must follow our tracks.

—William Tecumseh Sherman, 1864

Contents

Sherman's Ghosts

From Georgia to FM 3-24

On November 15, 1864, one of the most celebrated and controversial campaigns of the American Civil War began when sixty thousand Federal troops under the command of General William Tecumseh Sherman marched out of the burning city of Atlanta into central Georgia. Disregarding conventional military wisdom that an advancing army should not break contact with its line of communications and supply, Sherman had ordered his troops to evacuate the city they had only recently captured and sever the Western & Atlantic Railroad link that connected them to the Union's nearest supply depot at Chattanooga, Tennessee. Apart from the reduced provisions his soldiers carried with them, Sherman's army was now dependent for its survival on what they could take from the local population in the hostile Confederate heartlands of the Deep South.

Sherman's destination, though few of his soldiers realized it at the time, was the city of Savannah, three hundred miles away on the Atlantic coast, where he hoped to be resupplied by the Union Navy and then proceed northward into Virginia to assist his great friend Ulysses Grant, whose armies were locked in a brutal deadlock with Robert E. Lee's Army of Northern Virginia at the Confederate capital, Richmond. But Sherman also had very specific strategic intentions regarding Georgia itself. For more than a month, Sherman's army marched through the state known as the granary of the South, seizing or destroying vast quantities of food and provisions, demolishing and burning public and private property, and leaving a trail of devastation fifty to sixty miles wide. On December 21, Sherman's army captured Savannah in a triumphant conclusion to the "March to the Sea." In February the following year, Sherman led his army northward into South Carolina.

Here the destruction was more extensive and more explicitly punitive, as his soldiers burned and looted their way through the state that they regarded as the spiritual home of secession before moving on to North Carolina, where the march finally came to a halt in Goldsboro on March 23, 1865. On April 16, the Confederate general Joseph E. Johnston surrendered ninety thousand troops to Sherman at the Bennett Farm near the state capital, Raleigh, thus removing the last major Confederate army from the Civil War. By that time Sherman's seven-hundred-mile rampage had already begun its transformation into a military legend. In the North, it was acclaimed as a strategic masterstroke that transformed Sherman into a national hero. In the South, Sherman was vilified as a brutal military destroyer, a nineteenth-century Genghis Khan who violated the principles of "civilized warfare" and chose to make war on civilians and noncombatants.

This image of Sherman as the Great Destroyer has been handed down to posterity and reinforced in films, such as *The Birth of a Nation* and *Gone with the Wind*, as part of the "Lost Cause" mythologies of Southern victimhood, which present Sherman as the iconic symbol of Yankee barbarity. Today Sherman's army is still remembered throughout the South as the instrument of vengeful destruction described in the narrative voice-over spoken by Waylon Jennings in the Paul Kennerley song "They Laid Waste to Our Land": "With hate in their hearts, they moved in a line, cutting a scar through God's blessed country fifty miles wide / Burning, looting and gutting our land like vultures."

Sherman's sinister reputation is not confined to the Civil War. More than any military campaign in history, Sherman's March has become a byword for wartime devastation and cruelty. "In the twentieth century the name of Sherman has taken on an incantatory quality; speak it, and all the demons of destruction appear," writes the cultural historian Charles Royster.[1] Other historians have depicted Sherman as the spiritual father of total war, the general whose campaigns broke with the polite conventions of nineteenth-century warfare and paved the way for the new forms of military barbarism that followed. In his history of the conduct of war, the former British general and military historian J.F.C. Fuller singled out Sherman as the architect of the "moral retrogression" in warfare that he regarded as a particularly malign consequence of the American Civil War, the "leading exponent of this return to barbarism," who "broke away from the conventions of nineteenth century warfare, and waged war as ruthlessly as Calvin had waged it with the word."[2] In a more recent study of battlefield tactics in the Civil War, the British historian Paddy Griffith similarly condemned "Sherman's doctrine of warfare against civilians" as "one of the more vicious military theories of modern times."[3]

Sherman's many admirers have taken a more positive view of the man and his achievements. Some have pointed out the discrepancy between his frequently extreme and intemperate pronouncements and his more restrained actions. Few generals are more quotable, and few of Sherman's many aphorisms are more widely quoted than his famous extemporaneous insistence that "war is all hell," more often rendered as "war is hell"—an observation that has been endlessly repeated by politicians and soldiers as a justification for intensifying war's hellishness. Yet Sherman's defenders have argued that Sherman's campaigns of devastation were not "total" but a proportionate and relatively unbloody use of military force that was justified on military grounds. In a hagiographic biography written in the 1920s, the British military theorist Basil Henry Liddell Hart hailed Sherman as the unacknowledged genius of the Civil War, whose campaigns anticipated the Nazi blitzkrieg tactics in World II and their subsequent adaptation by General George Patton during his 1944 campaigns in Normandy. For Liddell Hart, Sherman was the "first modern general," whose methods presented a *less* destructive alternative to the meat-grinding battles of World War I.

In his study *The American Way of War*, Russell Weigley described the Civil War as a transformative moment in U.S. military history, in which Sherman's "strategy of terror" in Georgia and the Carolinas complemented Grant's "strategy of annihilation" in Virginia.[4] Whereas Grant's bludgeoning offensives in the spring of 1864 introduced a new strategic concept in American warfare, the "annihilation of armies," Weigley argued, the "deliberate effort to undermine civilian morale through terrorization" practiced by Sherman and his fellow general Philip Sheridan had the effect of "enlarging the sphere in which American soldiers saw civilians as possible military targets."[5]

In a personal journey along the route of Sherman's marches in 1984, the Southern writer and journalist James Reston Jr. attempted to trace a line of descent between Sherman's campaigns and the Vietnam War. For Reston, Sherman was "the first general of modern human history to carry the logic of war to its ultimate extreme, the first to scorch the earth, the first consciously to demoralize the hostile civilian population in order to subdue its hostile army, the first to wreck an economy in order to starve its soldiers."[6]

Generals who terrorize civilians and seize or destroy their property are not usually lionized for such actions. Napoléon's reputation was not enhanced by the brutal counterinsurgency campaigns waged by his armies in occupied Europe. The German and Japanese generals whose armies burned and destroyed towns and villages in the Soviet Union and China during World War II are generally regarded as war criminals rather than heroes, even in their own countries. Yet Sherman has attained an illustrious place in American history *because* of his campaigns of destruction rather than in spite of them, and his words and actions have often been cited as an inspiration by his successors in the wars that followed. To the popular historian Victor Davis Hanson, "Sherman . . . invented the entire notion of American strategic doctrine, one that would appear so frequently in the century to follow: the ideal of a vast moral crusade on foreign soil to restructure a society through sheer force of arms."[7]

At first sight, the notion of a "vast moral crusade" as the essence of America's "strategic doctrine" does not correlate with "strategies of terror" directed against noncombatants, but these two notions have by no means been incompatible. From the Civil War to the "terror wars" of the new century, the U.S. military has bombed cities and residential areas, burned homes, villages, forests, and crops, poisoned wells and rice paddies, destroyed food supplies, and used physical destruction as an instrument of coercion and intimidation against civilians as well as armed combatants. Such practices are hardly uniquely American. Yet few countries have the same ability to present even the most destructive wars as benign and even altruistic endeavors fought on behalf of universal values and principles. As the 2010 *National Security Strategy of the United States* puts it, America has "spilled American blood in foreign lands—not to build an empire, but to shape a world in which more individuals and nations could determine their own destiny, and live with the peace and dignity they deserve."[8] This image of U.S. military power is regularly disseminated on Veterans Days and at public ceremonies honoring the military, at museums, war memorials, and military cemeteries.

The elevated moral aura that so often surrounds American war making is not merely the result of propaganda or deliberate obfuscation, though it may fulfill both purposes. But physical destruction in American warfare is often seen as a necessary precursor to a more positive Americanized future—a tendency famously summed up by the response of a U.S. officer to a question about the bombardment of the village of Bén Tre during the Vietnam War: "It became necessary to destroy the village in order to save it." During the American occupation of the Philippines, U.S. soldiers were building roads, schools, and medical clinics in one part of the archipelago while simultaneously razing "insurgent" villages in another. Even as U.S. bombers were incinerating Japanese cities and killing tens of thousands of civilians during World War II, the U.S. armed forces were preparing one of the most progressive military occupations in history. More recently in Iraq, the United States launched a war that was supposedly intended to transform a dictatorship into an exemplary American-style democracy, in which the U.S. military was killing, arresting, and in some cases torturing real or imagined Iraqi insurgents by night, while teams of soldiers instructed Iraqis on local democracy and the formation of neighborhood associations during the day.

In recent years, the belief that American military power is a force for good and that what is good for America is good for everyone else has been called into question by a succession of wars that have generated a great deal of destruction without producing the positive outcomes that were predicted when they began. In two invasions and occupations, in Iraq and Afghanistan, U.S. military power has failed to achieve decisive victories against militarily weaker opponents, and these less than satisfactory results have prompted an ongoing debate within and beyond the U.S. military establishment about the way in which America fights its wars. On one hand, there are the "population-centric" counterinsurgency (COIN) doctrines propagated by General David Petraeus and the Marine Corps counterinsurgency manual FM 3-24, which challenge the military to concentrate less on the physical destruction of the enemy and more on protection of civilians, reconstruction, and "military operations other than war." Others have argued that an excessive concern with minimizing bloodshed and avoiding civilian casualties has weakened the ability of the U.S. military to carry out its core task of "killing people and breaking things" in order to achieve a decisive military victory.

These debates would not have been entirely unfamiliar in what Sherman called "the great problem of the Civil War." The ideas and practices that he developed in an attempt to solve that problem touch on many issues that have remained pertinent to American wars. The strategic use of physical destruction to change the attitudes and behavior of civilians and noncombatants, the conduct of military occupations, the blurred distinctions between combatants and noncombatants in irregular warfare, collective punishment as an instrument of counterinsurgency, postwar stabilization, the political and psychological dimensions of modern warfare—all these components of the American wars of this new century were also present in the war that Sherman once fought.

To what extent were Sherman's campaigns a "modern" form of warfare or an anachronistic regression? Whom did he attack and why? Is it true, as Russell Weigley and so many others have argued, that Sherman's strategy of terror in the South paved the way for the bombing of Dresden and Hiroshima, the free-fire zones of Vietnam, or the My Lai massacre? If so, how? What exactly did that strategy consist of and to what extent have America's subsequent wars followed the template that Sherman created? His campaigns have already generated a voluminous literature, and I do not claim to have uncovered any new historical material about them. I am not a Civil War historian, and this is not a conventional military history, partly because Sherman's campaigns were not a conventional military campaign, and also because my primary concern is not with military operations, strategies, and battles but with the broader impact of war—and American war in particular—on civilians. For many years now, I have written about the U.S. military and American wars, most often from a critical perspective.

If this book might be categorized as an antimilitarist military history, it is also to some extent a companion or counterpoint to my earlier history of terrorism, *The Infernal Machine*. The U.S. Department of Defense defines terrorism as "the calculated use of unlawful violence or threat of unlawful violence to inculcate fear; intended to coerce or to intimidate governments or societies in the pursuit of goals that are generally political, religious, or ideological." There is much of this definition that could be applied to what Sherman tried to do in Georgia and the Carolinas. This does not mean that I wish to indict Sherman as a terrorist—a futile and essentially meaningless exercise. But Sherman embodies a very specific use of military force as an instrument of coercion and intimidation that has often been replayed by the U.S. military and also by other armies. Understanding what he did and what his armies did and didn't do can therefore tell us a great deal, not only about the Civil War and American war making, but also about the evolution of modern war into attacks of unprecedented violence against civilians. I would like to hope that the following study can contribute to widening this understanding, not only by those who fight wars, but also by those who would like to stop them from being fought.

PART I

The March

1

The Iron Hand of War

When General P.G.T. Beauregard, the first commander of the newly formed Confederate Army, ordered the batteries at Charleston harbor to open fire on the U.S. Army garrison at Fort Sumter on April 12, 1861, few Americans on either side predicted the ferocity and duration of the conflict that was about to unfold. It was a moment that had often been imagined on both sides, not only because an "effusion of blood" was seen by Northerners and Southerners alike as the only means of resolving an abrasive political confrontation that had dragged on for decades, but also because many men and women on both sides had come to regard war itself as a beneficial and cathartic event. In July 1861, the *Rome* (Georgia) *Weekly Courier* hailed the "salutary influence of the war upon the popular mind in all the civil, moral, and social relations of life," and predicted that it would have an uplifting and reinvigorating impact on an egotistical and materialistic Southern society.

Similar views were expressed in the North. In a lecture to the Alumni Society at the University of Pennsylvania in November 1861, the physician and professor of medicine Alfred Stillé described the "hideous features" of war as an antidote to the "progressive decline of national virtue" and the "national degradation" of the prewar years. Sounding more like an early-twentieth-century Italian futurist than a nineteenth-century physician, Stillé hailed the societies of the past whose creative energies had been released

11

by "warlike engines," in which the "flash, and blaze, and roar, and the tears of blood they wring from human hearts, prepare a harvest of heroic deeds, of soaring thoughts, of generous and humane sentiments . . . which raise a nation higher than before in the scale of mental and moral power."[1]

Such romanticism was an indication of the prevailing concept of war in nineteenth-century America at the outbreak of the "War of the Rebellion" or the "War Between the States," as it later became known in the South. Both sides anticipated a European-style war whose outcome would be decided by set-piece battles between orderly lines of uniformed armies, with cavalry charges and stirring demonstrations of élan.

Yet there were those on both sides who imagined a different kind of war. "I only pray God may be with us to give us strength to conquer them, to exterminate them, to lay waste every Northern city, town and village, to destroy them utterly," wrote one Tennessee woman to a friend in May 1861. "All the means legitimate in civilized warfare must be freely employed," declared the *Chicago Tribune* in April that year. "If necessary to burn, kill and destroy, let there be no hesitation. Temporizing is out of place, and, in the end, more destructive of life than vigorous and decisive measures." That same month, a Boston preacher, Reverend Andrew Leete Stone, urged Union armies to "widen the streets through riotous cities" and "Raze the nests of conspirators with ax and fire. . . . Let the country burn this ulcer out."[2]

Such views did not reflect the official position of the recently inaugurated administration of Abraham Lincoln, whose election the previous year had triggered the secessionist revolt. As the war unfolded, Lincoln remained initially committed to a policy of moderation and restraint that was intended to win back the population of the South to the Union through persuasion rather than coercion. The day after the fall of Fort Sumter, the president issued a call for 75,000 volunteers to "repossess the forts, places, and property which have been seized from the Union," while simultaneously reassuring Southerners that these efforts would "avoid any devastation, any destruction of, or interference with, property, or any disturbance of peaceful citizens in any part of the country."[3]

By "property," Lincoln also meant that Southerners could keep their slaves—a concession that he was willing to make in order to woo ambivalent citizens and border states with large slave-owning populations from joining the Confederacy. By the time Sherman led his armies into Georgia three years later, Lincoln had reached very different conclusions, and American society had become familiar with a very different kind of war than the one that so many Americans had anticipated.

The Unwinnable War

The U.S. Department of Defense currently defines *strategy* as "a prudent idea or set of ideas for employing the instruments of national power in a synchronized and integrated fashion to achieve theater, national, and/or multinational objectives." At the beginning of the Civil War, the respective "national" strategic objectives of the two sides were clear enough. In order to win the war, the Confederacy had to avoid losing it and sustain itself for long enough to obtain recognition from the major European powers and force the North to accept the existence of the Confederate States of America (CSA). To restore the Union, the Federal government had to invade the South and decisively defeat its armies. On paper at least, the North had more "instruments of national power" at its disposal to achieve these objectives. With a population of 20,275,000 whites, compared with 5,500,000 in the South, the Union would never run short of soldiers, and its factories and workshops would always be able to outproduce the largely agricultural South in terms of war matériel.

The balance of forces was not as unequal as it seemed. To subdue the South, the Union was obliged to conquer a vast territory of more than 750,000 square miles that included two distinct theaters of war more than a thousand miles apart in terrain often barely accessible, poorly mapped, or not mapped at all. In addition, the fact that the South had 4 million slaves at its disposal meant that virtually the entire white male population of military age was available to fight, while public support for the war in the North was often lukewarm and inconsistent. Whereas the Union was obliged to operate across extended "exterior lines," the Confederate armies were fighting, for the most part, inside their own territory, in defense of their lands and homes.

At the beginning of the conflict, the U.S. Army consisted of just over sixteen thousand soldiers and naval personnel, in addition to volunteer state militias that could be called upon in times of national emergency, although the militias' main priorities were the defense of America's coasts and frontiers and the expansion of the Western frontier. Within a year, Lincoln's "ninety-day men" had become a combined army and naval force of seven hundred thousand, while the CSA's forces grew from a hundred thousand to just short of four hundred thousand. In total, approximately nine hundred thousand men served in the Confederate Army and nearly 2 million on the Union side in the course of the war.

American history provided no obvious strategic models for fighting a war on such a scale. Apart from the 1846–48 Mexican-American War, the army had not fought a major conflict since the War of 1812 against the British. The American officer class was steeped in European military strategies disseminated at West Point and other military academies, which emphasized the Napoleonic "decisive battle" and the principle defined by Antoine-Henri, Baron Jomini, the foremost exponent of Napoleonic military doctrine in the early nineteenth century, that "the best means of accomplishing great results was to dislodge and destroy the hostile army, since states and provinces fall of themselves when there is no organized force to protect them."[4] In the aftermath of Fort Sumter, the Union Army was commanded by General Winfield Scott, the seventy-five-year-old hero of the Mexican-American War, who proposed to defeat the South through a naval and land blockade that would "envelop" the Confederacy and cut its commercial links to the outside world.

Scott's "Anaconda plan," as the Northern press called it, was never formally adopted, though Lincoln did proclaim a blockade that became increasingly effective as the war wore on. Initially, however, the Confederacy was the more successful of the two protagonists; it was able to field a more effective and motivated army that quickly learned to equip itself by blockade running and rapid development of a homegrown armaments industry. In the summer of 1861, Lincoln's volunteer army was routed at the First Battle of Bull Run, also called the First Battle of Manassas Junction, on July 21, 1861, fueling Confederate expectations that the Union would quickly fold.

Instead, the war continued to intensify as the two armies clashed repeatedly in the bloodiest battles ever fought on American soil. On April 6–7, 1862, at Shiloh, or Pittsburg Landing, 23,746 soldiers from both sides were killed in two days. In a single twelve-hour period on September 17, 1862, some 22,000 Union and Confederate troops were cut down at the Battle of Antietam Creek—the single most catastrophic day in all of America's wars. At Gettysburg in 1863, the death toll was 43,000 over three days. Tens of thousands of soldiers died away from the battlefield, in field hospitals, army camps, and overcrowded prisoner-of-war stockades. In all, 623,026 soldiers and fighting men died, and 471,427 were wounded on both sides.

This death toll was even more shocking in that it had no obvious impact on the outcome of the war, as tactical victories failed to translate into strategic outcomes for either side. For the first

Battles without victory: Confederate dead at Antietam, Alexander
Gardner. Courtesy of the Library of Congress.

two years, the North built its strategy on the conquest of the Confederate capital, Richmond, and Union armies made various skill-
fully executed incursions into Virginia that were thwarted by
nimble Confederate generalship and the excessive caution of Federal commanding officers. Few Union generals were more inflicted with "the slows" than the gifted George B. McClellan,
who replaced Winfield Scott as commander in chief of the Union
armies in November 1861. In March 1862, the "Little Napoleon"
took charge of the Army of the Potomac during the Peninsula
Campaign. After an extraordinarily well-executed amphibious
operation, which eventually placed some 120,000 Union troops
south of the Confederate capital, McClellan was roundly defeated

in late June and early July at the Seven Days Battles, and his army was forced to withdraw. Impatient with this progress, Lincoln appointed General John Pope as commander of the Army of the Potomac, and replaced McClellan with General Henry W. "Old Brains" Halleck, the commander of the Department of the Mississippi, as overall commander in chief of the Union armies.

A dogged administrator and the army's foremost military intellectual, Halleck proved himself to be no less ponderous as a field commander than his predecessor, but he nevertheless forged a crucial relationship with Brigadier General Ulysses S. Grant, commander of the Army of the Tennessee, that was to change the strategic direction of the war. In February 1862, Grant's forces captured the key Confederate outposts of Fort Henry and Fort Donelson on the Tennessee and Cumberland Rivers, creating a springboard for further operations along the vital Mississippi waterway and into central Tennessee.

Grant's ascendancy coincided with McClellan's fall from grace. When Pope was defeated at the Second Battle of Bull Run, McClellan was reinstated to take charge of the defense of Washington. He was then sacked again in November for his failure to follow up his victory at Antietam; he was replaced as commander of the Army of the Potomac by Major General Ambrose Burnside. When Burnside launched his army into a bloody defeat at Fredericksburg, he too was replaced, by General Joseph "Fighting Joe" Hooker, who proved equally ineffectual against the armies of Lee and Thomas "Stonewall" Jackson at Chancellorsville in May 1863.

In June Lincoln appointed General George G. Meade as the Army of the Potomac's fifth commander in less than a year; Meade repulsed the Confederate Army in the great Union victory at Gettysburg the following month. That same month, Grant captured the strategic fortress-city Vicksburg, on the Mississippi River, in a dazzling campaign that electrified the Northern public and established complete Union control over the Mississippi from

Saint Louis to New Orleans. The fall of the Confederacy's "Gibraltar" confirmed Grant as Lincoln's foremost "fighting general" and shifted the focus of the war to the Western theater. In March 1864, Grant was promoted to lieutenant general and Union general in chief. By that time, the tide of war appeared to be moving irresistibly in the North's favor. The South was now cut in half; Union armies had seized key enclaves on the Atlantic coast; and Union armies were advancing ever deeper into the Mississippi Valley and Tennessee. Yet despite these reversals, the Confederacy was far from defeated, and the inability of the two sides to achieve a decisive victory on the battlefield had begun to change the strategic direction of the war.

Beyond the Battlefield

The Civil War was an internal conflict between two groups of Americans, and it was also a relatively new kind of war whose implications were only just becoming apparent in the nineteenth century. "It was a war between the States, or better still, a war between two nations," wrote the Georgia scientist and prominent proslavery theorist Joseph LeConte. "For each side it was really a foreign war . . . let it be distinctly understood, that there never was a war in which were more thoroughly enlisted the hearts of the whole people—men, women, and children—than were those of the South in this. To us it was literally a life and death struggle for national existence."[5]

Such support was not as universal as LeConte and others imagined; the popular truism "a rich man's war but a poor man's fight" expressed a more ambivalent attitude toward the conflict among the Southern lower orders that its more fervent supporters rarely acknowledged. The North viewed the war in similarly existential terms. The violence of such wars tends to spill out beyond the battlefield, and the Civil War was no exception. The historian James McPherson has estimated that as many as fifty thousand civilians may have died of violence, hunger, and disease in sieges of towns and cities or punitive raids and reprisals by soldiers and guerrillas. During the siege of Vicksburg, women and children lived for weeks in snake-infested caves dug into the fortified hills, living on dogs, cats, horses, and rats during the daily artillery barrages from Grant's armies. In the Shenandoah Valley in Virginia and in Missouri, Kentucky, and Tennessee, Federal troops and Union loyalists fought a vicious tit-for-tat war with Confederate guerrillas and bushwhackers, in which farms, towns, and villages were burned and their inhabitants made homeless or reduced to poverty and starvation. In the divided state of Missouri, Union troops and pro-Union irregulars, the Kansas "Jayhawkers," traded blows with Confederate raiders in a war of reciprocal murder and atrocity in which the dividing line between civilians and combatants often disappeared.[6] Thousands of fugitive slaves, or "contrabands," died in the refugee camps established behind Union lines, which often lacked food, shelter, and basic sanitation.

The Civil War also exposed Americans for the first time to the environmental devastation of war. Forests were stripped and cut down to make breastworks, trench fortifications, and chevaux-de-frise or set on fire in the course of battles. Armies burned crops and slaughtered livestock to deny food to their opponents or reduce besieged cities to starvation. Entire districts in the South were laid waste by foraging Union armies, who burned and stripped barns and fences and consumed grain and livestock, but also by Confederate soldiers, who frequently foraged with a voracious intensity that was indistinguishable from that of their enemies.[7] In 1864, the Confederate general Richard Taylor was so shocked by the predatory behavior of his troops in Alabama and the lower Mississippi that he compared them to medieval brigands and threatened to have offenders shot as common highwaymen. In

1863 Colonel C. Franklin complained to Jefferson Davis that guerrillas in Missouri had "transferred to the Confederate uniform all the dread and terror which used to attach to the Lincoln blue. The last horse is taken from the widow and orphan, whose husband and father has fallen in the country's service. No respect is shown to age, sex, or condition."[8]

This panorama of devastation was not simply a result of the visceral passions of civil war. Although the war was a "national" war between two rival societies or "civilizations," it was also a war in which the economic resources of the two antagonists were more essential than ever before. The huge Civil War armies depended on the mass production of muskets, cannons, gunpowder, ammunition, uniforms, tents, belt buckles, swords, horseshoes, and digging tools, and also on the transportation of men, animals, and war matériel from one battle zone to another.

No previous war had relied so heavily on railroads to shunt armies and supplies to and from areas of military operations, sometimes directly to and from the battlefield.[9] At the beginning of the war, there were thirty thousand miles of railroad track in America, more than the rest of world put together, and this system was quickly co-opted for military purposes by both sides. A more recent invention, the electric telegraph, also played a key role in the war, enabling the respective high commands to remain in contact with advancing armies to a degree that had not previously been possible. As a result, railroad lines and junctions, telegraph wires and installations, and waterways became strategic objectives as both sides conducted campaigns along the railroads that supplied them, tried to cut off the supply lines of their adversaries, and besieged towns by breaking up track and railroad installations, cutting telegraph wires, and burning bridges.

Raiding was a well-established component of Native American warfare long before European colonization, and American colonists had adopted the practice during various Indian wars since the sixteenth century. In 1778 George Washington ordered General John Sullivan to inflict "total destruction and devastation" on Iroquois villages in Cherry Valley, New York, in retaliation for the massacre of U.S. militia in Wyoming, Pennsylvania. Abandoning their baggage trains to increase their mobility, Sullivan's men burned 1,200 homes in forty villages, till their commander told Congress there was "not a single town left in the country of the five nations."[10] Washington's support for such tactics earned him the nickname "Town Destroyer" among the Iroquois.

From the autumn of 1862 onward, these tactics were used by both sides. The Confederate government authorized cavalry raids behind Union lines in an attempt to disrupt Union supply routes in Kentucky, Tennessee, and Mississippi. Over the next few months, Confederate raiders, such as Nathan Bedford Forrest, Braxton Bragg, and John Hunt Morgan, carried out a string of hit-and-run attacks on railroad links and Union supply depots. On December 20, 1862, under the command of General Earl Van Dorn, 2,500 Confederate cavalrymen galloped onto the main street of Holly Springs, Mississippi, which Ulysses Grant had transformed into a supply depot for his operations against Vicksburg, and proceeded to burn and dynamite warehouses, railroad carriages, and munitions depots, causing $1.5 million in damage and forcing Grant's army to abandon its offensive and retreat to Memphis. The Union responded in the same vein. In the spring of 1863, Colonel Benjamin Grierson led 1,700 Union cavalry on a six-hundred-mile raid through Mississippi and Louisiana, destroying railroads and railroad cars, ripping up track, and burning storehouses in order to divert Confederate attention from Grant's movements against Vicksburg.

Civilians inevitably bore the consequences of such operations as well, and the impact of the war on the civilian population was not only an incidental by-product of attacks on economic resources and communications. In a war between two relatively evenly matched antagonists able to recover from even the most devastating

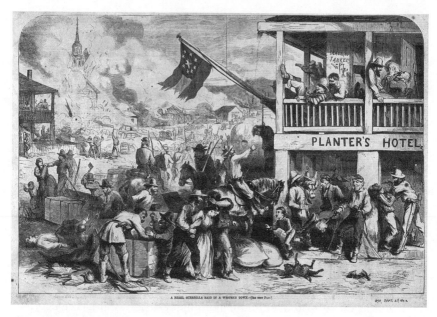

Hard war: a rebel guerrilla raid in a Western town, September 27, 1862, Thomas Nast. Courtesy of the Library of Congress.

battlefield defeats, the morale and will to fight of the enemy's non-combatants as well as its soldiers was increasingly seen by both sides as a key target for destruction. For the South, Northern public opinion was a mostly remote abstraction that it sought to influence through periodic raids and incursions into the North or by inflicting demoralizing defeats on its armies in battle. Union armies, by contrast, experienced the attitudes of the civilian population as a military problem that directly threatened their security during their occupation of the South. Lincoln's conciliatory policy toward the South reflected the administration's assumption that support for secession was lukewarm and shared by only a small percentage of the population.

As Federal troops penetrated the South, they encountered passive and sometimes active hostility from the civilian population, which led them to very different conclusions. "These people, safe in the knowledge of our conciliatory principles, talk their secessism as boldly as they do in Richmond," complained Captain Charles Wills of the 103rd Illinois Infantry from Alabama in the summer of 1862. "Many of our officers have given up all hope of our conquering them and really wish for peace. For myself . . . I believe I'd rather see the whole country red with blood, and ruined altogether, than have this 7,000,000 of invalids (these Southerners are nothing else as a people) conquer, or successfully resist the power of the North. I hate them now, as they hate us."[11]

Such anger was partly due to hostility toward the Union, which many civilians openly expressed to soldiers like Wills. But the tendency to regard civilians and soldiers as a common enemy was also exacerbated by the armed resistance that Union armies encountered from nonuniformed combatants as they occupied the South, which frequently transformed occupation into a hazardous activity. In the second half of the nineteenth century, the concept of irregular "people's war" fought by partisans and guerrillas was a relatively recent innovation, dating back only to the Napoleonic Wars, that was still regarded with horror by many European armies. In *The Art of War*, Antoine de Jomini nostalgically compared the lost era of eighteenth-century warfare in which "the French and English guards courteously invited each other to fire first," with "the frightful epoch when priests, women, and children throughout Spain plotted the murder of isolated soldiers."[12] American armies were already familiar with this "frightful epoch" through their own campaigns against the British in the Revolutionary Wars and the guerrilla resistance to Winfield Scott's invasion of Mexico. But the extent of guerrilla warfare in the Civil War appeared to many Union soldiers to be an unprecedented and entirely undesirable phenomenon. In the Shenandoah Valley, in

Tennessee, Missouri, and the Mississippi Valley, Union troops came under constant and sustained attacks from bushwhackers and other partisans who shot at passenger trains and steamboats, attacked isolated outposts, killed sentries and stragglers, and terrorized pro-Union civilians, burning their homes and killing them.

Guerrilla warfare was particularly fierce in the divided state of Missouri, where Union soldiers and pro-Union Jayhawkers fought a vicious war of tit-for-tat murders and atrocities from the earliest days of the war. Many of the leading Union generals, including Ulysses Grant, John Pope, and John Schofield, began their careers in Missouri, and their attitudes toward the South were often shaped by their disgust with a civilian population that they regarded as complicit in such attacks, a disgust summed up in a letter from two soldiers from Warsaw, Missouri, in August 1863: "There is one kind of people that is asleep with one eye open and only wait an opportunity to murder loyal people without mercy and these men are the ones that walk up to a federal soldier with outstretched hand and a smile on their face and say they have always stayed at home and never done anything."[13] Frustrated Union commanders increasingly chafed against the "sickly inoffensive war" promoted by the administration and advocated harsh measures in response to guerrilla attacks and acts of sabotage; these included martial law, summary executions, fines, and the burning of homes or whole neighborhoods. In August 1861, Lincoln publicly revoked the draconian martial law proclamation enacted by the commander of the Department of the West, John C. Frémont, in Missouri, which called for the emancipation of all slaves of disloyal citizens and the confiscation of their property. Over the coming year, the Union political and military leadership concluded that much of the South was not going to be won over by conciliation and that if Southerners would not willingly return to the Union, then they must be made to do it.

Hard War

In July 1862, Lincoln sarcastically dismissed complaints from Union loyalists in Louisiana that Union troops were protecting slaves and imposing restrictions on local trade; he asked them if they expected him to wage war "with elder-stalk squirts, charged with rose water." That same month, Lincoln responded to Robert E. Lee's invasion of Maryland by drawing up a preliminary Emancipation Proclamation, which declared his intention to free all slaves in Confederate states that did not return to the Union by January the following year. The Emancipation Proclamation was intended to preempt the possibility of international recognition of the Confederacy and pave the way for the formation of black regiments. But it also confirmed the government's new willingness to wage "hard war" with an "iron hand" against the South. Writing to Grant in April 1863, Henry Halleck observed, "The character of the war has changed very much with the last year. There is now no possible hope of reconciliation with the rebels. . . . There can be no peace but that which is forced by the sword. We must conquer the rebels or be conquered by them."[14]

The changed mood in Washington was reflected in new powers given to Union commanders to confiscate or destroy Southern property, including slaves, farms, factories, and cotton.[15] Lincoln also authorized his commanders to take many of the draconian measures proposed by the discredited John Frémont the previous year in response to guerrilla attacks against Federal troops, measures that he had previously opposed. These measures still fell considerably short of some of the more bloodthirsty and exterminatory proposals emanating from some Northern politicians and the press, but the impact of the new policy was nevertheless felt throughout the South. On July 26, 1862, the commander of the newly formed Army of Virginia, General John Pope, issued General Order No. 11, authorizing all male inhabitants to declare allegiance to the United States or be removed beyond army lines. Pope also authorized his troops to "subsist upon the country" and take food from the local population in return for vouchers by which "loyal citizens" would be reimbursed after the war, as well as to burn any houses from which they were fired upon. In April 1863, Union troops devastated the district of Deer Creek, Mississippi, in an attempt to clear the area of guerrillas, after which the expedition's commanding officer, Brigadier General Frederick Steele, reported, "We burnt every thing & took all the Horses, Mules & Niggers that we came across."[16]

In May 1863, Grant's army occupied Jackson, the capital of Mississippi, during his operations against Vicksburg and spent thirty-six hours destroying railroad track, cotton warehouses, and factories to cut the city off from the Southern hinterland. Visiting shortly afterward, the English officer and Confederate sympathizer Lieutenant Colonel Arthur James Lyon Fremantle found that its "numerous factories have been burned by the enemy, who were of course justified in doing so." But Freemantle also accused Grant's forces of having "wantonly pillaged nearly all the private houses. They had gutted all the stores, and destroyed what they could not carry away. . . . I saw the ruins of the Roman Catholic church, the priest's house, and the principal hotel, which were still smoking, together with many other buildings that could in no way be identified with the Confederate Government. . . . The whole town was a miserable wreck, and presented a deplorable aspect."[17]

Southern newspapers routinely raged against the "Yankee Vandals" who carried out such raids and urged their own armies to respond in kind. In June 1863, the *Charleston Courier* called on Robert E. Lee's invading armies in Pennsylvania to "wage war, even as it has been waged against us, sparing neither public nor private property, but ravaging and destroying in every direction." Lee did not respond to these exhortations and placed his troops under strict orders to pay the local population for food and supplies. These orders were more or less obeyed, but such restraint was not always present. Confederate bushwhackers had no compunctions about shooting at passenger trains or passenger-carrying steamboats on the Mississippi. John Singleton Mosby, the Confederate lawyer-turned-guerrilla known as the Gray Ghost, ordered the shelling of Union trains even when they had women and children aboard, on the grounds that he "did not understand that it hurts women and children to be killed any more than it hurts men."[18] On August 20, 1863, more than four hundred Confederate raiders led by William Clarke Quantrill occupied the town of Lawrence, Kansas, and proceeded to murder more than four hundred unarmed men and boys before looting and burning much of the town.

On July 30, 1864, Confederate cavalry numbering 2,800 under the command of Brigadier General John McCausland raided the town of Chambersburg, Pennsylvania, in retaliation for a punitive antiguerrilla campaign conducted by the Union general David "Black Dave" Hunter in the Shenandoah Valley during the summer, which culminated in the destruction of the town of Lexington, Virginia. McCausland ordered Chambersburg's inhabitants to pay compensation, and when they proved unable to provide it his men burned some 550 buildings, creating what the *Richmond Enquirer* called "a blaze that will arrest the view of the Northern people, and illustrate the destruction of villages, homesteads, and towns in every Southern state."

Such raids were sporadic, if only because the Confederacy lacked the capacity to carry them out on a regular basis. For the Union, on the other hand, physical destruction was not only intended to punish civilians for their real or alleged collusion in guerrilla attacks; it also became an instrument of pacification and subjugation. Such destruction was generally aimed at property rather than people, but it could nevertheless have devastating consequences for those on the receiving end. As Philip Sheridan, one of the toughest Union generals and an implacable proponent of destructive raiding, observed in his memoirs, "Death is popularly considered the maximum of punishment in war, but it is not; reduction to poverty brings prayers for peace more surely and more quickly than does the destruction of human life, as the selfishness of man has demonstrated in more than one great conflict."[19]

Sheridan destroyed a great deal of Southern property. He rejected the concept of war as a "duel" in which "lines of men shall engage each other in battle, and material interests be ignored" and insisted that it was legitimate to extend "deprivation and suffering" to "those who rest at home in peace and plenty" yet still supported the war from a distance. The Lincoln administration's hard-war policy was based on similar assumptions. Though the government never ceased to offer amnesties to Southerners who took the oath of allegiance, it was increasingly taken for granted that some sections of the population would have to be forced back into the Union if they could not be attracted to it. This was the general consensus in Washington in March 1864, when Ulysses Grant replaced Halleck as general in chief of the Union armies.

Grant's promotion took place at a time when the war had to all intents and purposes shifted irresistibly in the Union's favor. Large swathes of Southern territory were under Union occupation; the Confederate Army and Navy had experienced huge losses; some 33 percent of its nominally available troops were absent without leave; and the civilian population had seen its living standards drastically decline under the impact of war-induced inflation, high food prices, and the increasingly tight blockade. Yet despite these reversals, the Confederacy remained undefeated. Its heartlands in the Deep South were largely untouched, its capital remained unconquered, and it retained powerful and well-entrenched armies in both theaters. It was against this background that Grant was authorized to devise a new strategic plan that would bring the war to a conclusion, together with the man who was soon to prove himself the most destructive of all the Union raiding generals.

2

Uncle Billy's War

In the famous photograph taken by the Civil War photographer Mathew Brady in May 1865 at the height of General William Tecumseh Sherman's fame, Sherman is wearing a high white collar and uniform, his arms crossed, his receding hair wild and unkempt on his domed forehead, his posture ramrod straight. He is looking slightly to his left with a fierce, implacable expression, the embodiment of "grim-visaged war," as one of Grant's staff officers described him in Atlanta in September 1864, whose severe demeanor is enhanced by the black armband commemorating Lincoln's assassination, the sharp aquiline nose, hard-set mouth and hooded eyes, and the pronounced crease on his right cheek, which looks like a dueling scar. Brady's iconic image does not convey the contradictions of Sherman's complex personality—the thoughtful, literate, and highly intelligent man who was prone to fits of depression and self-doubt, the democrat who disliked and distrusted democracy, the racist who freed slaves, the ruthless soldier who often professed his loathing for war and preferred to avoid battle, the man who loved the South yet set out to bludgeon it into submission. The photograph was taken when Sherman had barely returned from the campaigns that had transformed him into the eccentric genius general of the North and the nemesis of the South, and he exudes confidence and willpower and the sense of a man who is conscious of his place in his country's history. Before the war, there was little to suggest that such an outcome

"Grim-Visaged War," Mathew Brady, May 1865. Courtesy of the National Archives (111-B-1769).

was likely; Sherman himself had come to believe that he was destined for obscurity and mediocrity, and even after the war began
his career came close to unraveling before it had even begun.

The Vagabond Soldier

The general whom one of his officers called "the most American
looking man I ever saw" was born on February 8, 1820, in the small
town of Lancaster, Ohio, the son of a successful lawyer who gave
him his unusual middle name in honor of the legendary Shawnee
chieftain. At the age of nine, his father died of fever, leaving his
widow with eleven children to support. To ease the burden on his
mother, "Cump" Sherman was handed over to the care of the attorney Thomas Ewing, a family friend and Whig Party senator.
Ewing secured his adopted son a place at the West Point military
academy at the age of sixteen, where he received the standard military education of the period, with a heavily Europe-oriented cur-
riculum that included courses on civil and military engineering,
fortifications, siegecraft, artillery and infantry tactics, and a great
deal of drill, in addition to more academic subjects such as miner-
alogy, geology, moral philosophy, and international and common
law, which Sherman described to his younger brother John as essential requirements for "the scientific officer."

One of Sherman's professors at West Point was Dennis Hart
Mahan, the father of the great admiral and naval strategist Alfred
Thayer Mahan. He taught courses on military and civil engineering and the science of war at the academy from 1832 to 1871.
Sherman does not say much in his memoirs about the impact of
West Point on his future thinking and career, except to boast of
the demerits he received as a result of the academy's insistence on
"neatness in dress and uniform, with a strict conformity to the
rules." Though he may not have paid much attention to his appearance, this most cerebral of American generals thrived academically,

and he also imbibed a strong sense of the military as a special caste and the ultimate guarantor of the laws and Constitution of the republic that shaped his worldview both during and after the Civil War.

In 1840 Sherman left the academy as a second lieutenant and received his first posting, to Florida, where between 1835 and 1842 the U.S. Army was engaged in a vicious guerrilla war against the Seminoles known as the Second Seminole War, in which ten thousand regular troops and thirty thousand volunteers fought a frustrating campaign against one thousand Seminole warriors, for whom the swamps and hummocks of the Everglades provided a natural fortress and hiding place. In 1841 Colonel William J. Worth turned the war in the government's favor by sending small units into the Everglades outside the normal hunting season, in the winter, to burn and destroy Seminole camps, canoes, crops, and food supplies rather than hunt their elusive combatants. These operations contain the outlines of Sherman's future campaigns in the Civil War and also in the West. Though he made little contribution to the Seminole campaigns, he described them with some enthusiasm to Ellen Boyle Ewing, the daughter of Thomas Ewing and his soon-to-be fiancée, as "a kind of warfare which every young officer should be thoroughly acquainted with, as the Indian is most likely to be our chief enemy in times to come."[1]

These less than glorious skirmishes in the Florida swamps were the closest Sherman came to actual combat before the Civil War. In 1842 he was stationed at Fort Moultrie, on Sullivan's Island outside Charleston, where he first became personally acquainted with Southern society. In 1843, he spent three months in Georgia and Alabama investigating claims made by state militias for the loss of horses in the First Seminole War, and while there he went on long rides through Georgia's former Cherokee country and drew topographical sketches of the same terrain "where in after-years I had to conduct vast armies and fight great battles."

Sherman had a keen eye for topographical detail, and his letters are filled with precise and vivid descriptions of landscapes and wildlife during his prewar journeys in Florida, the Deep South, the Gulf of Mexico, California, and the West. He also liked to paint. During his less than demanding duties at Fort Moultrie, he developed such a passion for painting and drawing that he even contemplated giving up the military to become a painter—a career direction that many Southerners would later come to wish he had chosen. Sherman's impressions of the South were generally positive. He enjoyed the social life at Charleston, the abundance of balls, and the attractive young women who attended them, and he was sympathetic toward the "peculiar institution" that sustained Southern society.

He was less enthusiastic about the military, which offered only limited prospects of promotion. Unlike Grant and many of his other West Point classmates, Sherman did not participate in the 1846–48 war with Mexico, and he was uncomfortably conscious afterward that "our country had passed through a foreign war, that my comrades had fought great battles, and yet I had not fired a single shot." In 1850 he married Ellen Ewing, and three years later he left the army after having obtained the rank of captain, largely as a result of pressure from his adopted family to find more remunerative employment. That same year, he moved to San Francisco to take up a position as manager of the local branch of a Saint Louis bank, where he was appointed major general of the California militia.

This appointment drew him into a bitter dispute between the state government and a self-styled Vigilance Committee over the deteriorating law-and-order situation in the city. True to his West Point education, Sherman took the side of the government and was ignored and humiliated, an experience that reinforced his instinctive conservatism, in which an almost religious reverence for the law and the Constitution was coupled with a deep suspicion of "mob rule" and "anarchy," and the politicians and newspapers who he believed often promoted these tendencies.

Sherman's letters and memoirs contain a cross section of the turbulent and dynamic mid-nineteenth-century American society that he inhabited, from Indians, aristocratic Mexican women, and slave-owning planters to California gold miners, frontier scouts, and settlers, as well as the hardworking Yankee middle classes of the great Northern cities that he was never able to feel part of. In 1856, an economic slump in California led his employers to close down his bank in San Francisco. In July 1858, the Shermans moved to Leavenworth, Kansas, where he was admitted to the Kansas bar, but this career path also turned out to be a dead end when the new lawyer was unable to generate sufficient work to feed his growing family.

These failures intensified Sherman's tendency to melancholy and self-pity, and his pessimism regarding his career prospects was not helped by the success of his younger brother John, who made a smooth transition from the law to the House of Representatives. In one of his many despondent moments, Sherman told his wife that he was "doomed to be a vagabond," and described himself as "a dead cock in the pit." In 1859, his luck changed when he secured a job as superintendent of a new military academy in Louisiana, and the following year he wrote to Ellen in a tone of resignation rather than satisfaction from the newly created Louisiana Seminary of Learning and Military Academy, "I must rest satisfied with the title of the 'Old Man,' the 'cross old schoolmaster.'"

War

The "cross old schoolmaster" was then forty years old and appeared to have reached the zenith of his less than dazzling achievements. Without the Civil War, Sherman might have spent the rest of his life churning out Southern cadets for the U.S. Army, but this did not mean that he relished the opportunity that the outbreak of war provided. On Christmas Eve, 1860, he was in his college rooms when he read that South Carolina had seceded. According to a Virginian friend and colleague, Sherman began crying and pacing the room and decried what he called an act of "folly, madness, a crime against civilization" that would force him to fight "against your people, whom I love best." Sherman insisted that the South could not prevail against "one of the most powerful, ingeniously mechanical and determined people on earth" but he nevertheless foresaw, unlike many of his contemporaries, that the war would be long and bloody.[2]

On January 18, 1861, he resigned his post as superintendent in protest at the seizure by Louisiana troops of the federal arsenal at Baton Rouge. After an emotional good-bye to his cadets and colleagues, he made his way back to Lancaster and then to Washington, at the invitation of his brother. In March he met Abraham Lincoln and was distinctly underwhelmed by what he perceived to be the president's complacent attitude toward the looming confrontation. Even after Fort Sumter, Sherman was not ready to offer his services to a government he believed was unwilling to fight the war the way it should be fought, and he turned down an offer from Lincoln's treasury secretary, Salmon Chase, to become chief clerk of the War Department. In May that year, he changed his mind at the behest of his family and became a colonel in the Thirteenth Regular Infantry, which played a minor role at the First Battle of Bull Run/Manassas Junction. Sherman was disgusted by the chaotic retreat of Lincoln's volunteer army, which he accused of having "degenerated into an armed mob."

Against his better judgment, he agreed to become brigadier general of a volunteer regiment in Kentucky, and in October he was unexpectedly promoted to commander of the Army of the Cumberland in Kentucky, when his predecessor resigned on health grounds. Sherman did not believe he was ready for high command, and the promotion nearly wrecked his career when he scandalized Lincoln's secretary of war Simon Cameron by declaring that at least two hundred thousand soldiers would eventually be needed to extend the war into the South. This prediction, as it turned out, was not inaccurate, but it was not what the North believed at the time. Sherman's case was not helped by his paranoid overestimation of the numbers of Confederate troops in Kentucky, which led him to believe that his own army was about to be overwhelmed.

These views caught the attention of the Northern press, which was frequently as eager to destroy the reputations of Union generals as it was to boost them, and led to a series of stories questioning his sanity. Reports from Sherman's headquarters of the manic behavior of the insomniac commander of the Army of the Cumberland did nothing to dispel such reports and eventually prompted his wife to travel to Louisville to rescue him from what was effectively a nervous breakdown. In November 1861, Sherman was relieved of his command and taken home to recuperate before being transferred to a remote post in Missouri, where he might easily have remained had it not been for the efforts of his wife, his brother, his stepfather, and his father-in-law, who lobbied intensively in Washington for him to be given another chance.

In February 1862, his old West Point classmate Henry Halleck sent him to Paducah, Mississippi, to organize the supply depot that Ulysses Grant had established for his campaign against forts Henry and Donelson. Here Sherman first demonstrated the logistical skills that would later shape his campaigns in the Deep South. Located twelve miles apart at the parallel Tennessee and Cumberland Rivers respectively, in barely mapped terrain with few roads, these two forts were a vital component of the Confederate defense of Tennessee. Placed by Halleck in charge of the District of Cairo, Sherman demonstrated the punctilious attention to detail of a consummate quartermaster and restored much needed order and organization to the Western army's chaotic supply chain. It was largely due to his efforts that Grant was provided with a constant flow of boats bearing food, supplies, and reinforcements when he needed them, in order to carry out his complex operations that provided the Union with its first major victories of the war, and this contribution restored Sherman's own confidence. His redemption was confirmed at the Battle of Shiloh on April 6, though only just. Initially taken by surprise by the Southern assault, he proved himself to be a courageous and inspirational general during twelve hours of ferocious combat, in which he was lightly wounded twice and had three horses shot from under him.

Sherman was praised by both Halleck and Grant for his contribution to the successful Union counterattack the next day, and Shiloh cemented his friendship with Grant that was to play such a decisive role in the campaigns that followed. Even more than Bull Run, Shiloh exposed the former lawyer and bank manager to the horrors of the conflict. "The scenes on this field would have cured anybody of war," he told his wife. "Mangled bodies, dead, dying, in every conceivable shape, without heads, legs; and horses!"[3] Sherman witnessed many such scenes in the course of the war, during his mixed record as a field commander. On December 27, 1862, he led a failed assault on the Confederate forts and trenches overlooking Chickasaw Bayou, north of Vicksburg, in which his forces took 1,776 casualties, compared to the Confederates' 187. At Chattanooga on November 25, 1863, he played only a supporting role in the successful Union assault on Confederate positions on Missionary Ridge, in which his forces became pinned down under heavy enemy fire as a result of a navigational error that left them in an exposed position.

If Sherman's record on the battlefield was less than outstanding in comparison with that of Robert E. Lee, Stonewall Jackson, or even Grant, he nevertheless displayed talents that were extremely useful to the Union cause. He was a tenacious and meticulous quartermaster in a war in which logistics were more important than ever. He was also a sharp analyst of the South with a keen understanding of the political and military dimensions of the war. Last but not least, he proved himself highly proficient at organizing and directing the movement of large numbers of troops on the march. All these qualities transformed the temperamental and self-doubting officer who nearly exited the war in Kentucky into Grant's right-hand man and the co-architect of the strategy that was to finally bring the war to an end.

This transformation was partly due to Grant's influence. In April 1863, Grant finally succeeded in moving his army from the west to the east bank of the Mississippi River, thus enabling him to strike at Vicksburg. Rather than remain tied to his new operational base at Grand Gulf, Grant opted to march his army across the country between the two main defending Confederate armies, at Vicksburg and the state capital of Jackson. To increase his mobility and tactical flexibility, Grant ordered his soldiers to carry only essential supplies and make up the balance by living off the country.

These tactics were not entirely unprecedented. In 1847 Winfield Scott led his army on a seven-hundred-mile march from Veracruz to Mexico City, relying mostly on supplies that his army bought from the local population along the route. But Sherman was so appalled by Grant's plan to move twenty thousand soldiers through hostile territory without supplies that he sent a courier in an attempt to get him to change his mind. Grant rejected Sherman's arguments. Moving rapidly east toward Jackson, he dispatched two corps—one of which was commanded by Sherman—in a feint movement northward toward Vicksburg, before capturing Jackson. Throughout this campaign, the Union armies drew their food and forage from the surrounding population while simultaneously dividing the Confederate defenders, providing no supply line that could be attacked but cutting the line of communication between Jackson and Vicksburg.

Grant's tactics were a revelation to Sherman. Not only had he demonstrated that a large army could subsist on the country without supplies, but his skillful manipulation of the Confederate armies offered a brilliantly executed example of how to make tactical gains over an opposing army by avoiding battle rather than pursuing it. Sherman's corps also participated in the destruction of factories, storehouses, and railroad lines at Jackson, while Grant moved toward Vicksburg. Sherman learned these lessons well. In July that year, he returned to Jackson following the fall of Vicksburg and completed the destruction of the city with such thoroughness that Union soldiers dubbed it Chimneyville.

Sherman's Torch

Unlike his superiors, Sherman never believed that the South could be brought back to the Union through a policy of conciliation. "The greatest difficulty in the problem now before the country is not to conquer but so conquer as to impress upon the real men of the South a respect for their conquerors," he wrote to his brother from Saint Louis in 1861. "When one nation is at war with another, all the people of the one are the enemies of the other; then the rules are plain and easy of understanding," he wrote to Secretary of the Treasury Salmon P. Chase from Memphis in August 1862. In a letter to Grant that same month, he promised to "make this war as severe as possible, and show no symptoms of tiring till the South begs for mercy; indeed, I know, and you know, that the end would be reached quicker by such a course than by any seeming yielding on our part."[4] In October he told his brother, "It is about time the North understood the truth. That the entire South, man, woman and child are against us."[5]

The "severity" that Sherman recommended was not dictated only by military considerations. He also regarded the war itself as a "salutary political schooling" that would eliminate "the modern anarchist doctrine . . . of secession" and force the South to accept the permanent authority of the federal government. "Obedience to the Law," he wrote to Halleck on September 17, 1863, ". . . is the lesson that this war, under Providence, will teach and enlighten American citizens." In these circumstances, "I would banish all minor questions, assert the broad doctrine that as a nation the United States has the right, and also the physical power, to penetrate to every part of our national domain, and we will do it . . . that it makes no difference whether it be in one year, or two, or ten, or twenty; that we will remove and destroy every obstacle, if need be, take every life, every acre of land, every particle of property, every thing that seems to us seems proper; that we will not cease till the end is attained; that all who do not aid us are our enemies, and that we will not account to them for our acts."[6]

By that time, such ideas were no longer as anomalous in Washington as they had once been, but Sherman's pronouncements sometimes went beyond the new parameters of hard war. In July 1862, he told one of his officers, "To secure the safety of the navigation of the Mississippi River I would slay millions. . . . For every bullet shot at a steamboat, I would shoot a thousand 30-pounder Parrotts into even helpless towns on Red, Ouachita, Yazoo or wherever a boat can float or soldier march."[7] In January 1864, an officer from the Army of the Tennessee in Huntsville, Alabama, asked him for clarification on the correct treatment of civilians under his jurisdiction with known "secesh" sentiments. In a detailed and learned reply, with references to precedents in European wars and civil wars, Sherman explained that noncombatants who "remain in their houses and keep to their accustomed peaceful business" should not be molested. Those who failed to observe such conditions, however, could be subjected to a range of punishments that included fines, imprisonment, banishment, or, in cases of espionage, death. Having "appealed to war," Southerners had only themselves to blame for whatever consequences befell, Sherman explained: "A people who will persevere in war beyond a certain limit ought to know the consequences. Many, many people, with less pertinacity than the South has already shown, have been wiped out of existence."[8]

Sherman's letters and statements contain frequent references to "extermination" as a remedy for this "choice." But despite his propensity for extreme statements, Sherman was frequently appalled at the treatment of Southern civilians by his own troops. In the summer of 1861 he was so disgusted by the thieving and vandalism carried out by Union soldiers during the frantic retreat from Bull Run that he complained to his wife that "every woman within five miles who has a peach stolen or roasting ear carried off comes to me to have a guard stationed to protect her tree, and our soldiers are the most destructive men I have ever known."[9]

In July the following year, during the march from Shiloh to Corinth, Sherman ordered his soldiers to cease "This demoralizing and disgraceful practice of pillage . . . else the country will rise on us and justly shoot us down like dogs and wild beasts."[10] These orders appear to have had little impact, according to another letter from his camp near Vicksburg in January 1863, in which he told his brother, "Our armies are devastating the land and it is sad to see the destruction that attends our progress—we cannot help it. Farms disappear, houses are burned and plundered, and every living animal killed and eaten. General officers make feeble attempts to stay the disorder, but it is idle." Like many Union officers, he was concerned that such behavior would erode the discipline of his own army, but he also regarded pillage and looting as morally abhorrent activities in themselves. "War is at best barbarism, but to involve all—children, women, old and helpless—is more than can be justified," he told one of his divisional commanders in the Yazoo River in April 1863.[11]

Sherman never entirely shifted from these views, but he nevertheless came to embrace a form of war that directly or indirectly targeted "children, women, old and helpless" in order to attack the Confederate Army and its government.

This evolution was to some extent a consequence of the war itself; the longer it continued, the more Sherman, like many Union officers, was disposed to win it through whatever means he believed necessary. His own experience of dealing with guerrilla warfare in the South reinforced his conviction that the Southern civilian population was collectively responsible for the war. Sherman's letters and public statements are filled with bitter invective against the civilians who he believed had "chosen" a war while remaining largely immune or indifferent to its worst consequences. His hardening attitude toward the South was not just a consequence of the death and injury that he routinely encountered, but may also have been shaped by personal tragedy. In September 1863, Sherman broke his own rule that campaigning officers should not bring their families to visit them in the field. He invited his family to join him at his XV Corps camp near the Big Black and Yazoo Rivers. During the visit his beloved nine-year-old son, Willie, caught typhoid fever and died in Memphis. Sherman always blamed himself for the death, and it is difficult to avoid the conclusion that he also blamed the war itself.

His personal motives notwithstanding, Sherman came to believe from a purely military perspective that the South could not be subjugated unless the civilian population also paid a price for its support of the Confederate government and army. In his letter to Halleck in September 1863, he declared in unequivocal terms that the war should be waged not just against those who actively resisted the Union, but also against Southerners who "stand by, mere lookers-on in this domestic tragedy, they have no right to immunity, protection, or share in the final results."

Despite such statements, Sherman still attempted for the most part to limit these efforts to public property rather than private homes, but his previous concern when his troops exceeded these boundaries was conspicuously absent by the summer of 1863. "Of necessity, in the war the commander on the spot is the judge, and may take your house, your field, your everything, and turn you all out, helpless to starve," he told a citizens committee from Warren County. "It may be wrong, but that don't alter the case."[12] In February 1864, Sherman led an even more destructive raid on the important railroad hub and arsenal of Meridian, 150 miles from Vicksburg, which became a prototype of his subsequent raid through Georgia. Following Grant's cue, Sherman ordered his corps commanders and staff officers to strip their supply wagons to the minimum and march without tents, carrying only essential supplies of artillery and ammunition. On February 3, he led 23,000 soldiers out of Vicksburg, accompanied by a herd of cattle, and proceeded to carve a ten-mile-wide trail of burned and destroyed buildings all along what was left of the railroad line to Jackson, before proceeding to Meridian.

Marching in two columns and supported by simultaneous diversionary operations in northern Mississippi and along the river, Sherman was able to prevent Lieutenant General Leonidas Polk's twenty-thousand-strong Army of Mississippi from massing against him. On February 14, his troops entered Meridian unopposed. Sherman spent the next five days displaying what Bruce Catton has called "a sinister zeal for destroying Southern property," wrecking the city with such thoroughness that he was able to report to Grant that "Meridian, with its depots, storehouses, arsenals, hospitals, offices, hotels, and cantonments no longer exists."[13] The Confederate general Stephen D. Lee was aghast at this prodigious application of "Sherman's torch," and questioned whether such methods violated "the warfare of the civilization of the nineteenth century?"[14] Sherman was generally indifferent to such criticisms. In his view, Southerners had "chosen" or "appealed to" war and therefore were obliged to accept its consequences—even if these consequences were decided by him. "To make war we must and will harden our hearts," he wrote to Assistant Secretary of War Charles Anderson Dana in the spring of 1864. "Therefore when preachers clamor and sanitaries wail, don't join in, but know that war, like the thunderbolt, follows its laws and turns not aside even if the beautiful, the virtuous and charitable stand in its path."[15]

Sherman often described war as if it were a force of nature that could not be controlled, but he was also conscious that its impact could be intensified or diminished according to necessity. In August 1864, he reminded his friend James Guthrie of the early period of the war "when I would not let our men burn fence rails for fire or gather fruit or vegetables though hungry. . . . We at that time were restrained, tied by a deep-seated reverence for law and property."[16] Such restraint was no longer required, he insisted. "The rebels first introduced terror as part of their system. . . . No military mind could endure this long, and we were forced in self-defense to imitate their example." Many armies in wartime have justified their own departure from military conventions on the grounds that their enemies had departed from them first. For Sherman, however, "terror" was not simply an instrument of military domination. "I believe in fighting in a double sense, first to gain physical results and next to inspire respect on which to build up our nation's power," he told a member of Grant's staff after the battle of Chattanooga.[17] And in the spring of 1864 he and Grant set out to impose this power decisively in a coordinated campaign in both theaters of war.

Atlanta

On March 20, 1864, Sherman and Grant met in the Burnet House hotel in Cincinnati to devise the coming spring campaign, at a time when the outcome of the war was by no means certain.

Despite steady Union gains over the past year, Union casualties far outnumbered those of the Confederacy; its army was also plagued by desertion, and the Lincoln administration was entering an election year in which the president could not take the support of the public or even his own party for granted.

Both Grant and Sherman were acutely aware that a Democratic victory in the November election might lead to a negotiated peace and the definitive breakup of the Union, as they plotted a simultaneous campaign in both theaters that would bring the Confederacy to its knees. In the East, the Armies of the Potomac and the James would advance on Richmond and attempt to draw Lee's Army of Northern Virginia into a position where the Union armies would be able to destroy it. While Grant's armies set out to "get Lee," the Union Army and Navy would attack the Confederacy at multiple points throughout Georgia, Mississippi, Alabama, and the Carolina coast.

As commander of the Military Division of the Mississippi following Grant's promotion, Sherman was entrusted with preventing Joseph Johnston's Army of Tennessee, the second of the CSA's armies, from coming to Lee's assistance from Georgia. On April 4, Sherman was ordered "to pursue Johnston's army, to break it up and to get into the interior of the enemy's country as far as you can, inflicting all the damage you can against their war resources." Over the next month, Sherman prepared for the coming campaign with characteristic thoroughness. On April 6, he commandeered all available rolling stock and food supplies south of Nashville exclusively for military use. For the next four weeks, an average of 130 locomotives hurtled down the heavily guarded railroad between the Union supply depot at Nashville and its forward supply base at Chattanooga, while horses, pack animals, and herds of cattle were shunted toward the front.

On May 4, some 120,000 Union soldiers crossed the Rapidan River in Virginia, and the following day they clashed with Lee's forces in the dense woodland known as the Wilderness, in a hallucinatory two-day battle of stunning savagery. Over the next six weeks, the two armies were engaged in what Grant later called "as desperate fighting as the world has ever witnessed," a series of ferocious and bloody battles in which the Union armies lost 65,000 men and Lee 35,000.

While this terrible war of attrition was unfolding in Virginia, Sherman began a very different campaign in Georgia. On May 7, the combined armies of the Cumberland, the Tennessee, and the Ohio left Chattanooga, Tennessee, and followed the route of the Western & Atlantic Railroad, which was to be their principal supply conduit. Established in 1773 as a result of a royal charter from King George III, Georgia, the last of the fifteen British colonies, now had one million inhabitants. They had not yet experienced the war firsthand, but their state now became the scene of a dramatic war of maneuver, as a hundred thousand infantry, artillery, cavalry, and engineers advanced cautiously down the railroad toward Atlanta and forced the Army of Tennessee to conduct a series of tactical retreats to avoid being outflanked.

Today it takes just over an hour to drive from Chattanooga to Atlanta. In the summer of 1864, it took Sherman's army more than two months to fight its way to the Chattahoochee River. Sherman generally tried to avoid direct frontal assaults on the well-defended Confederates and attempted to turn Johnston's flanks, while his adversary was equally determined to conserve his forces by avoiding a decisive confrontation. The Union advance was marked by constant skirmishing and vicious small-scale engagements at New Hope Mill, Pickett's Mill, Dallas, and Kennesaw Mountain, where Sherman ordered a rare and costly failed attack on strongly fortified Confederate positions on June 27. Though Confederate cavalry and guerrillas harried Sherman's armies and attempted to cut their railroad supply link, this damage was quickly repaired—under the direction of Sherman's brilliant chief of engineers, Captain Orlando Poe—with an improvisational ability that astonished the rebels, in one instance rebuilding a 780-foot-long trestle bridge across the Chattahoochee River in four days. Throughout this advance, Union soldiers foraged relentlessly to compensate for delays in the flow of supplies, and they burned buildings and houses in retaliation for acts of sabotage and guerrilla attacks. "We have devoured the land and our animals eat up the wheat and corn field close," Sherman wrote to his wife. "All the people retire before us and desolation is behind. To realize what war is one should follow our tracks."[18]

At the beginning of July, Union armies were only eight miles from Atlanta. By this time, Grant's advance on Richmond had stalled. After nearly two months of relentless slaughter that had earned Grant the nickname the Butcher among Northern Democrats, the two armies now faced each other across fifty-mile-long entrenchments around Richmond and the city of Petersburg, and the fighting now took the form of sporadic skirmishes and sharpshooting from the trenches. Once again the Confederate defensive line in Virginia had held, and the appalling casualties horrified the Northern public and boosted the Democratic Party's peace agenda.

As a result, the Lincoln administration's hopes of reelection rested on Sherman's campaign. On July 17, Jefferson Davis lost patience with Johnston's cautious defensive strategy and replaced him with Lieutenant General John Bell Hood. A brave but reckless commander who had lost a leg and the use of an arm and took opiates to kill the pain, Hood immediately threw twenty thousand troops against Union forces at Peachtree Creek on July 20, losing 4,746 men in the first of three attempts to drive Sherman's encircling armies back. The next day, Union batteries opened fire on Atlanta for the first time. On August 1, Sherman ordered his artillery commanders to "fire from ten to fifteen from every gun you have in position into Atlanta that will reach any of its houses. Fire slowly and with deliberation between 4 P.M. and dark."

On August 9, an estimated five thousand exploding shells and cannon shots fell on the city, whose population may have been as large as ten thousand, including refugees who had fled the Union advance. To escape the bombardment, many of its inhabitants were obliged to dig "bombproofs" and "gopher holes" beneath their gardens or by extending their cellars, as Union commanders targeted prominent buildings and used heated shells as incendiaries. Though Sherman told one of his generals that most civilians had "got out" of the besieged city, civilians were inevitably killed in these bombardments. "This seems to me a very barbarous mode of carrying on war, throwing shells at women and children," reflected a local bookseller named Samuel Richards.[19] One Atlanta woman wrote to her husband to report that "a little child was killed in his mother's arms," while another shell killed a neighbor and "his little daughter Lizzie whom you would have seen at our house."[20]

Sherman declared that he would make Atlanta "too hot to be endured" and transform it into a "used-up community by the time we are done with it." On September 1, Union troops captured Jonesboro, twelve miles to the south of Atlanta, closing the city's last connection to the interior. The following day, Hood's army abandoned Atlanta, and on September 4 Sherman sent an exultant telegram to Lincoln announcing that "Atlanta is ours, and fairly won." If Sherman had failed to "break up" the Army of Tennessee, he had nevertheless fixed it in place and captured a major railroad hub that was also a center for the homegrown Confederate armaments industry. The capture of the "Gate City" also effectively won the election for Lincoln. Then, having presented the president with this prize, Sherman took a decision that shocked and horrified many Southerners.

"See the Books"

Only five days after taking control of Atlanta, Sherman informed Hood that he had decided to reserve the city exclusively for military use and that it was "to the interest of the United States that the citizens now residing in Atlanta should remove, those who prefer it to go south, and the rest north." This was not the first time civilians were forcibly evacuated during the Civil War. On August 25, 1863, Sherman's father-in-law, Brigadier General Thomas Ewing, ordered the depopulation of three counties in Missouri in retaliation for Quantrill's raid on Lawrence. Some twenty thousand people were driven from the county and their homes burned, an expulsion that was justified by General John Schofield, then commander of the Department of the Missouri, on the grounds that "all the inhabitants [were] practically the friends of the guerrillas." On July 7, during the advance on Atlanta, Sherman ordered General Kenner Garrard to arrest four hundred mostly female mill workers and their children from two factory towns near Roswell, outside Atlanta, whose factories produced a fabric used to make Confederate tents and uniforms. In Sherman's opinion, their workers were "as much governed by the rules of war as if in the ranks."[21] Accordingly, he ordered Garrard to remove them "no matter what the clamor, and let them foot it, under guard, to Marietta, whence I will send them by cars to the North." Though Sherman specified that the women and their families were to be transported to a "country where they can live in peace and security," they were taken by rail to Louisville, where they eventually wound up in a female military prison.

The evacuation of Atlanta was justified on different grounds. From Sherman's perspective, the continued presence of civilians was both a security threat to his own troops and an additional drain on the food supplies available to his army. Hood reluctantly agreed to comply in an angry letter the following day, in which he accused Sherman of deliberately shelling civilians and condemned the evacuation order as an affront to "the name of God and humanity" and an "unprecedented measure" that "transcends, in studied and ingenious cruelty, all acts ever before brought to my attention in the dark history of war." This prompted an acrimonious exchange in which Sherman denied that his decision was unprecedented and accused the Confederacy of "hundreds" of similar actions.[22]

Sherman insisted that it was not cruelty but "kindness to these families of Atlanta to remove them now, at once, from scenes that women and children should not be exposed to," because his army did not have the capacity to feed them. He also rejected the accusation that he had deliberately shelled civilians and accused Hood of having placed his defensive parapets at Atlanta so close to civilian houses that it was impossible for his artillery to distinguish between military and nonmilitary targets, then concluded with the following scornful riposte: "In the name of commonsense, I ask you not to appeal to a just God in such a sacrilegious manner. You who, in the midst of peace and prosperity, have plunged a nation into war—dark and cruel war—who dared and badgered us to battle. . . . If we must be enemies, let us be men, and fight it out as we propose to do, and not deal in arch hypocritical appeals to God and humanity. God will judge us in due time, and he will pronounce whether it more humane to fight with a town full of woman and the families of a brave people at our back or to remove them in time to places of safety among their own friends and people."

In a long rejoinder, Hood insisted that "there are a hundred thousand witnesses that you fired into the habitations of women and children for weeks, firing far above and miles beyond my line of defense" and accused Sherman of "subjugating free white men, women and children" in order to "place over us an inferior race, which we have raised from barbarism to its present position"— reference to the presence of black soldiers in the Union army. Sherman denied that there were "negro allies" in his army and maintained that "I was not bound by the laws of war to give notice of the shelling of Atlanta, a fortified town, with magazines, arsenals, foundries, and public stores; you were bound to take notice. See the books."

Perhaps the most remarkable aspect of this exchange is that it even took place at all. Victorious generals have never been obliged to explain or justify their decisions to their opponents, and this was just as true in the nineteenth century. Hood's references to "the laws of God and man" and Sherman's reference to the "books" both evoked a corpus of customs or usages of war inherited from the European military tradition, which attempted to limit the impact of war on noncombatants. The work of eighteenth-century legal scholars such as the Swiss jurist Emmerich de Vattel and the French philosopher Jean-Jacques Rousseau received a new impetus in the second half of the nineteenth century as armies, governments, and jurists debated a wide spectrum of military activities that included the treatment of civilians by occupying armies, the appropriation and destruction of private and public property, the conditions under which cities could be bombarded, and the legitimacy of reprisals and other forms of collective punishment in response to guerrilla warfare.

These debates were reflected in the foundation of the International Committee of the Red Cross in 1863, as well as in the Civil War. On April 24, 1863, Lincoln promulgated General Orders No. 100: Instructions for the Government of Armies of the United States in the Field, which laid down a code of conduct for Union commanders in Southern territory.[23] Drawn up by Francis Lieber, a prominent legal scholar of Prussian origin, the "Lieber Code" was the first comprehensive attempt by any government in history to establish the mutual rights and responsibilities of soldiers and civilians in wartime, and many of its provisions were subsequently incorporated into the Hague Conventions regarding the Laws and Customs of War on Land, in 1899 and 1907. The Lieber Code's insistence that "men who take up arms against one another in public war do not cease on this account to be moral beings, responsible to one another and to God" was balanced by its recognition of the principle of military necessity, which was invoked to list a number of conditions in which these moral principles could be disregarded. Thus Article 18 declared: "When a commander of a besieged place expels the noncombatants, in order to lessen the number of those who consume his stock of provisions, it is lawful, though an extreme measure, to drive them back, so as to hasten on the surrender."

Sherman clearly regarded his decision to remove the population of Atlanta as justifiable according to this criterion, and this interpretation was supported in a letter from Halleck that same month: "Not only are you justified by the laws and usages of war in removing these people, but I think it was your duty to your own army to do so. . . . Let the disloyal families of the country, thus stripped, go to their husbands, fathers, and natural protectors, in the rebel ranks; we have tried three years of conciliation and kindness without any reciprocation; on the contrary, those thus treated have acted as spies and guerrillas in our rear and within our lines. Therefore the safety of our armies . . . requires that we apply to our inexorable foes the severe rules of war."[24]

Sherman's conception of militarily necessity evinced his belief that war imposes its own priorities, which do not correspond with those of peacetime. Hood's condemnations were soon followed by an impassioned plea from James Calhoun, the mayor of Atlanta, and two councillors, who asked him to reconsider his evacuation order, which "would involve extraordinary hardship and loss" for a population whose members included pregnant women and women with husbands in the army and no one to look after them. In response Sherman wrote that his orders "were not designed to meet the humanities of the case" and included one his most famous pronouncements, when he declared "You cannot qualify war in harsher terms than I will. War is cruelty, and you cannot refine it."[25]

He also suggested that Calhoun's appeal for mercy had an element of bad faith from a city whose population had previously supported the war and helped make it possible:

Now that war comes home to you, you feel very different. You deprecate its horrors, but did not feel them when you sent car-loads of soldiers and ammunition, and moulded shells and shot, to carry war into Kentucky and Tennessee, to desolate the homes and of hundreds and thousands of good people who only asked to live in peace in their old homes, and under the Government of their inheritance. But these comparisons are idle. I want peace, and believe it can only be reached through union and war, and I will ever conduct war with a view to perfect and early success.

That, as far as Sherman was concerned, was the crux of the matter. Not only had the Confederacy brought such treatment on itself, but Atlanta's role in wartime production meant that its population was also a legitimate military target. Not only was war a form of cruelty that could not be "refined," but the escalation of its "horrors" was an instrument of "perfect and early success" and was therefore more merciful and humane in the long run. The Lieber Code expressed a very similar idea when it declared, "The more vigorously wars are pursued, the better it is for humanity. Sharp wars are brief." And Sherman's reply to Calhoun closed with a rhetorical flourish that held out the prospect of reconciliation in exchange for the South's obedience: "But, my dear sirs, when peace does come, you may call on me for any thing. Then I will share with you the last cracker, and watch with you to shield your homes and families against danger from every quarter. Now you must go, and take with you the old and feeble, feed and nurse them, and build for them, in more quiet places, proper habitations to shield them against the weather until the mad passions of men cool down, and allow the Union and peace once more to settle over your old homes at Atlanta."

Despite his ruthlessness, Sherman still rejected the suggestion that his conduct of the war constituted what would later be called a "war crime" as a personal insult and an insult to his government.

When Hood published extracts from this correspondence in a Macon newspaper, Sherman sent the complete exchange, together with his letter to Calhoun, for publication in Northern newspapers to make sure that his position was understood. In the North, the response was generally positive. "General Sherman says to the Mayor of Atlanta what every true heart in the land confirms and approves," observed *Harper's Weekly*. In the South, Sherman's words were as iniquitous as his actions and transformed him into a hate figure in whom the *Macon Telegraph* saw "all the attributes of man . . . merged in the enormities of the demon, as if Heaven intended in him to manifest depths of depravity yet untouched by a fallen race."

"Making Georgia Howl"

The South would soon have many more reasons to despise Atlanta's conqueror. By the end of September, the city had been emptied of its inhabitants, but Sherman was beginning to have second thoughts about maintaining Atlanta as a military base and retaining a railroad supply line that ultimately extended some 470 miles to Louisville, Kentucky, via Chattanooga and Nashville, much of which passed through hostile territory and was vulnerable to attacks by marauding Confederate cavalry raiders in addition to Hood's roving forty-thousand-strong army. To keep the railroad link open required the continued deployment of large numbers of troops that would undermine the offensive momentum that his armies had acquired, at a time when Grant's armies were already bogged down in Virginia.

Grant suggested in a telegram that Sherman might link with General Edward Canby, the Union commander at New Orleans, and carry out a joint attack on the city of Columbus. Instead Sherman proposed to march his army through central Georgia "hauling some stores, and depending on the country for the balance" with a view to attacking Macon, Augusta, or Savannah, depending on the Confederate response, because "either horn of the dilemma will be worth the battle."[26] On September 26, Grant recommended that Sherman take his army back into Tennessee to counter a possible invasion of the state by Hood or Nathan Bedford Forrest's cavalry.

On September 29, Sherman dispatched a large force under command of the "Rock of Chickamauga," General George H. Thomas, to defend Tennessee against Hood. Two days later, he informed Grant of his intention to "destroy Atlanta and march across Georgia to Savannah or Charleston, breaking roads and doing irreparable damage." This plan became more defined as Hood attempted to lure his army out of Atlanta by cutting the railroad link to Chattanooga. These efforts were partly successful, and Sherman was obliged to venture out of the city to keep his supply line open. But he had no intention of chasing Hood's army indefinitely. On October 10, he suggested to Grant that he "strike out with our wagons for Milledgeville, Millen, and Savannah." This expedition was not designed to capture these cities, because "until we can re-populate Georgia, it is useless for us to occupy it; but the utter destruction of its roads, houses, and people, will cripple their military resources. . . . I can make this march, and make Georgia howl!"

In another telegram two days later, Sherman dismissed the idea of pursuing Hood or defending the railroad: "We cannot remain on the defensive. With twenty-five thousand infantry and the bold cavalry he has, Hood can constantly break my road. I would infinitely prefer to make a wreck of the road and of the country from Chattanooga to Atlanta, including the latter city; send back all my wounded and unserviceable men, and with my effective army move through Georgia, smashing things to the sea." Grant was not averse to a campaign of devastation in principle. That same month, Philip Sheridan was ordered to transform the Shenandoah

Valley into a "barren waste" in an attempt to cut off the flow of food to Confederate guerrillas and Lee's army. On October 7, Sheridan reported the destruction of over two thousand barns and seventy mills, the seizure of four thousand head of livestock, and the killing or distribution of more than three thousand sheep to troops. He boasted that "the Valley, from Winchester up to Staunton, ninety-two miles, will have little in it for man or beast."[27]

Sherman's proposals were not dissimilar, but both Grant and Lincoln were anxious that a three-hundred-mile march through hostile territory might unravel in the face of concerted local resistance. Sherman was already acting as though his plan were a fait accompli. On October 19, he told his chief commissary in Atlanta, General Amos Beckwith, to begin preparations for "my big raid," in which his army would "abandon Atlanta, and the railroad back to Chattanooga, to sally forth to ruin Georgia and bring up on the seashore." In a letter to Halleck that same day, he outlined his intention to carry out a movement that was "not purely military or strategic but will illustrate the vulnerability of the South." The following day, he clarified these "psychological" and symbolic intentions still further when he told General Thomas that his campaign would "demonstrate the vulnerability of the South and make its inhabitants feel that war and individual ruin are synonymous terms."

These observations are an indication of the extent to which Sherman's strategic thinking had moved beyond the Napoleonic concept of the decisive battle. In his standard textbook, *An Elementary Treatise on Advanced-Guard, Out-Post, and Detachment Service of Troops*, Sherman's former tutor at West Point Dennis Hart Mahan argued that "carrying the war into the heart of the assailant's country, or that of his allies, is the surest plan of making him share its burdens and foiling his plans."[28] Sherman's plans were in keeping with these recommendations. Though he shared Grant's belief that the military victory was dependent on the destruction of Lee's Army of Northern Virginia, he identified the inhabitants of the South as a military target in their own right, whose "ruin" would transmit a wider psychological message to the whole population.

The benefits of this course of action were by no means obvious to his superiors in Washington, who were accustomed to more conventional military objectives. Anticipating these objections, Sherman fired off two more telegrams to Grant on November 1, in which he insisted that it was "useless" to pursue Hood. "If I turn back, the whole effect of my campaign will be lost." The following day, Grant conceded that pursuing Hood would mean "giving up all we have gained in territory" and told his friend to "go on as you propose." On November 6, the triumphant Sherman promised "to act in such a manner against the material resources of the South as utterly to negate Davis's boasted threat and promises of protection. If we can march a well-appointed army right through his territory, it is a demonstration to the world, foreign and domestic, that we have a power which Davis cannot resist. This may not be war, but rather statesmanship."

Sherman now accelerated his preparations, as trains shuttled back and forth between Atlanta and Chattanooga, carrying sick and wounded soldiers and surplus artillery and equipment, and bringing new supplies for the coming campaign. Amid the pandemonium and the purposeful movement of soldiers, wagons, and animals, civilians who had not yet left the city crowded onto the last trains with their household pets and what furniture they were able to carry or bribe the guards to let them take on board. On November 8, Sherman issued his Special Orders No. 120, which informed his troops that they had been organized "into an army for a special purpose, well known to the War Department and to General Grant . . . that . . . involves a departure from our present base, and a long and difficult march to a new one. All the chances of war have been considered and provided for, as far as human sagacity can."

Sherman's troops were instructed to take with them only the minimum of supplies and provisions. Servants, noncombatants, and refugees were to be sent back to Tennessee. Each corps was to carry provisions for ten days and forage for three days in its supply wagons, while soldiers were expected to "forage liberally on the country" to make up the rest. While quartermasters and commissary officers continued to accumulate supplies and equipment, teams of soldiers destroyed everything in Atlanta and its surrounding towns that could be of use to the enemy. Using an improvised battering ram and a grappling hook invented by the indefatigable chief of engineers, soldiers knocked down foundries, factories, and railroad installations and tore up a hundred miles of track. On November 12, the telegraph link was cut, leaving his army, as Sherman later put it, "detached from all friends, dependent on its own resources and supplies."

Over the next few days, fires broke out in the business district of Atlanta and eventually destroyed some five thousand homes, creating a conflagration that was visible for miles around. Some fires were caused by pillaging soldiers; others were an accidental consequence of the ongoing destruction. On the morning of November 15, the first of Sherman's columns marched eastward out of the deserted city along the Decatur road. The following day, at seven in the morning, Sherman himself left the smoking ruins of Atlanta with the Fourteenth Corps along the Decatur road, accompanied by the strains of military bands.

Sherman and his soldiers left the city in a buoyant mood. He later wrote, "The day was extremely beautiful, clear sunlight, with bracing air, and an unusual feeling of exhilaration seemed to pervade all minds—a feeling of something to come, vague and undefined, still full of venture and intense interest." The British *Army & Navy Gazette* observed that Sherman "has done either one of

the most brilliant or one of the most foolish things ever per-
formed by a military leader," while the *London Herald* predicted
that the coming campaign would determine whether Sherman
was to become "the scoff of mankind, and the humiliation of the
United States for all time" or whether his name would be "written
on the tablet of fame." Georgia newspapers predicted that Sherman had committed a tactical error that would result in the destruction of his army at the hands of Confederate guerrillas. In a
visit to Macon shortly before his departure, Jefferson Davis exhorted the population of Georgia to ensure that Sherman's armies
would meet the same fate as Napoléon's Grand Army during its
retreat from Moscow—causing Grant to ask sarcastically whether
the Confederate president would be providing the snow. Over the
next month, the hollowness of these aspirations became painfully
apparent, as Sherman's armies showed the South what his "statesmanship" meant.

3

The Destruction Machine

Throughout history, warring armies have burned and destroyed crops and property in order to reduce besieged cities to starvation, to punish rebellion and defiance, to deny food to their opponents, or to prevent invading armies from living off the land. In 1069–70, the Normans adopted a policy of "harrying the North" in response to a baronial rebellion in Yorkshire that was supported by a Danish invasion. The twelfth-century chronicler William of Malmesbury describes how William the Conqueror "ordered both the towns and fields of the whole district to be laid waste; the fruits and grain to be destroyed by fire or by water" in a campaign of "fire, slaughter and devastation" that left "the ground, for more than sixty miles around, totally uncultivated and barren, remaining bare even to this present day."[1]

"Ravaging" expeditions in which foraging was indistinguishable from plunder were a well-established tactic of medieval European warfare, one that was often radically at odds with the prevailing mythology of knightly chivalrous war. The late twelfth-or early thirteenth-century *Chanson des Lorrains* describes a typical spectacle of military depredation that would not have been unfamiliar to Sherman's armies:

> The incendiaries set the villages on fire, and the foragers visit and sack them; the terrified inhabitants are burnt or led apart with their hands tied to be held for ransom. Everywhere alarm bells

ring, fear spreads from side to side and becomes widespread. On all sides one sees helmets shining, pennons floating, and horsemen covering the plain. Here hands are laid on money; there cattle, donkeys and flocks are seized. The smoke spreads, the flames rise, and the peasants and shepherds flee in panic in all directions.[2]

During the Hundred Years War, the armies of King Edward III carried out raiding expeditions known as *chevauchées* in northern France, in which villages, churches, and monasteries were burned and their inhabitants killed. In 1355 Edward's son Edward, better known as the Black Prince, led an army of six thousand to eight thousand English and Gascon soldiers on a seven-hundred-mile circular raid into the Languedoc from Bordeaux to Narbonne. Marching three columns abreast, young Edward's forces attacked more than five hundred villages, towns, and fortified places, amassing more than a thousand wagons laden with booty and bringing back prisoners for ransom, while French knights helplessly observed their progress.

Campaigns of devastation aimed at civilian life and property were also a feature of the more stately conventions of warfare in early modern Europe. In Ireland, Sir Arthur Chichester described operations in 1593 along Lough Neagh in which "We have killed, burnt and spoiled all along the lough within four miles of Dungannon. . . . We spare none of what quality or sex soever, and it has bred much terror in the people, who heard not a drum nor saw not a fire there for a long time."[3] In 1686 Louis XIV attacked the Piedmontese Protestant community called the Vaudois, or Barbets, where many French Huguenots had taken refuge from Catholic persecution. When the Vaudois turned to guerrilla war, the French army carried out mass arrests in the countryside and destroyed or confiscated food and animals till the French commander Marshall Catinet reported, "This country is completely desolated, there are no longer any people or livestock at all."[4]

The most notorious act of devastation in ancien régime Europe took place during the War of the League of Augsburg (1688–97), when Louis XIV set out to establish a defensive cordon of "dead zones" adjoining the French frontiers to protect his kingdoms from invasion. In December 1688, the French minister of war François-Michel Le Tellier, the marquis of Louvois, ordered the French military commander in the Rhenish Palatinate "to completely ruin all the places that you leave along the lower and upper Neckar so that the enemy, finding no forage or food whatever, will not try to approach there."[5] More than a thousand towns and villages were destroyed in these campaigns, with such thoroughness that the "devastation of the Palatinate" was still remembered in the region more than a century later.

Such campaigns were not an aberration in the nineteenth century. During the Peninsular War, General Arthur Wellesley, the future Duke of Wellington, ordered his army to burn crops, villages, and fruit trees in a wide swathe of territory in front of the defensive lines of Torres Vedras that his troops erected around Lisbon—to deny food to the advancing French. These measures eventually forced the half-starved French army to fall back, and they may also have resulted in the deaths of some fifty thousand Portuguese civilians. They nevertheless earned the praise of Napoléon, who complimented Wellesley on his ability to "destroy his enemy without fighting."

Napoléon's armies frequently relied on *le système de maraude* or *le système devastateur* in the countries they conquered—stripped their populations of food and other provisions to maintain their armies. Devastation was used as a punitive measure between 1830 and 1847 during the conquest of Algeria, where French troops under the command of General Thomas Bugeaud carried out destructive raids, or *razzias*, in which crops, orchards, granaries, and villages were burned to suppress indigenous resistance. These measures were described by Alexis de Tocqueville, the great liberal political thinker, as "unfortunate necessities that any people wishing to make war on the Arabs must accept."[6]

At first sight, these precedents make it tempting to regard Sherman's campaigns as a mere continuation of a tradition that is as old as war itself. For Southerners, indeed, Sherman's march was a retrograde throwback to an earlier form of "uncivilized" war that was legitimate only against "savages." But if some of the actions of Sherman's army would not have surprised William the Conqueror or Sir Humphrey Gilbert, his campaign was also recognizably modern in its targets and its strategic intentions. And what makes Sherman's march through Georgia so resonant in the wars that followed is the fact that a democratic state regarded a campaign of strategic devastation against its own citizens as a legitimate instrument of psychological subjugation and politico-military domination.

The Flying Column

The transformation of Sherman's march into a paradigm of military destruction has often been enhanced by evocative metaphors that have variously compared his army to a storm or a typhoon, an expression of divine wrath and retribution, or a "wild Halloween brawl," as Bruce Catton once described it. The novelist E.L. Doctorow described Sherman's army as "a great segmented body moving in contractions and dilations at a rate of twelve or fifteen miles a day, a creature of a hundred thousand feet. It is tubular in its being and tentacled to the roads and bridges over which it travels. It sends out as antennae its men on horses. It consumes everything in its path. It is an immense organism, this army, with a small brain."[7]

Sherman himself wrote of his intention to transform his army into "a mobile machine, willing and able to start at a minute's notice, and to subsist on the scantiest food." By the time he left Atlanta, this "machine" had been carefully streamlined in order to achieve the very specific objectives that he had designed for it. The army that Sherman took with him into central Georgia was less than half the size of the one that he had originally brought with him from Nashville, consisting of four corps reduced to a combined total of roughly 54,000 men, in addition to 5,015 cavalry under command of the rambunctious and egocentric General Hugh Judson Kilpatrick. In order to ensure the maximum "celerity," its supply train was limited to a total of 2,500 wagons, including 600 ambulances, which carried ammunition, and enough food and forage for twenty days, in addition to 14,500 horses, 19,500 mules, and 5, 500 head of cattle to be slaughtered as required. Artillery was also reduced to a minimum, and individual pieces were drawn by teams of four horses rather than the usual three.

To reduce the loads still further, heavier wall tents were limited to officers only; enlisted men were reduced to the light fly sheets they carried with them, each of which formed one half of a pair to make a tent. Apart from their rubber blankets, soldiers carried three days' rations and forty rounds of ammunition in their pockets and knapsacks. A rigorous medical selection process in Atlanta ensured that only the healthiest and strongest soldiers were allowed on the march. To give himself maximum tactical flexibility, Sherman divided his army into two parallel wings, marching roughly twenty miles away from each other. The Fourteenth and Twentieth Corps of the Army of the Cumberland occupied the left, under the command of the New Yorker Major General Henry W. Slocum. On the right marched the Fifteenth and Seventeenth Corps of the Army of the Tennessee, commanded by the devoutly Christian Major General Oliver O. Howard.

With Hood's army absent in Tennessee, Georgia was defended by an ad hoc conglomeration of Confederate forces that included four brigades of the ill-trained and inexperienced Georgia State Militia, various hastily scooped up and under-strength regiments dispersed throughout the state, in addition to fewer than 2,000 cavalry under the command of General Joseph "Fighting Joe" Wheeler, making a total of some 13,000 fighting men. These forces could not hold back an army of nearly 60,000 veteran soldiers, but Sherman was no less aware than Grant that any extended delay would quickly exhaust his army's supplies of food and provisions and leave it vulnerable to hit-and-run attacks. In a state crisscrossed with rivers, creeks, and swamps, determined resistance from even small concentrations of troops might bring his army to a halt.

Sherman's organization and deployment of his army were carefully designed to avoid such bottlenecks. Both wings were preceded by ax-wielding "pioneers," whose task was to rebuild destroyed bridges, clear blocked roads, and cut down trees to "corduroy" the swamps and muddy roads with rows of timber to allow wagons to pass. Each corps included a contingent from Orlando Poe's corps of engineers, equipped with wagons carrying the canvas canoes and light planks that were used to replace destroyed bridges with pontoon bridges up to nine hundred feet long. These preparations transformed his army into two astonishingly mobile "flying columns" that were capable of marching at an average speed of ten to fifteen miles a day with very few stragglers.

From the early hours of the morning until often late in the evening, Sherman's soldiers marched almost continuously in fifty-minute stretches broken by ten-minute rests, with a forty-minute break for lunch at midday, in a line that sometimes stretched for twenty miles, including the cattle and supply trains. In May 1862, it took the overcautious Henry Halleck three weeks to march a hundred-thousand-strong army five miles to capture the city of Corinth. It took Sherman's army less than a month to reach the outskirts of Savannah on December 10. In that time, his army crossed fifteen creeks, streams, and rivers; constructed pontoon bridges at an average of 230 feet per crossing; and chopped down trees to corduroy more than a hundred miles of mud and swamp while fighting constant skirmishes with Confederate cavalry.

This irresistible progress was a testament to Sherman's meticulous planning and organization and also to the skill and motivation of what was then one of the finest and most experienced armies in the world. With Judson "Kill Cavalry" Kilpatrick's horsemen acting as messengers, the two wings invariably arrived when and where they were supposed to, while stripping food from the countryside through a remorselessly effective foraging system. Under Sherman's chief quartermaster, General George L.C. Easton, foraging was carried out with such speed and efficiency that supply wagons barely paused during the march as new quantities of food and other goods were absorbed and distributed among them. Each morning, brigade commanders dispatched foraging parties of approximately fifty men, who were sent out before daylight with details of where the army would be camping at the end of the day. Fanning out five to six miles or more from the main body of the army, these organized teams, as well as more autonomous foragers known as bummers, returned in the early evening or late at night to the next camp, mounted on mules, cows, or horses or in requisitioned buggies and wagons loaded with corn, molasses, sweet potatoes, turkeys, ducks, chickens, and meat, all of which were handed over to the brigade commissary officers.

The success of this system was partly due to Sherman's prewar travels in the South. His exceptional memory for landscape and topographic detail meant that he knew exactly what to expect before leaving Atlanta, and he brought with him a copy of the 1860 census containing precise details of the population and economic resources of every county in the state. As he later boasted to his wife, "No military expedition was ever based on sounder or surer data."[8] The rapid progress of his armies was also due to his own skillful generalship. Whether poring over maps with his staff officers or pacing the campfire in his dressing gown and drawers into the early hours of the morning, Sherman was constantly thinking about the campaign and planning ahead, able to switch tactics and direction in accordance with shifting developments on the ground, with the assistance of his experienced and capable corps commanders, who knew exactly what was expected of them.

As in the Meridian campaign, Sherman divided his army in order to confuse his enemies about his intentions. On leaving Atlanta, the left wing followed the Decatur road through Covington and Madison toward the state capital of Milledgeville—a line of march that seemed to suggest the city of Augusta as its ultimate objective. The right wing, meanwhile, headed farther south through Jonesboro and McDonough, leaving open the possibility of an attack on Columbus or Macon. From a conventional military perspective, any of these cities constituted a potential target. Augusta was the site of the largest gunpowder factory in the CSA; Columbus was the site of the Columbus Arsenal and Armory, the Confederate Quartermaster Depot, and the Naval Iron Works; while Macon contained a number of factories and workshops dedicated to military production.

Rather than commit his troops to a prolonged siege of fortified cities, Sherman chose to bypass them, forcing his opponents to disperse their forces and constantly guess his ultimate direction, using Kilpatrick's infantry as an instrument of deception. On approaching Macon, Kilpatrick's men carried out a feint attack to the very outskirts of the city, while the right wing wheeled north to converge with the left at the state capital of Milledgeville. From there the two armies diverged once again, and Kilpatrick was transferred to the left wing, where he carried out a similar feint toward Augusta, skirmishing with Joseph Wheeler's cavalry at Waynesboro before resuming the march toward Savannah.

By the time it became clear to the Confederacy that both wings were headed toward Savannah, it was too late to do anything about it. With the main Confederate army pinned down in Virginia, only John Bell Hood's forty-thousand-strong Army of Tennessee posed a significant threat to Sherman's forces, a threat that was removed when Hood decided to take his army out of Georgia and invade Tennessee. Successive defeats at Franklin on November 30 and Nashville on December 15–16 decimated Hood's army and eliminated any last possibility that Sherman might have to diverge from his route to defend the state.

As a consequence, Sherman was able to move through Georgia almost at will, using Kilpatrick's cavalry to shield his army from Wheeler's probing attacks. Apart from cavalry skirmishes and occasional sharpshooting attacks, his army faced no significant resistance. The only significant battle of the march took place near the small town of Griswoldville on November 22, when a 1,500-man brigade of the Fifteenth Corps under Brigadier General Charles C. Walcutt easily repulsed a pointless assault by 4,500 ill-trained militia and Georgia state troopers, many of whom consisted of adolescent boys and old men, in which 51 rebels were killed and 471 wounded. On December 10, Sherman's armies reached the swampy outskirts of Savannah and found that the city's defenders had broken open the dikes and flooded the rice fields. Three days later, the Second Division of the Fifteenth Corps stormed the Confederate outpost of Fort McAllister, overlooking the Ogeechee River, thus enabling the Union Navy to resupply Sherman's armies and reopen the "cracker line"—as Union soldiers called their supply line, after the hardtack crackers that were an essential part of their rations.

The dikes were quickly repaired by Poe's unstoppable engineers, and as the waters receded Sherman's army prepared to besiege a city that was defended by ten thousand Confederate troops under the command of Lieutenant General William J. Hardee.

Sherman warned Hardee to surrender and threatened to inflict the "the harshest measures" on the city's population if he was obliged to mount a siege. On the night of December 20, Hardee's forces quietly slipped out of the city across a makeshift causeway, and the following day the Union army entered Savannah. On Christmas Eve, its triumphant commander sent a telegram to Lincoln offering him the city and its cotton as a "Christmas present." Sherman's previous failures were forgotten as the North celebrated a campaign that appeared to confirm the imminent collapse of the Confederacy. Behind him, the March to the Sea had left a trail of misery and destruction that confirmed his reputation as the nemesis of the South and which, to many Southerners, did not seem like war at all.

Smashing Things

In his memoirs Sherman later described the March to the Sea somewhat dismissively as a "mere change of base" that was intended to put his army in a position to assist Grant in Virginia. While this objective certainly figured in his calculations, this explanation does not accord with the motives in his letters and telegrams that preceded the march. Unlike Scott's march on Mexico City in 1847, Sherman's march was not simply intended to get from one place to another, but to eliminate Georgia's war resources and break its communication links to the rest of the South. These objectives were pursued with the same mechanical and workmanlike precision that characterized other aspects of the campaign.

Between Atlanta and Savannah, Sherman's soldiers tore up 317 miles of the Central Georgia Railroad, including the vital junction at Millen where the lines from Savannah, Augusta, Atlanta, and Macon converged, in addition to demolishing and burning railroad depots, warehouses, station buildings, and bridges. In

what was already a well-established procedure, sections of
track were hoisted up simultaneously by hundreds of soldiers,
and the wooden ties burned to make a bonfire on which rails were
softened and twisted around trees or bent into bow shapes—
"Sherman's neckties"—so they couldn't be used again.

After severing the railway and telegraph connections within
the state and between Georgia and the rest of the South, Sherman
did not need to actually capture the cities that the Confederacy was
so anxious to defend. The effectiveness of this strategy was demonstrated by the complete collapse of gunpowder production at
the Augusta powder factory during the march. Factories, cotton
storehouses and cotton gins, flour and salt mills, workshops, tan-
neries, and sawmills with any direct or potential military purpose
were also destroyed. Sherman's soldiers also targeted Georgia's
agricultural production, burning barns and storehouses containing food supplies that they didn't need for themselves, and shooting or bayoneting livestock that they couldn't take with them.
Thousands of exhausted mules and horses were put down with
the blow of an ax or a bullet so that they couldn't be used by the
enemy, and bloodhounds used to pursue slaves were also shot, often at the request of the slaves themselves.

This ongoing slaughter of animals added to the general desolation that accompanied Sherman's army. One Confederate officer
described how "the whole region stunk with putrefying carcasses,
and earth and air were filled with innumerable turkey buzzards
battening upon their thickly strewn death feasts." Sherman's
marching orders in Atlanta had specified that destruction should
be limited to public property and subject to approval from commanding officers. In the early stages of the march, however, soldiers burned property as they saw fit; Georgians were able to
measure the progress of the Union armies by the spreading fires.

"As far as the eye could reach, the lurid flames of burning
buildings lit up the heavens. I could stand out on the veranda and

for two or three miles watch them as they came on," remembered one Georgia woman.[9] During a sixty-five-mile journey to her home in the village of Gordon in Washington County in late December through the "Burnt Country" left by Sherman's troops, Eliza Frances Andrews, the daughter of a local judge, passed through a bleak world of trampled fields, damaged or destroyed property, and slaughtered animal carcasses in which "the dwellings that were still standing all showed signs of pillage, and on every plantation we saw the charred remains of the gin-house and packing screw, while here and there lone chimney-stacks, 'Sherman's Sentinels,' told of homes laid in ashes."[10]

Such testaments tend to give a somewhat misleading picture of universal destruction, which was subsequently embellished further in popular memory. "No one, without being there, can form a

Destruction: *Sherman's March to the Sea*, F.O.C. Darley, lithograph, c. 1883. Courtesy of the Library of Congress.

proper idea of the devastation that will be found in our track," wrote Chaplain Bradley of the Twenty-Second Wisconsin. "Thousands of families will have their homes laid in ashes, and they themselves will be turned beggars in the street. We have literally carried fire and sword into this once proud and defiant land." Yet Sherman's army did not burn every house they came upon, and the majority of Georgian homes, both rich and poor, were not affected by "voluntary incendiarism," which was more likely to be limited to barns, storehouses, and outbuildings.

House burning became less frequent as the march went on, and Sherman's officers were mostly able to keep the destruction within officially designated parameters, which restricted arson to certain public buildings or as a response to acts of resistance or sabotage. At the former state capital, Louisville, Federal troops vandalized and burned much of the town to the ground after a bridge was set on fire by retreating Confederates. On November 29, Andrew J. Boies of the Thirty-Third Massachusetts Volunteer Infantry found what was "once a flourishing town, but today it is a heap of ruins."[11]

A Michigan surgeon described how cotton sheds on the road out of Parks Mill along the Oconee River were "purified by fire. The smoke ascends to the skies bearing aloft the prayers of the Yanks for success & the curses of the rebs for our defeat." Plantation mansions and other symbols of the Southern social order, such as slave auction blocks, prisons, and courthouses, were often singled out for vandalism and destruction, and not always with the orderly precision that Sherman expected from his army. At the genteel state capital of Milledgeville, soldiers trashed the statehouse and trampled its book collection before holding a riotous and drunken mock-legislative meeting in which they revoked Georgia's order of secession. In the town of Madison, in Morgan County, Captain David Conyngham, an officer in Sherman's army and a correspondent with the *New York Herald*, witnessed soldiers dancing on pianos before breaking them up with axes and burning them.[12]

From the point of view of local farmers and householders, foraging was also a form of destruction, and its impact was often exacerbated by pillage and theft, as soldiers robbed silver plate, cutlery, jewelry, silk dresses, pistols, family heirlooms, and watches. In some cases, soldiers beat up and tortured male home owners and slaves to find out where they had hidden valuables, tying ropes around their necks and nearly strangling them to make them talk. Such actions were officially prohibited, but they were not easy to prevent. Though Georgians often went to great lengths to hide their animals, provisions, and valuables in swamps or slave quarters, foragers became adept at locating concealed hiding places in gardens or even cemeteries, prodding at lawns and flower beds with bayonets or ramrods. The most remorseless and skilled foragers were the bummers, who achieved folkloric status in the North. These were ordinary Union soldiers who were assigned to foraging expeditions but often operated on their own in civilian clothes or composite military and civilian outfits. Captain George Whitfield Pepper, a chaplain in Sherman's army, described a typical bummer as "a ragged man, blackened by the smoke of many a pine knot fire, mounted on a scrawny mule, with a gun, a knapsack, a butcher knife and a plug hat, stealing his way through the pine forests far out on the flanks of a column."[13]

According to Pepper, such men subjected the population of Georgia to a "class of devastations" of which "the North has little conception," which included "deliberate and systematic robbery for the sake of gain" and the "wanton destruction of property which they could not use or carry away." Conyngham describes a typical "scene of ruin and pillage" that was often repeated: "Boxes were burst open; clothes dragged about; the finest silks, belonging to the planters' ladies, carried off to adorn some negro wenches around camp; pictures, books, furniture, all tossed about and torn in pieces."[14]

Such behavior was subject to harsh punishments, at least in theory, but Sherman's own officers sometimes complained that he did not discipline his troops with the necessary rigor, and many of his soldiers assumed that they had their commander's tacit approval or interpreted private pillage as the destruction of war matériel. As Conyngham observed with only a modicum of irony, "To draw a line between stealing and taking or appropriating everything for the subsistence of an army would puzzle the nicest casuist," for even plates, jewelry, or watches "were things that rebels had no use for. They might possibly convert them into gold, and thus enrich the Confederate treasury."[15]

All these events formed part of what George Pepper described as "one vast sheet of misery. The fugitives from ruined villages or desolated fields, seek shelter in caves and dens. Cities sacked, towns burned, populations decimated are so many evidences of the desolations of war."[16] These "desolations" also included the destruction of forests and woodland for firewood and timber to make corduroy roads, in addition to the depredations of Wheeler's cavalrymen and assorted Confederate deserters, who seized food and animals with such voracity that Georgians often loathed them as much as Sherman's soldiers. Nevertheless, this devastation was not as apocalyptic as has sometimes been depicted. Evocations of the "sixty-mile swath of destruction" left by Sherman's armies in books and films such as *Gone with the Wind* often conjure up images of a blackened land containing nothing but charred ruins. But compared with the behavior of some twentieth-century armies, Sherman's soldiers were relatively restrained and subject to sufficient discipline to keep their worst instincts in check—most of the time.

From Savannah Sherman sent an audit of destruction to his superiors, which claimed that his armies had seized 6,871 mules and horses, 13,294 head of cattle, 10.4 million pounds of grain, and 10.7 million pounds of fodder and had inflicted $100 million in damages on the Georgian economy, only $80,000 of which he attributed to "simple waste."[17] It is difficult to know how Sherman arrived at these financial calculations or how they were recorded, and the casual reference to "simple waste" suggests they were not as accurate as he claimed. But the destruction of war material was only one component of a campaign that he later stated was intended "to whip the rebels, to humble their pride, to follow them to their innermost recesses, and make them fear and dread us. Fear is the beginning of wisdom."[18] The "demonstration" of the power of the Federal army and government was partly intended to intimidate and overawe the civilian population, but it also contained some of the ingredients of what the Pentagon now calls information warfare.

In a letter to Halleck from Savannah, Sherman wrote that "this war differs from European wars in this particular: we are not only fighting hostile armies, but a hostile people, and must make old and young, rich and poor, feel the hard hand of war, as well as their organized armies. I know that this recent movement of mine through Georgia has had a wonderful effect in this respect. Thousands who had been deceived by their lying newspapers to believe that we were being whipped all the time now realize the truth, and have no appetite for a repetition of the same experience."[19]

The belief that Southern morale or willpower played a decisive role in the Confederate war effort was not limited to Sherman; Southern newspapers frequently issued strident patriotic appeals calling for a collective act of will that would compensate for their defeats and overcome the North's superior material resources. Such appeals were often accompanied by false and inaccurate claims to encourage the population to believe that victory was possible. Sherman's campaigns were specifically designed to crush such expectations, by bringing the "hard hand of war" to the neighborhoods and homes of Southerners. This purpose was clearly understood by many of his soldiers. "Evidently it is a material element in this campaign to produce among the people of Georgia a thorough conviction of the personal misery which attends war, and of the utter helplessness and inability of their 'rulers,' State or Confederate, to protect them," wrote Major Henry Hitchcock, a New York lawyer attached to Sherman's staff as a military secretary. Echoing his commander, Hitchcock described the devastation of Georgia as a "lesson" that "has been well taught and by many has been thoroughly learned" and insisted that "no other teaching can enlighten those who have been drugged & stupefied with the lies & brag of Jeff. Davis and his organs."[20]

There is no doubt that this "lesson" was understood. Many Georgians were stunned by the size of Sherman's army; this was the first time many of them had ever seen Union troops. "They say you are retreating, but it is the strangest retreat I ever saw," one old man told George Pepper at the town of Millen. "Why, dog bite 'em, the newspapers have been lying in this way, all along. They are always whipping the Federal armies, and they always fall back when the battle is over."[21] Sherman regarded destruction as a form of "teaching" and a demonstration of the power of his government, but there were also limits to the amount of pain he was willing to inflict on the population. Though he declared on more than one occasion that it would be necessary to kill three hundred thousand men in order to stabilize the South, neither he nor his government attempted to put such proposals into practice.[22] During the Spanish Civil War, advancing Nationalist troops carried out many massacres and executions of their real or suspected political enemies as they marched northward in a systematic campaign of terror intended to impose what one of Franco's generals described as "mastery" over the population. Sherman also set out to terrorize and overawe Southern civilians, but his campaigns were also intended in the long run to reincorporate the Southern population into the Union as equal citizens, even in the state that he and many of his soldiers held primarily responsible for the war.

The Smoky March

Even before capturing Savannah, Sherman had always intended to join Grant's armies in Virginia via the Carolinas. As the first state to secede from the Union, South Carolina and its planter aristocracy were particularly despised by Sherman and many of his soldiers. "With Savannah in our possession, at some future time if not now, we can punish South Carolina as she deserves," he told Grant on December 17. "I do sincerely believe that the whole United States, North and South, would rejoice to have this army turned loose on South Carolina, to devastate that State in the manner we have done in Georgia."[23] After briefly considering the possibility of bringing Sherman's armies from Savannah to Virginia by sea, Grant once again agreed to give Sherman his head, and the latter began preparing for a campaign that was more challenging than Georgia.

With its swamps and waterlogged lowlands, nine major rivers and innumerable streams and creeks, South Carolina presented formidable obstacles to an invading army and the state was also better defended. A total of 33,450 Confederate infantry, cavalry, and militia were deployed in South and North Carolina, which included the Army of Tennessee, made up of the remnants of Hood's battered army and Hardee's garrison from Savannah, under the command of Sherman's reinstated adversary Joseph Johnston in addition to cavalry and militia.

Sherman undertook his preparations for what Grant called his "January project" with characteristic thoroughness. His chief quartermaster and commissary officers were ordered to the Union-controlled city of New Bern in North Carolina to oversee a buildup of supplies, and his engineers repaired the stretch of the Atlantic and North Carolina Railroad that was under Union control to ensure that provisions were waiting for his army when it arrived. As in Georgia, Sherman's men were instructed to carry only minimal supplies and live off the land, but this time his officers were deprived of their wall tents and obliged to use the same bivouacs as enlisted men in a campaign that promised to be more explicitly punitive than its predecessor. "The truth is, the whole army is burning with an insatiable desire to wreak vengeance on South Carolina," he wrote to Halleck on Christmas Eve. "I almost tremble at her fate, but feel she deserves all that seems in store for her."[24]

Heavy rains delayed his army's departure, so that it was not until February 1 that Sherman set out once again, with 60,000 infantry and cavalry, 40,000 animals, and 3,000 wagons equipped with twenty days' rations. Following his modus operandi in Georgia, Sherman continued with his "horns of a dilemma" strategy and again divided his army into two wings, marching within supporting distance of each other. For the first two days, all four corps marched toward Augusta between the Savannah and the Salkehatchie Rivers. On February 3, the Seventeenth Corps veered right and crossed the flooded Salkehatchie. Wading waist- and sometimes shoulder-deep in icy water and holding their rifles and cartridge belts above their heads, Federal troops drew Confederate fire while their companions outflanked the Confederate positions in floats and rafts, enabling the rest of the army to erect pontoon bridges and cross behind them.

The two wings continued to make their way through the swamps and water channels at an astonishing pace, dragging wagons that sometimes sank in the mud and water and had to be unloaded and reloaded by up to seventy-five men. Once again, Sherman's pioneers and engineers played a vital role in making this rapid

progress possible, hacking their way through swamps, laying corduroy roads, and erecting pontoon bridges, as the left wing feinted
toward Augusta while the right moved east toward Charleston,
which was already blockaded by the Union Navy. This rapid progress astounded Sherman's adversary Joe Johnston, who later wrote
that "there had been no such army in existence since the days of
Julius Caesar," but it was facilitated by poor judgment by General
Beauregard, the overall commander of Confederate forces in the
Carolinas. As Major George Nichols, one of Sherman's staff officers, observed, "Beauregard committed the gross error of attempt-
ing to defend cities of no strategic importance" instead of using the
terrain to his advantage and concentrating his forces along the
Salkehatchie River.[25]

Having crossed the river, Sherman's forces now proceeded to
inflict on South Carolina the punishment they believed it deserved. In December Halleck had urged Sherman to raze Charleston to the ground, as Rome did to Carthage, and leave "a little
salt . . . sown upon its site," in order to "prevent the growth of future crops of nullification and secession."[26] In the event, Sherman
did not enter Charleston. Instead Union forces tore up some fifty
miles of the South Carolina Railroad track west of Branchville on
February 11, thereby cutting off Charleston from the interior and
leaving it to surrender to the navy while both wings continued
toward the state capital, Columbia. No sooner had Sherman's soldiers entered South Carolina than they began burning towns,
farms, and plantations. On February 13, David Conyngham entered Orangeburg to find "the smoking ruins of the town, the
tall, black chimneys looking down upon it like funeral mutes,
and . . . old women and children, hopeless, helpless, almost fren-
zied, wandering amongst the desolation."[27] At Barnwell all public
buildings were burned, including the courthouse and the Ma-
sonic Hall, as well as various private homes, leaving "only the

chimneys standing like grim sentinels," as one local resident de-scribed it, and causing Sherman's cavalry commander Kilpatrick to rename the town "Burnwell."

As in Georgia, Sherman's orders specified that only houses that had been abandoned were to be burned, but these orders were not always obeyed. "I never saw so much destruction of property be-fore," wrote Charles Wills. "Orders are as strict as ever, but our men understand they are in South Carolina and are making good their old threats. Very few houses escape burning, as almost ev-erybody has run away from before us, you may imagine there is not much left in our track. Where a family remains at home they save their house, but lose their stock, and eatables."[28]

Another Union veteran described how "the army burned ev-erything it came near in the state of South Carolina, not under orders but in spite of orders. . . . Our track through the state is a desert waste." Crops, railroads, plantations, courthouses, public records offices, libraries, and plantations were burned, vandalized, or destroyed in the course of the "smoky march," and the homes of the despised slave-owning South Carolina "chivalry" were sin-gled out for special punishment. On the west bank of the Ashley River, a favorite summer retreat for wealthy Charlestonians, nu-merous mansions were burned and looted. At one plantation near Hartsville, in Darlington County, soldiers ransacked drawers, trunks, and closets, stealing money, jewelry, and clothes from own-ers and servants, before making a bonfire of Bibles and hymnals.

Similar scenes were enacted all along the forty-mile-wide strip that the two wings of Sherman's army passed through. "Where our footsteps pass, fire, ashes, and desolation follow in their path," observed Nichols in his diary. "The sufferings which the people will have to undergo will be most intense. We have left on the wide strip of country we have passed over no provisions which will go any distance in supporting the people," wrote Major Thomas Os-born, Sherman's chief of artillery.[29] George Pepper recalled,

"Wherever a view could be had from high ground, black columns of smoke were seen rising here and there within a circuit of twenty or thirty miles. Solid built chimneys were the only relics of plantation houses after the fearful blast had swept by. The destruction of houses, barns, mills, &c., was almost universal."[30]

As in Georgia, Sherman's soldiers foraged relentlessly and destroyed or spoiled what they did not need, emptying granaries and spilling their contents into the street and slaughtering livestock till farms and public roads were littered with butchered cattle, hogs, and mules. Even more than in Georgia, foraging became a justification for vandalism and theft, as soldiers broke into houses, destroying furniture, paintings, and photographs and the contents of libraries with malicious relish, sometimes torturing slaves and white householders to make them reveal the whereabouts of valuables and goods. In some cases, valuables were shipped to the North from Charleston—including a melodeon looted from a church by one of Sherman's generals. The Confederate general Richard Taylor disgustedly described a visit to Washington shortly after the war, filled with demobilized soldiers and "hundreds of volunteer generals . . . gorged with loot" accompanied by women "resplendent in jewels, spoil of Southern matrons."[31]

Some of this loot undoubtedly came from Georgia and the Carolinas. The Carolinian novelist William Gilmore Simms described the looting and vandalism of wealthy South Carolina homes, in which "choice pictures and works of art, from Europe, select and numerous libraries, objects of peace wholly, were all destroyed. The inhabitants, black no less than white, were left to starve, compelled to feed only upon the garbage to be found in the abandoned camps of the soldiers."[32] At one plantation near Barnwell, a Mrs. Alfred Proctor Aldrich described how her house was visited by successive waves of Union soldiers who "ate like hungry wolves," then broke bureaus and wardrobes with their bayonets, hunting for gold, silver, and jewelry, tearing open feather beds, and smashing furniture and musical instruments. "We have marched through the heart of South Carolina, living off the country as we went, destroyed everything before us, including houses, cotton-gins, leaving many a woman and child in a state of starvation," wrote Andrew Boies on March 25. "It will beat all the raids that we have made yet. It will take years to put it back into shape, as it was when we first marched into it."[33]

As in Georgia, Sherman's soldiers also ruined newspaper offices and printing presses. Though the destruction was generally confined to property, there were incidents in which slaves and white householders were murdered by soldiers in the course of robberies and foraging expeditions. Such actions were not official policy, and Union officers tried to prevent pillaging, carrying out impromptu inspections of soldiers' knapsacks, camps, and wagons and in some cases returning stolen goods to their owners. But many of Sherman's soldiers believed that South Carolina deserved everything it got and rationalized their actions in terms identical to those used by their commanding officer. As one Ohio sergeant wrote, "Every house, barn, fence and cotton gin gets an application of the torch. That prospect is revolting, but war is an uncivil game and can't be civilized."[34]

The Burning of Columbia

The targeting of cities was always an important component of the Union's hard-war policy, whether because of their significance as industrial centers and transportation hubs or as symbols of Confederate political power. For many Southerners, the most shocking and visible evidence of the war's destructive power was the transformation of towns and cities, which had previously been regarded as symbols of civilized progress and material prosperity, into the ruined "chimneyvilles" that dotted the South. With the advent of photography, Americans were presented with images of urban devastation that would later become so familiar to the twentieth century—hollowed-out roofless buildings, piles of rubble, and protruding chimneys at Charleston, Vicksburg, Richmond, Atlanta, and other cities. When Sherman's army entered Atlanta, the spectacle of destruction shocked even his own soldiers. "I had often heard of the terror of bombardment of a crowded city, but I never realized it before," wrote the Union surgeon J.C. Patton, who observed buildings "torn in every shape that can be imagined," trees cut down and fences destroyed, "in short every kind of mischief done by these iron missiles."[35]

By the time the Union army abandoned the city in November, some 35 percent of it had been burned down or destroyed, either by Hood's retreating army or by Sherman's soldiers. When the first refugees returned at the end of November, they found what one eyewitness called "an ocean of ruins" inhabited by roving packs of feral dogs, where "the putrid carcasses of dead horses and mules met the eye, while the stench that exhaled from them filled the air, producing a loathing on the part of all who ventured into the city, unutterably disgusting."[36] Similar scenes accompanied the progress of Sherman's vengeful army through the Palmetto State. Though the destruction of Charleston did not fit Sherman's war plans, Union naval bombardments were sufficient to destroy 1,500 out of 5,000 homes, leaving what the Northern reporter Sidney Andrews described as "a city of desolation, of vacant homes, of widowed women, of deserted warehouses, of weed wild gardens . . . of miles of grass grown streets."[37] The most "Carthaginian" act of urban destruction during Sherman's march through the Carolinas took place on February 17, 1865, when his army occupied Columbia.

Before the war, Columbia was a prosperous city of some 8,000 residents, half of whom were slaves. With gas lighting and three railroads, it was a city that the celebrated Carolinian diarist Mary

Chestnut described as "the place for good living, pleasant people, pleasant dinners, pleasant drives." By the time the city surrendered to Sherman's troops, its population had grown to 24,000, including many evacuees and young women sent from the countryside to what was considered to be a safer environment. Though it contained some factories that had been reconfigured for military purposes, Columbia was essentially an administrative center whose significance to Sherman's army was largely due to its political symbolism as the capital of the "cradle of secession."

The day before entering the city, Sherman told General Oliver Howard to "occupy Columbia, destroy the public buildings, railroad property, manufacturing and machine shops; but [we] will spare libraries, asylums, and private dwellings." He was nevertheless aware that many of his soldiers wanted to go further than this—a sentiment summed up in their reworking of the song "Hail, Columbia," with its refrain "Hail, Columbia, happy land! / If I don't burn you, I'll be damned." The city was already beginning to burn on the morning of February 17, when the local plantation owner General Wade Hampton III ordered his retreating cavalry to set fire to bales of cotton in the street. For the rest of the day, fires continued to spread as Union troops poured into the city and proceeded to burn buildings on their own account. Many soldiers were given alcohol by the local population in a misconceived attempt to pacify their conquerors, but these efforts had the opposite effect.

In the course of the night, much of the city was burned to the ground, as drunken soldiers and freed slaves rampaged through the streets in a wild spree of looting, burning, and vandalism, driving much of the population into the streets. "Streams of pale women, leading their terrified children, with here and there an infant in arms, went by, they knew not whither, amid the fierce flames," wrote Columbia resident Reverend Anthony Toomer Porter. "The streets were filled with soldiers mounted and on foot, in every stage of drunkenness. . . . Shouts of derision and blasphemy filled the air. Cries of 'There are the aristocrats!' 'Look at the chivalry!' were yelled into the ears of these defenseless women. Men seemed to have lost their manhood, and the mere beast was in the ascendant."[38]

At the Ursuline convent, soldiers broke into the chapel in search of the chalice, ransacked the dormitories of the convent school, and broke into pupils' trunks before the convent was eventually burned. Union officers made some attempts to put these fires out and control their troops, but numerous eyewitnesses saw soldiers setting fire to private homes and public buildings and cutting fire-engine hoses with bayonets. "I myself saw men with balls of cotton dipped in turpentine enter house after house," wrote Reverend Porter. "Some would take bottles of turpentine, throw the liquid round about, and then set it on fire." Other eyewitnesses described how Union soldiers threw grenades and "fireballs" at the women and children who spent the night in the park to escape the fires or because their homes had been destroyed.

By morning Columbia had become a scene of urban devastation with which the twentieth century would become familiar—a city, as Conyngham described it, "wrapped in her own shroud, the tall chimneys and blackened trunks of trees looking like so many sepulchral monuments, and the woe-stricken people, that listlessly wandered about the streets, its pallid mourners. Old and young moved about seemingly without a purpose. Some mournfully contemplated the piles of rubbish, the only remains of their late happy homesteads."[39]

The "burning of Columbia" has always been one of the most egregious crimes attributed by Southerners to Sherman's army. Sherman blamed the fires on the burning of cotton by Wade Hampton's cavalry and pointed out that his men had tried to prevent it and had distributed food to the homeless population. These claims were rejected by William Gilmore Simms, who fled to the city after the sacking of his plantation. In a detailed account of the sacking of Columbia that was published in installments in a tri-weekly newspaper, the *Columbia Phoenix*, within weeks of the withdrawal of Sherman's forces, Simms maintained that Sherman's army had been under "perfect discipline" throughout the destruction of the city and that "General Sherman knew what was going on, yet kept aloof and made no effort to arrest it, until daylight on Saturday."[40]

If Sherman did not specifically order the city's destruction, he took few precautions that might have prevented it and showed few regrets afterward. "Though I never ordered it and never wished it," he wrote later, "I have never shed many tears over the event, because I believe it hastened what we all fought for, the end of the

". . . like so many sepulchral monuments." Ruins seen from the capital, Columbia, South Carolina, 1865. Photographed by George N. Barnard. Courtesy of the National Archives (165-SC-56).

war." Many of his soldiers agreed. Even Conyngham believed that the destruction of the city had an exemplary impact on the population of the state, so that "white table-cloths were suspended from windows, with 'Have mercy on me!' for a legend, and the fiery spirit of South Carolina was tamed effectually."[41]

These pleas frequently fell on deaf ears, as Sherman's soldiers continued to burn their way through the state. "From Columbia to Blackstocks, there was scarcely a dwelling left. Horses, barns, ricks, shanties, fences, ploughs, all shared the same fate, while the carcases of horses, mules, cows, hogs, sheep, strewed the earth; killed in the most barbaric wantonness of power," wrote the Columbia physician Daniel H. Trezevant.[42] At Mary Chestnut's hometown of Camden, the local newspaper reported that Sherman's army had "run through the gamut, from impertinence to outrage, from pilfering to wholesale spoliation. Many families have been stripped of everything they had in the world." Whether ordered or not, this destruction was in keeping with Sherman's concept of devastation as a form of statesmanship and as a means of long-term pacification and punishment, but some of it was also directed toward more immediate purposes.

"Not War but Murder"

In Carolina as in Georgia, the population was mostly unmoved by appeals from Southern politicians, generals, and newspapermen to wage guerrilla warfare against Sherman's invading army. Nevertheless sixty-four bummers were found dead during the march toward Savannah, and others disappeared, presumably killed by cavalrymen or by local inhabitants. In South Carolina, Confederate cavalrymen executed foragers on sight, sometimes leaving them by the side of the road with their throats cut and a note declaring DEATH TO FORAGERS. In both states, Sherman's columns came under sporadic fire from bushwhackers and sharp-shooters, and the absence of more concerted resistance was partly due to the measures that Sherman took to prevent it.

As military governor of Memphis, Sherman was a stern advocate of collective punishment in response to acts of sabotage or sharpshooter attacks on Union steamboats on the Mississippi. On September 23, 1862, a Union packet steamer came under fire from the vicinity of a small town, Randolph, that was under his jurisdiction. In response Sherman ordered Colonel Charles C. Walcutt, commander of the Forty-Sixth Ohio Infantry Regiment, to burn the town. Walcutt carried out these orders so well that Sherman was able to inform Grant afterward with his usual brusqueness in such matters, "The regiment has returned and Randolph is gone."

Sherman's marching orders in Atlanta instructed his officers to inflict "a devastation more or less relentless" in response to acts of resistance or sabotage, and these orders were carried out on various occasions. In one incident, Sherman ordered the destruction of a farm at Buffalo Creek near Milledgeville in retaliation for the burning of a nearby bridge. When Henry Hitchcock suggested that it was unfair to punish someone who might not have been responsible, Sherman replied that individual responsibility was not the issue. "If they find that burning bridges only destroys their own citizens' houses, they'll stop it. . . . In war everything is right that prevents anything."[43]

Such views were by no means anomalous, either in the Civil War or in the broader context of nineteenth-century warfare. To most nineteenth-century armies, partisans and guerrillas who fought without uniforms or identifying marks were bandits, re-voltés, and Francs tireurs rather than legitimate combatants and were not protected by the usages of war. During the Napoleonic Wars, French armies took leading citizens hostage and sometimes fined or shot them in retaliation for guerrilla attacks, and carried out indiscriminate reprisals against the civilian population that included the burning of their homes and villages and exemplary massacres. In his *Narrative of the Peninsular Campaign*, the British general Sir William Francis Patrick Napier stated, "An insurrection of armed peasants is mere anarchy," and so "the right to burn their villages must rest on the principle of necessity."[44]

The Union Army's response to bushwhacking and guerrilla warfare belonged to the same tradition. When one of Philip Sheridan's most popular officers was murdered during his October campaign in the Shenandoah Valley, reportedly by Confederate guerrillas, Sheridan ordered General George Armstrong Custer to burn every home within a five-mile radius.[45] Sherman generally ensured that reprisals and acts of punitive destruction were proportional to the acts that had provoked them—in his own mind, at least. During the Atlanta campaign, he decreed that anyone who attempted to damage the railroad or telegraph lines should be "shot without mercy" or deported to Honduras or Santo Domingo, and he ordered his officers to notify the population along the line of march that his army would "of necessity strip the country and destroy all things within reach" in response to any disruption in his supply line.[46]

In South Carolina, he decreed that any killings of foragers would be followed by the execution of Confederate prisoners. When a Union soldier was found dead near the town of Cheraw in South Carolina, with a DEATH TO FORAGERS placard around his neck, a group of prisoners was ordered to draw lots to see who would be executed, and an aging Methodist preacher named Small drew the black-marked slip and was shot by a reluctant firing squad.

Sherman was particularly outraged by the Confederate tactic of burying shells or "torpedoes" as mines along the roads or along railroad tracks. In his memoirs, he describes how he came across "a handsome young officer, whose foot had been blown to pieces by a torpedo planted in the road," waiting for a surgeon to amputate his leg at the knee along the road to Savannah. "There had been no resistance at that point, nothing to give warning of danger, and the rebels had planted eight-inch shells in the road, with friction-matches to explode them by being trodden on," Sherman recalled. "This was not war, but murder, and it made me very angry."[47] In response he ordered a group of Confederate prisoners to clear the rest of the road with picks and shovels. These soldiers "begged hard, but I reiterated the order, and could hardly help laughing at their stepping so gingerly along the road."

In the event, none of the prisoners was killed. Looking back on this episode, Sherman declared, "Prisoners should be protected, but mercy is not a legitimate attribute of war. Men go to war to kill or be killed if necessary and should expect no tenderness. . . . But it was, I think, a much better show of tenderness for me to have the enemy do this work than to subject my own soldiers to so frightful a risk." This indignation ignored the fact that he himself sometimes ordered his soldiers to pile branches on top of bent railroad ties to conceal shells that would blow up anyone trying to retrieve them. If Sherman was not always morally consistent, neither was he as implacable as he was sometimes depicted. In Sandersville, Georgia, he watched Confederate cavalry set fire to stacks of fodder just outside the town and use civilian buildings for cover during their retreat. Even though these actions breached the rules that he had imposed, he did not inflict "general devastation" on the town and told a preacher who pleaded on behalf of the female population and their families, "I don't make war on women and children." For the most part, Sherman's resort to collective punishment and reprisals in response to irregular warfare was focused, selective, and pragmatic, geared toward the achievement of his military objectives and the security of his troops.

Endgame

This pragmatism was also evident in his use of physical destruction as an instrument of pacification and subjugation. On March 7, the advance units of the Twentieth Corps crossed the state line into North Carolina, and the bulk of Sherman's army followed the next day. Some of the worst environmental destruction of the campaign took place in North Carolina, as soldiers set fire to the pine forests and resin pits that formed the basis of South Carolina's turpentine and tar industry, causing huge fires that illuminated their progress, till one Union stretcher bearer described how Sherman's army was visible at night only "by glimpses under the smoke and muffled by the Niagara-like roar of the flames as they licked turpentine and pitch."

Sherman's soldiers were generally more restrained in North Carolina, the last state to join the rebellion, than they had been in South Carolina, and Sherman made more effort to restrain them, especially as it became clearer that the war was coming to an end. On February 2, Union troops captured Wilmington, depriving the Confederacy of its last port. On March 11, Sherman's army reached Fayetteville, where it proceeded to destroy the Confederate arsenal, various foundries, and the offices and paper mills of the town's three newspapers. After pausing to reoutfit his troops and evacuate the wounded soldiers and slaves who had joined his army, Sherman took his army over the Cape Fear River on pontoon bridges and continued its inexorable advance.

Once again Sherman confused the Confederate defenders, sending four light divisions toward the state capital, Raleigh, in the northwest while the bulk of his army converged in two separate wings on Goldsboro, which was defended by the remnants of Joseph Johnston's Army of Tennessee and other Confederate units. On March 19, Johnston's forces sallied out of Goldsboro and attacked Slocum's left wing near the town of Bentonville. A three-day battle produced the bloodiest fighting since Sherman's army had left Atlanta, before Johnston's army was driven back at the cost of 2,600 casualties. Sherman called off a follow-up attack by General Joseph Mower's brigade that might have captured Johnston's entire army, but this error, if such it was, soon became irrelevant as Sherman's forces entered Goldsboro on March 23 without resistance, where it joined Schofield's Army of the Ohio to form a combined force of 90,000 men.

With Union armies tearing through its territory from multiple directions, the Confederacy was now close to collapse. On March 22, Major General James Harrison Wilson, the twenty-three-year-old chief of cavalry in Sherman's Military Division of the Mississippi, led 13,480 cavalrymen on a 525-mile raid into Georgia, capturing the cities of Columbus and Macon and destroying their factories, arsenals, railroads, and rolling stock.[48] On April 1, Grant finally broke through the Confederate defensive line southwest of Petersburg, forcing Lee's army to abandon Richmond two days later. On April 9, Sherman told his wife that he was preparing to march on Raleigh to confront the remnants of Johnston's army. "Poor North Carolina will have a hard time, for we sweep the country like a swarm of locusts," he wrote. "Thousands of people may perish, but they now realize that war means something else than vain glory and boasting. If Peace ever falls to their lot they will never again invite War."[49]

That same day, Robert E. Lee surrendered to Grant at Appomattox, and Sherman finally turned off the destruction machine. On April 13, his troops occupied Raleigh, and the following day he issued Special Field Orders No. 55, which ordered his troops to refrain from "further destruction of railroads, mills, cotton, and produce . . . without the specific orders of an army commander" and ensure that "the inhabitants will be dealt with kindly, looking to an early reconciliation." Even after the assassination of Abraham Lincoln on April 15, these orders were obeyed. On April 26,

Joe Johnston surrendered his army at Bennett Farm, near Durham, and the Civil War was to all intents and purposes over, and so too was the seven-hundred-mile march that Sherman described as "by far the most important in conception and execution of any act of my life."[50]

4

Civilians and Soldiers

For a conquered population in wartime, the first sight of an invading or occupying army in their streets and cities provides definitive proof of its own defeat and the overwhelming power of the victors. In August 1914, many Belgians heard the advancing German army long before they saw it, through the rhythmic pounding of hobnailed boots on the roads. The American journalist Richard Harding Davis described the arrival of the first German units in Brussels as "something uncanny, inhuman, a force of nature like a landslide, a tidal wave, or lava sweeping down a mountain."[1] On April 27, 1941, the French consul in Greece, Xavier Lecureuil, witnessed SS troops marching through the port of Patras "with a heavy but quick step, human 'robots' forming two rectangles of iron, they give an impression of invincible force."[2]

In the course of America's wars, civilian populations throughout the world have witnessed the arrival of victorious U.S. armies. In 1805, U.S. Marines and assorted mercenaries briefly occupied the city of Derna in Cyrenaica during the First Barbary War, the first time that the U.S. flag was flown over a foreign city. Since then U.S. armies have marched as conquerors, liberators, occupiers, and sometimes as a combination of all three through an extensive list of foreign capitals and cities that includes Mexico City, Manila, Berlin, Rome, Palermo, Tokyo, Paris, Seoul, Santo Domingo, Port-au-Prince, and Baghdad. In some cases, U.S. soldiers have been greeted with kisses, flowers, and celebrating crowds; at other times, with sullen defiance, anger, and resentment, followed by bullets and bombs.

Many Southerners regarded the "Yankee ruffians" and "Yankee Vandals" who marched through their previously inviolable heartlands as a foreign army. In 1861 the *Raleigh Banner* described Lincoln's armies as "the sewers of the cities—the degraded, beastly outscourings of all quarters of the world."[3] For many Georgians and Carolinians, their first sight of Sherman's army was a terrifying and also awe-inspiring spectacle. Grace Elmore, the daughter of a wealthy Carolinian family in Columbia, watched Sherman's army take an entire day to pass her front gate in the state capital like a "a huge serpent trailing its mighty length throughout our land, the maker of famine and desolation wherever it goes."[4] Another Columbia resident, Mrs. Harriott H. Ravenel, described how "the immense column of men, cannon and baggage wagons filed past us, on its way to North Carolina . . . like a world in arms" following the burning of the city. "The utter helplessness of a conquered people is perhaps the most tragic feature of a civil war or any other sort of war," remembered the Georgia female suffragist Rebecca Latimer Felton, who was visiting her grandmother in Crawfordville when Sherman's army feinted toward Macon.[5]

Cinematic references to Sherman's campaigns in *The Birth of a Nation* and *Gone with the Wind* portray Sherman's army as a conquering horde or an irresistible juggernaut, trampling everything in its path. In D.W. Griffiths's racist epic, a homeless and terrified Georgia woman huddles with her children in the countryside while Sherman's triumphant army marches below them, accompanied by the caption "While the women and children weep, a great conqueror marches to the sea." This image of Sherman the Great Destroyer overwhelming a defenseless civilian population with ruthless Yankee power has remained essential to the Lost Cause myth. But the encounters between soldiers and civilians in Georgia and the Carolinas produced a strikingly wide range of responses on both sides, some of which are common to all wars, and some of which can tell us a great deal, not only about the prevailing norms and expectations of wartime during the Civil War, but also about the interactions between the U.S. army and civilians in the wars that followed.

A Hostile People

Most civilians encountered Sherman's army for less than twenty-four hours, but the meeting was often a harrowing ordeal, as a seemingly endless line of soldiers marched past and often into their homes, stripping them of the food and possessions that their predecessors had not taken. "Like demons they run in!" wrote Dolly Sumner Lunt Burge, a New England native and widow of a Southern husband, about Union soldiers at her plantation near Covington, Georgia. "My yards are full. To my smoke-house, my dairy, pantry, kitchen, and cellar, like famished wolves they come, breaking locks and whatever is in their way." By the time the last remnants of Sherman's army had left the next day, Lunt Burge claimed to have been left "poorer by thirty thousand dollars than I was yesterday morning. And a much stronger Rebel!"[6]

Many Georgians and Carolinians were terrified of the "Vandal Sherman" long before they saw his army. "Yesterday I broke down— gave way to abject terror under the news of Sherman's advance with no news of my husband," wrote Mary Boykin Chestnut on January 14, 1865. Grace Elmore agonized over whether it was sinful to commit suicide to avoid being "maltreated" by Union soldiers as the "Sherman horror" approached Columbia. Sherman was amused by the dread reputation that preceded his army, but he also recognized its usefulness. "The soldiers and people of the South entertained an undue fear of our Western men and, like children, they invented such ghostlike stories of our prowess in

Georgia, that they were scared by their own inventions," he recalled. "Still, this was a power and I intended to utilize it."[7]

With most military-age men in the army or in hiding to avoid military service, this power was directed mostly at women, children, the elderly, and their slaves and servants, the ones who remained on farms and plantations. Among the white population, the reactions to the Federal army covered a wide gamut of fear, anger, sullen defiance, and resignation or stunned disbelief. One Union soldier mocked the local inhabitants who "look and act scornful and indignant to think that the Yankees should have dared to tread the sacred soil of Georgia." An Illinois soldier from the Seventeenth Corps passed an "old man to right of road—arms folded, looking over his silent home and desolate fields!" as the Union army crossed the Oconee River in Georgia. Another described householders watching their homes being looted "with grim despair depicted on their countenances."

Rich plantations were always more likely to suffer such depredations, but poverty did not guarantee immunity. Union soldiers were often shocked at the primitive living conditions of the Southern "white trash" they encountered. Nevertheless foragers stripped even the humblest farms and shacks and sometimes burned them, particularly in South Carolina. Nor was age always respected. Sherman had declared his intention to make "old and young" feel the weight of war, and elderly people were sometimes selected for special treatment because of their vulnerability, rather than in spite of it. Caroline Ravenel, a resident of Anderson, South Carolina, described how soldiers threatened to hang her grandmother if she did not reveal where her family had concealed its valuables, and went on to hang her sixty-year-old uncle from his bedstead, pulling him up and down various times before beating him with a shovel in an attempt to make him talk.[8]

Such practices were fairly common, according to George Pepper, who described a typical routine in which Sherman's bummers "come to a house where an old man may be found . . . they assume that he has gold and silver hidden, and demand it. If he gives up the treasure cheerfully he escapes personal violence. If he denies the possession of the treasure and they . . . do not believe him they resort to violent means to compel him to surrender." Children were also exposed to the "hard hand of war" in various ways. In Atlanta, young children were killed during the Union bombardment and lost their homes when Sherman expelled the civilian population from the city. Some became refugees a second time when his army marched into central Georgia. "Sherman is swooping down through Georgia from mountains to coast, scattering frightened women and children in his path, like a swooping eagle among a flock of doves," reported the scientist Joseph LeConte, a Georgia refugee working in Columbia who returned to his plantation in December 1864 to evacuate some of his relatives before the Union army reached them.[9]

As in all wars, children were entirely dependent on the adults who looked after them. When their parents went hungry, they also went hungry. When their homes were destroyed, they also became homeless. Three days after the capture of Atlanta, James Comfort Patten saw a mother skinning a dead cow by the side of the road as his unit marched into the city, while her six-year-old daughter held "a piece of the raw meat in her hands devouring it with the eagerness of a starving dog."[10] If children were not deliberately targeted, it was nevertheless a tacitly accepted consequence of Sherman's strategy of war that terrorizing and inflicting hardship on them would increase the pressure on their parents and families, especially those who had fathers and brothers fighting in the war. Many children witnessed the destruction and vandalism of their homes.

On February 22, 1865, soldiers sacked Otranto Plantation, part of modern Berkeley County, in South Carolina. The plantation was occupied by an entirely female household consisting of

Mrs. Louise Porcher, her two daughters and two aunts, and their servants. One of Mrs. Porcher's daughters watched soldiers sack the house and outbuildings, driving off and killing livestock. "It was awful to hear the screams of cattle and hogs as they were chased and bayoneted, and the scatter and terror of the sheep was terrible to see," she later remembered. "Even my pet calf . . . was killed; and dear old Aaron, our house cat, was cruelly run through with a bayonet, right before my eyes."[11]

In Columbia, female pupils at the burned Ursuline convent were turned out into the street while Union soldiers ransacked their trunks and possessions. One of them later described how she and her companions followed the nuns and a priest with "up-turned crucifix" into the burning streets in a "sorrow-stricken cortege" with "the schoolgirls, some of them little things, clinging to their older companions in terror, lest they might be torn away."

Rebel Women

Such episodes cannot be attributed entirely to out-of-control soldiers acting on their own behalf. Sherman's strategy of intimidation was intended to break the morale of the Southern population, and to that end the horrors were often specifically directed against the white female population. A ghoulish caricature in *Frank Leslie's Illustrated Newspaper* on May 17, 1862, entitled "The Rebel Lady's Boudoir" shows a wealthy Southern woman reading a letter from her soldier husband in a room decorated with the skulls and bones of Union soldiers. Union soldiers in the South often commented on the hostility they encountered from females. Sherman himself, despite his fondness for Southern women in his prewar military postings, was no exception. "I doubt if history affords a parallel to the deep and bitter enmity of the women of the South," he wrote to his wife from Vicksburg in June 1863. "No one who sees them and hears them but must feel the intensity of their hate."[12]

There is no doubt that many Southern women were ardent supporters of the Confederacy, regardless of whether or not they owned slaves or even approved of the "peculiar institution." "If every man did not hasten to battle, they vowed they would themselves rush out and meet the Yankee vandals. In a land where women are worshipped by the men, such language made them war-mad," wrote one English immigrant to Arkansas who enlisted in the Confederate Army. At Richmond, one observer reported that "ladies are postponing all engagements until their lovers have fought the Yankees."[13] The diarist Mary Boykin Chestnut was disgusted by slavery, but she nevertheless wrote that the Carolinian men who had not joined the army "are wasting their time dancing attendance on me. I can not help them. Let them shoulder their musket and go to the wars like men."

The Southern press also regarded the female population as a military asset and frequently exhorted the "women of the South" to use their influence to send more men to the front and stem the rate of desertions. Female support for the war was expressed through Ladies Aid societies and Soldiers' Relief or Ladies Clothing associations, which made socks and uniforms for soldiers or prepared food parcels for them. When the Union Army invaded and occupied the South, its soldiers were frequently shocked at the extent of female hostility, as women spat at and insulted occupying troops, refused to walk under the Union flag, or threw stones and even fired on the invaders. Retreating through the town of Winchester, Virginia, in June 1862, one Massachusetts officer reported that women "fired at us from windows and then hand grenades and bottles of fulminating powder and hot water and even chamber pots were used as missiles." In New Orleans in 1862, General Benjamin "Beast" Butler outraged Southerners when he issued General Orders No. 28, which declared that any woman who spat at or insulted his troops would be treated as "a woman of the town plying her avocation," i.e., as a prostitute.

Sherman's army often encountered such hostility during its marches. In Georgia, one divisional commander and his staff were insulted by women using "language which no well bred ladies use." At Milledgeville a woman threw a stone at passing soldiers from a second-story window. Other women openly berated soldiers as they passed. The twenty-six-year-old Charlestonian Emma Holmes, who was working as a governess on a South Carolina plantation when Sherman's army arrived, harangued soldiers for the best part of an hour on the iniquities of making war on women and children, and proudly related afterward that one admiring officer had called her "the best rebel he had ever met." Union soldiers were often amused by such behavior and sometimes deliberately provoked rebel women to "hear them roar," as one soldier put it.

Others were angered by it and locked some of the more vocal "secesh" women in cupboards or cellars to shut them up. One woman who shouted at a group of foragers was dumped in a barrel of molasses. In South Carolina, General Smith D. Atkins told a female house owner, "We shall soon see the women of South Carolina as those of Georgia with tears in their eyes begging crusts from our men for their famishing children. O it was glorious to see such a sight . . . you women keep up this war. We are fighting *you*."[14] If the open defiance of so many rebel women in Georgia and the Carolinas, which Southern accounts of Sherman's march often celebrated, suggested that there were limits to how far Union soldiers were prepared to go to intimidate them, their obvious commitment to the Confederacy also prompted many soldiers to call their nonbelligerent status into question. Told by a teenage girl at Sandersville that the Union army "had no right to punish helpless women who had never done anything, etc., etc.," Henry Hitchcock asked her "where her young men friends were gone" and whether she had used her "influence" to keep them at home. When his interlocutor replied that she had not, Hitchcock told her, "Then you have done all you could to help the war, and have not done what you could to prevent it."

Many women in Georgia and the Carolinas had already experienced the "hard hand of war" indirectly, long before Sherman's soldiers arrived on their doorsteps, and some had lost their earlier enthusiasm for it. In her diary, Mary Boykin Chestnut describes how her enthusiasm for the Confederate cause was tempered by her growing depression and despondency at the growing numbers of men who came back wounded or not at all and by her horror at the sight of wounded Confederate veterans in local hospitals.[15] In South Carolina, George Pepper met wealthy Carolinian ladies who told him "they had lived on bread and water for two months at a time—others that they had seen meat but once a week." Many women in the path of Sherman's army now found themselves deprived of some or all the food they needed to feed their families and their slaves. Others lost their only source of income. At the novelist Alice Walker's birthplace at Eatonton, Georgia, Orlando Poe destroyed a textile factory that made Confederate tents and uniforms, even though its twenty to thirty female workers begged the Federals to spare it. At the village of Saluda, South Carolina, Conyngham observed female factory workers "weeping and wringing their hands in agony, as they saw the factory, their only means of support, in flames."

Despite Sherman's orders not to enter private houses, the more relentless foragers searched through beds and blankets for hidden goods even when sick women and children were lying in them. On December 1, 1864, Sue Sample visited her aunt's house next door to her plantation in Georgia with her sister-in-law and found that "the beds were torn open, feathers all out. The bedsteads were chopped to pieces, books stolen, and not a thing left worth sleeping on."[16] Such acts went beyond the destruction of war resources or simple thieving. In some cases, soldiers singled out women for particularly vindictive acts of destruction, which included slashing paintings and furniture or destroying daguerreotypes and other objects of particular sentimental value. Pianos were a common target and were often deliberately destroyed or chopped up with axes after their female owners had been forced to play them.

Such behavior is not an aberration in the history of war. Both conquering and defeated armies have often inflicted particular forms of violence and intimidation against women, whether motivated by a desire for vengeance, a demonstration of male power and virility, or the emasculation of their menfolk. The wartime dispatches of the Soviet journalist Vasily Grossman describe the frequent fury and amazement of Red Army soldiers in Nazi Germany at the prosperity and normality they encountered, which became a justification for violent retribution against the civilian population and women in particular.[17] Some of the vandalism carried out by Sherman's soldiers was undoubtedly motivated by similar anger at the comfortable domestic worlds they encountered, which intensified their resentment toward the women who in their view had incited rebellion while escaping its consequences.

Such sentiments have often provided a context for sexual violence. In a society where (white) female honor and purity were sacrosanct, the prospect of mass rape by Yankee "mudsills" was a persistent theme in the Southern press. In November 1864, the *Macon Telegraph* urged Southern men to "hasten to the front . . . to die for home, altars and female purity" and prevent Sherman's army from "subjecting our wives, daughters and sisters, to the brutal lusts of an infidel, coarse, and fiendish horde."[18] Sherman's army was often accused of putting these fantasies into practice. As Federal troops closed in on Savannah, the *Louisville Times* claimed that Sherman "left in his track hundreds of violated women and deflowered maidens." On December 7, 1864, a letter from Milledgeville to the *Richmond Dispatch* accused Sherman's troops of systematic "violence towards the ladies. At least six or seven suffered the last extremity. One young girl became crazed in consequence, and has been sent to the asylum. Other ladies were stripped of their garments, and in such a plight, compelled to play the piano." On December 17 the *Macon Telegraph* reported that Southern women were now exposed to "the lustful appetites of the hell-hounds" and the "cesspools of Northern infamy and corruption."

Much of this was rumor and fabrication. Sherman later claimed that there were only two reported cases of rape, one of which took place at Winnsboro, South Carolina, on February 27, 1865, when a black woman was raped by two soldiers of the Thirty-Eighth Ohio Volunteers, who were court-martialed and sentenced to ten and four years' hard labor. In another incident in South Carolina, Sergeant Arthur McCarty of the Seventy-Eighth Ohio Regiment was court-martialed for the rape of a girl near Bennettsville and drummed out of the army. There were other cases that Sherman may or may not have been aware of. At Milledgeville, Mrs. Kate Latimer Nichols, the twenty-seven-year-old wife of a Confederate captain, was raped by two soldiers while lying sick in bed and later died in a mental institution. At Aiken in South Carolina, a detachment of Wheeler's cavalrymen were told by a weeping Baptist minister that a group of Union soldiers had just raped his daughter. Wheeler's men caught seven of the men responsible and cut their throats, leaving them with a sign that read THESE ARE THE SEVEN.

There were numerous testimonies of rape carried out by Union soldiers during the calamitous occupation of Columbia. Daniel Trezevant described how soldiers broke into the home of a Mrs. Thomas B. Clarkson Jr. and "forced her to the floor for the purpose of sensual enjoyment" before raping her maid instead.[19] There are also accounts of Federal soldiers gang-raping black women and of naked black women's bodies lying in the streets of Columbia bearing "such marks upon them as would indicate the most detestable of crimes," as one eyewitness put it.[20] According to William Gilmore Simms, "The poor negroes were terribly victimized by their assailants, many of them . . . being left in a condition little short of death. Regiments, in successive relays, subjected scores of these poor women to the torture of their embraces."[21]

Simms was a prominent advocate of slavery whose sympathy for the "poor negroes" can certainly be called into question, but similar events were reported elsewhere. According to South Carolina resident Mrs. Sarah Trapier, "A gentleman in our neighborhood assured us that not a female slave on his plantation (with a single exception) was allowed to retain that which should have been dearer to her than her life." The full extent of rape during Sherman's marches will never be known; many women would have been too ashamed to report it, and some incidents would have gone unrecorded, particularly on isolated farms or when they involved black slaves rather than upper-class white women. Sexual relations between female slaves and Union soldiers were also consensual—up to a point. Conyngham observed "negro wenches, particularly good-looking ones, decked in satin and silks, and sporting diamond ornaments," who accompanied Union soldiers returning from foraging expeditions. The South Carolina naturalist and Lutheran minister Reverend John Bachman remembered how soldiers descended on his house and "stole the ladies' jewelry, hair ornaments, etc., tore many garments into tatters, or gave the rest to the negro women to bribe them into criminal intercourse."

Nor were relations between the army and the white female population always so acrimonious. In many cases, Sherman's officers responded positively to requests from women to guard their homes, and some soldiers spontaneously offered to protect their property from their own comrades. In South Carolina, one soldier nearly died when an elderly woman begged him to save furniture and a photograph of her husband from the house that the

Northern views of Sherman's army: "The Halt: A Scene in the Georgia Campaign," Thomas Nast, 1866. Courtesy of the Library of Congress.

army had just burned. A Mrs. Alfred P. Aldrich described how a soldier threatened to burn down her house at Barnwell unless she told him where her silver was, only to be stopped by a Union officer who "repeatedly expressed his disapprobation of war, and his sorrow for what was going on around him" and ordered the soldier to "let the lady alone."

Sherman's soldiers often expressed their amazement and disgust at the "ugliness" of rural white women, and were appalled by their propensity for swearing and their unladylike habit of chewing tobacco. But many of Sherman's battle-hardened soldiers also admired the "pretty smart pieces" they encountered during the march, finding their elegance and femininity a pleasing contrast to the brutal campaigns they had endured, a reminder of the female world of wives, mothers, and sisters that they had left behind them. Some formed temporary and even permanent relationships with white women and married them after the war.

Such events do not belong to the image of Sherman's march depicted in *Gone with the Wind*, when Scarlett O'Hara shoots a lascivious Union intruder on her stairwell. But for all their anger toward the "hostile people" and the women whom some soldiers blamed for the war, Sherman's army remained for the most part a controlled and disciplined army, whose treatment of women was in keeping with the moral conventions of nineteenth-century society. Such an army might be willing to chop up pianos, raid smokehouses, and steal cows and chickens, but it generally stopped short of resorting to sexual violence either as a right of conquest or as a weapon of war.

The Jubilee

Southern condemnations of Sherman's "Vandal army" were often reinforced by the many instances of vandalism and destruction of private libraries and scientific laboratories carried out by Sherman's soldiers. Descriptions of soldiers trampling on books at the Milledgeville statehouse or making bonfires of books on South Carolina plantations support a wider depiction of the Civil War as a confrontation between a refined, cultured, and lettered Southern civilization and the materialistic, utilitarian North. But there was always another side to this "civilization," which tended to be ignored in subsequent Southern condemnations of Sherman's march. On December 4, the pious Grace Elmore passed the prisoner-of-war compound of Camp Sorghum, near Columbia, on the way to a classical music recital and recorded her pleasure on witnessing "one fellow riding a rail and another bucked and gagged, hoped they were native born Yankees and not poor foreigners."[22]

In addition to her vituperative outbursts of hatred toward a Yankee enemy she regarded as "a blot upon the whole creation," Elmore's diaries are also laced with racial contempt for "the negro," whom she called "the most inferior of the human race, far beneath the Indian or Hindu." The feminist Rebecca Latimer Felton, who so plaintively evoked the experience of defeat, stridently advocated the lynching of black males for real or imagined sexual relations with white women in the Reconstruction years and once told a group of farmers, "If it takes lynching to protect woman's dearest possession from drunken, ravening human beasts, then I say lynch a thousand a week if it becomes necessary."[23] Lynching continued to take place even during Sherman's advance. On March 15, 1865, a slave named Saxe Joiner from Unionville, South Carolina, wrote to two white women in the house where he worked and offered to conceal them in a "safe place" from the approaching Union Army. There was nothing to suggest that Joiner's intentions were anything but honorable, but he was nevertheless accused of inappropriate behavior and imprisoned in a local jail, before a lynch mob dragged him from the courthouse and hanged him.

For tens of thousands of slaves, Sherman's army brought freedom, or at least the possibility of it, from this world of whippings, bloodhounds, lynchings, violence, and terror on which the Southern social order depended. Even before Sherman's army reached them, plantation owners were uncomfortably conscious that the "breath of Emancipation" had reached their slaves, and some owners removed "bad negroes" to more distant plantations to prevent them from trying to escape to the Union lines. Some slaves, particularly house servants, remained loyal to their masters and mistresses and suffered at the hands of Sherman's army, but many recognized the opportunity presented to them and seized it. At Madison, a slave owner pleaded with an elderly black couple not to leave the plantation with the Union Army on the grounds that he had always treated them kindly. The couple agreed that he had, but nevertheless explained, "We must go, freedom is as sweet to us as it is for you."[24]

Hitchcock records an incident at a plantation near Covington, Georgia, where Sherman pressed a reluctant old slave for his views on the war. He eventually responded, "Well, Sir, what I think about it, is this—it's mighty distressin' this war, but it 'pears to me like *the right thing couldn't be done* without it." Hitchcock concluded, "The old fellow hit it, exactly."[25] For some slaves, the arrival of Sherman's army provided an opportunity for vengeance as well as freedom. At the rice plantation of Gowrie, one of several plantations owned by the wealthy South Carolina Manigault family, slaves fled to Savannah on flatboats following the arrival of Sherman's army on Christmas Eve, while soldiers proceeded to seize ten thousand bushels of rice before burning the plantation house, the steam thresher, and a rice-polishing mill.

In February, Sherman's army reached the sumptuous Manigault plantation of Middleton Place, near Charleston, where slaves broke open the vaults of the family graveyard and scattered the bones about the landscaped grounds, while soldiers burned the mansion and destroyed its library and gardens in what Gabriel Manigault called an act of "Gothic barbarity." Manigault's father, Charles, was appalled at what he regarded as the disloyalty of his slaves when Sherman's army reached two more Manigault plantations, New Hope and Silk Mill, near Charleston, and slaves seized family portraits and paintings from the plantation house and nailed them to the walls of their own quarters or left them in the rain, "to shew their hatred of their former master & all his family."[26]

Other slaves provided Sherman's army with information of military value, told soldiers where their masters and mistresses had hidden livestock and valuables, or simply refused for the first time in their lives to obey orders. As they marched through Georgia and the Carolinas, Sherman's soldiers were frequently greeted by ecstatic crowds of slaves, who danced and sang and kissed them. At Milledgeville, a New Jersey soldier described "old negroes and young negroes, males and females, house servants generally, blessing us—cheering us—laughing—crying—praying—dancing and raising a glorious old time generally, even trying to hug the men as they go along." In a letter to his wife, General Oliver Howard described freed slaves following his troops on the road to Lafayetteville with "bundles on their heads, children in arms, men on mules, women in old wagons & many with little to eat. They will do anything, suffer anything for freedom."

Many slaves saw the arrival of the Union army as the fulfillment of the biblical Day of Jubilation, the Jubilee promised in Leviticus 25: 8–13, where God exhorts the Israelites every fiftieth year to "proclaim liberty throughout all the land unto all the inhabitants thereof: it shall be a jubile unto you; and ye shall return every man unto his possession, and ye shall return every man unto his family." Sherman had mixed feelings about this reception. His own attitudes toward slavery were strongly imbued with white supremacism. "All the Congresses on earth can't make the negro anything else than what he is; he must be subject to the white man, or he must amalgamate or he must be destroyed," he told his wife on July 11, 1860.[27]

Whatever his personal views, Sherman was obliged to implement Lincoln's Emancipation Proclamation, and he recognized its military usefulness at a time when the Confederacy was desperate enough to consider the previously inconceivable step of drafting black soldiers for its own army. At the same time, Sherman did not want his army to be encumbered by a refugee population that might slow its progress. His general policy was to inform slaves that they were free and advise them to remain on their plantations, while offering the more able-bodied men the opportunity to become paid pioneers—but not to carry weapons—

with his army. Hundreds of freed slaves accepted this offer and worked as servants and laborers during the march. As many as twenty thousand black men, women, and children nevertheless ignored his instructions to remain on their plantations and followed his advancing columns.

The attitudes of Sherman's soldiers toward the slaves were a microcosm of the Union itself. Some soldiers were passively or actively racist, like the German soldier who told a Southern woman near Atlanta, "Fight for the nigger! I'd see 'em in de bottom of a swamp before I'd fight for 'em." Two or three black soldiers were killed by Union soldiers in Savannah. At Robertsville, South Carolina, a white resident reported that Sherman's bummers were murdering black men driving wagons on the roads and seizing their loads. According to Conyngham, many other freed slaves "died in the bayous and lagoons of Georgia" of hunger because "when food was getting scarce, we turned them adrift, to support ourselves or perish."[28] On December 8, during the approach to Savannah, Major General Jefferson C. Davis, commander of the Fourteenth Corps, ordered his troops to pull up a trestle bridge between Ebenezer and Lockyer creeks, leaving five hundred to six hundred slaves stranded. Dozens drowned trying to swim or make their way across in homemade rafts to escape the approaching Confederate cavalry, while others were returned to slavery or killed.

Davis was a notorious racist, who once described the refugee columns as "useless creatures . . . encumbering the trains and devouring the subsistence along the line of march so needed for our soldiers."[29] But such attitudes were not universal. One soldier with the Fourteenth Corps described the slaves who joined the march at Jacksonboro as "a nuisance to the army; but we could not drive them back, as they were seeking their freedom, and so they trudged on after us and we divided our rations with them." One semiliterate private wrote, "I can afoard to go hungry somb times if it will help to free the slaves." Many officers and soldiers—including Sherman himself—were deeply moved by the reception they received from the freed slaves and the accounts of slavery they heard, and some, like the fervently abolitionist George Pepper, were fascinated by Southern black culture and attended church services or asked slaves to sing and dance for them.

In effect, Sherman's army inadvertently became an instrument of the social revolution that Lincoln's proclamation had authorized. On January 16, 1865, Sherman co-wrote Special Field Order No. 15 in Savannah with Lincoln's secretary of war Edwin Stanton, which set aside four hundred thousand acres of coastal land in South Carolina and Florida for freed slaves to settle and cultivate as they pleased. This policy of "forty acres and a mule," as it came to be known, was undertaken largely as a temporary measure, in order to reduce the numbers of slaves accompanying Sherman's army, but the dispensation of white-owned land to freed blacks in the South was nevertheless an extraordinarily radical gesture in its context, which Michael Fellman has called "the single most revolutionary act in race relations during the Civil War."[30] Within six months, the "Sherman lands" were settled by some forty thousand freedmen, before the policy was revoked by Lincoln's successor, Andrew Johnson.

Not surprisingly, Sherman was highly regarded by Southern blacks. Presented by Stanton with stories circulating in Washington that he was racist and discriminatory, Sherman summoned a deputation of leading black dignitaries to testify on his behalf, all of whom spoke in his favor. In *The Souls of Black Folk*, W.E.B Du Bois looked back on the "Conqueror, the Conquered, and the Negro" as the three essential components of Sherman's "raid through Georgia" and concluded, "Some see all significance in the grim front of the destroyer, and some in the bitter sufferers of the Lost Cause. But to me neither soldier nor fugitive speaks with so deep a meaning as that dark human cloud that clung like remorse on the rear of those swift columns, swelling at times to half their size, almost engulfing and choking them."[31]

The "dark human cloud" was also celebrated in "Marching Through Georgia," a song written for Sherman by the Connecticut songwriter and fervent abolitionist Henry Clay Work, with its rousing depiction of his troops as an army of liberation carving "a thoroughfare for freedom and her train / Sixty miles of latitude, three hundred to the main." Many marching armies have sung that song in very different circumstances, and many have done so without understanding the line "How the darkies shouted when they heard the joyful sound!" or the meaning of the chorus, "Hurrah! Hurrah! We bring the Jubilee." But just as the "peculiar institution" calls into question the very idea of Southern civilization, so the crowds who followed Sherman's army invest the destruction that it inflicted on Southern society with a poignancy

Refugee "contrabands" following Sherman's army. *Harper's Weekly*, 1865. Courtesy of the Library of Congress.

and a moral ambivalence that has rarely, if ever, accrued to a similar campaign.

"American Barbarism"

In *The Trojan Women*, Euripides denounces the victorious "spear-carrying Greeks" as barbarians because of their vindictive treatment of women and children after the Trojan armies have been defeated. Both during and after the Civil War, Sherman was also denounced by Southerners as a coward and a barbarian who made war against "defenseless women and children." On the one hand, Sherman's campaign was seen as an expression of brutal and brutish Yankee warfare, which violated the chivalrous "Celtic" warrior code that supposedly defined the Southern military tradition. At the same time, the campaign was depicted as a retrograde anachronism, an accusation that was often accompanied by references to the "Vandal Sherman" and historical comparisons between his army and the Goths, the Thirty Years War, the French Army in the Palatinate, or the "savage" warfare of the American West.

When the Reverend William W. Lord pleaded with Sherman not to "burn and pillage" the town of Winnsboro in South Carolina on the grounds that it "sheltered only helpless women and children," Sherman testily replied, "Burn and pillage be damned! My soldiers may do as they please!"—to which the reverend responded that this was "an eleventh-century answer to a nineteenth-century appeal."[32] In 1881 the South Carolina rice planter Daniel Heyward recalled a meeting in Savannah with Robert E. Lee after the war, in which he asked Lee, was Sherman "justified under the usages of war, in burning as he passed through South Carolina, the homes of our women and children, while our men were in the field, fighting him bravely?" According to Heyward, Lee replied "in a voice more emphatic than I ever heard him: 'No sir! No sir! It was the act of a savage, and not justified by the usages of war.'"[33]

Such accusations were not limited to Southerners. In December 1864 the New York correspondent for *The Times* of London condemned the "American barbarism" of the Civil War and suggested that "the war had lost its original character, and is fast degenerating into a savage contest"—a development that he primarily blamed on Union invaders in the South who had first decided to engage in "hostilities against women and children, and forgo the decencies and amenities of civilization in [their] treatment of the helpless inhabitants of conquered cities."

The idea that Sherman's campaigns represented a form of moral atavism reflected a widespread assumption that warfare between "civilized nations" had undergone a process of moral advancement in the nineteenth century, regarding the protection of civilians and noncombatants. Such preoccupations were not new. The "laws on truces and peace" drawn up by Pope Gregory IX in the thirteenth century included pilgrims, monks, peasants, and the "naturally weak"—women, children, widows, orphans, and their animals, goods, and lands—among those who merited such protection. Emmerich de Vattel's hugely influential *The Law of Nations; or, the Principles of Natural Law* (1758) states, "Women, children, feeble old men, and sick persons, come under the description of enemies, and so we have certain rights over them, inasmuch as they belong to the nation with whom we are at war, . . . but these are enemies that make no resistance; and consequently, we have no right to maltreat their persons or use any violence against them, much less to take away their lives."[34]

The principle of civilian immunity was firmly embedded in the West Point tradition to which Sherman belonged and was reiterated in the Lieber Code, which declared that among civilized nations "protection of the inoffensive citizen of the hostile country is the rule; privation and disturbance of private relations are the exceptions." Lieber acknowledged the international consensus in the nineteenth century in establishing a distinction between the "private citizen belonging to a hostile country and the hostile country itself," in which "the unarmed citizen is to be spared in person, property, and honor as far as the exigencies of war will admit." Article 37 specifically mandated Union commanders to "acknowledge and protect, in hostile countries occupied by them, religion and morality; strictly private property; the persons of the inhabitants, especially those of women: and the sacredness of domestic relations," while Article 44 proscribed "all wanton violence committed against persons in the invaded country, all destruction of property not commanded by the authorized officer."

At the same time, Lieber also established conditions under which these principles might not be binding. It was, for example, legitimate for the "citizen or native of a hostile country" to be "subjected to the hardships of the war." Though "wanton" violence and physical destruction were not permitted, military necessity may make an exception of "all destruction of property, and obstruction of the ways and channels of traffic, travel, or communication, and of all withholding of sustenance or means of life from the enemy." Lieber also distinguished between "loyal citizens," whom commanders were obliged to protect, and rebels or "disloyal citizens," on whom "the commander will throw the burden of the war, as much as lies within his power."

Much of what Sherman's army did in Georgia and the Carolinas fell within these parameters, or at least it was possible to argue that it did. Had the Union lost the war, Sherman might well have been put on trial for war crimes, and he might have cited Lieber in his defense. His lawyers could have argued that most of the destruction carried out by his army was not "wanton" but was directed at military resources, communications, and matériel of potential use to the enemy. They might have cited Article 17, which declared that "war is not carried on by arms alone" and that it could therefore be lawful in certain circumstances "to starve the hostile belligerent, armed or unarmed, so that it leads to the speedier subjection of the enemy." They could have argued that his army needed to take food from the population in order to survive and also to prevent it from being exported to Confederate armies, that many of the more extreme actions carried out by his soldiers were in contravention of Sherman's orders, and that the burning of Columbia was not his decision and that he tried to prevent it.

Even if this hypothetical court ruled that what Sherman's army did was legal, it is difficult to imagine that it would have ruled that it was moral or even that Sherman would have offered such a defense. He might have argued, as he often did, that the rules, laws, and moral codes that regulated civilian society in peacetime were not necessarily the same as those prevailing in war and that the actions of his army in Georgia and the Carolinas were not de-signed "to meet the humanities of the case." Sherman might also have reminded his accusers that Confederate bushwhackers fired on passenger trains and steamboats and killed or beat up Union loyalists and burned their homes. He might have mentioned Cham-bersburg or Lawrence. Sherman could also have quoted the Con-federate "Gray Ghost," J. Singleton Mosby, who justified shelling Union trains even when they had women and children aboard on the grounds that he "did not understand that it hurts women and children to be killed any more than it hurts men."[35]

In the course of the war, men killed men in their hundreds of thousands, as artillery and the new rifled muskets wreaked terri-ble carnage on the battlefield. In his memoir of Grant's cam-paigns in Virginia, Lieutenant Colonel Horace Porter describes the "unutterable horror" of the Battle of the Wilderness: "Forest fires raged; ammunition-trains exploded; the dead were roasted in the conflagration; the wounded, roused by its hot breath, dragged themselves along, with their torn and mangled limbs, in the mad energy of despair, to escape the ravages of the flames; and every bush seemed hung with shreds of blood-stained clothing. It was as though Christian men had turned to fiends, and hell itself had usurped the place of earth."[36]

The Civil War contained an abundance of such horrors, which Sherman himself often described with disgust. Few Americans on either side questioned the right of soldiers to shoot, bayonet, maim, and bludgeon their opponents to death in battle, but neither the Union nor the Confederate Army was expected to steal and pillage, terrorize women and children, and violate "the sacredness of domestic relations" through the destruction of private property. Then as now, the American soldier was expected to behave as "an officer and a gentleman" and limit the use of force as much as possible to armed combatants. We have already seen how Sherman, Sheridan, and other Union generals came to disregard such limitations, but how did Sherman's soldiers come to terms with the peculiar forms of destruction that his marches entailed?

The Citizen Army

Southerners often described Sherman's army as a rabble, a mob, whose behavior was sometimes attributed to the numbers of soldiers from the urban slums in its ranks. But the Army of the West included men from a variety of social backgrounds, from comfortable New England middle-class families and recently arrived German immigrants who barely spoke English to Midwestern farm boys and East Coast Irishmen. By the time they reached Atlanta, many of them had already fought and marched for more than a thousand miles, in some cases without boots or shoes, barefoot or with their feet wrapped in cloth and gunnysacks. They were tough, supremely fit, and imbued with a strong sense of their own invincibility and the infallibility of their commander, and also with an egalitarian spirit that owed much to the fact that more than 50 percent of captains and 90 percent of lieutenants had once served as enlisted men.

Observers commented on the motley appearance of Sherman's army. Their put-together Confederate and Union uniforms, sometimes with mixed boots, top hats, and even women's bonnets, contrasted strikingly with the scrupulously well-turned-out Eastern armies. In Beaufort, South Carolina, one observer described Sherman's "western marauders . . . strange, rough-looking, unshaven, and badly dressed: they seem like a gang of coal-heavers" and "roaring out songs and jokes, making sharp comments on all the tidy civilians, and over-flowing with merriment and good-nature."[37]

Most of Sherman's soldiers had "seen the elephant," as Civil War soldiers called combat, both before and during the Atlanta campaign. Many had seen their comrades, friends, relatives, and neighbors maimed or killed. Some soldiers were undoubtedly hardened by the experience of war. At Jonesboro during the siege of Atlanta, the Third Brigade of Sherman's Fourteenth Corps scaled Confederate redoubts and shot or bayoneted soldiers who tried to surrender. Soldiers capable of such actions were not likely to quibble about slaughtering livestock or burning barns and houses. For many of its participants, the March to the Sea was a relief from the danger of battle. Charles Wills called the march "the most gigantic pleasure excursion ever planned." Another soldier from Slocum's corps cheerfully recorded in his diary, "Destroyed all we could not eat, stole their niggers, burned their cotton & gins, spilled their sorghum, burned and twisted their R. Roads and raised Hell generally."[38]

Some soldiers took a vindictive pleasure in the destruction they inflicted and the distress of the local population. A resident of Winnsboro in South Carolina described soldiers "like truants out of school" cheerfully tossing unwanted molasses and foodstuffs

into the streets in a "high carnival" of destruction. In Georgia a
soldier, confronted with a sobbing woman who pleaded with him
not to take her last chickens after a day of depredations, replied,
"Madam, we're going to suppress this rebellion if it takes every
last chicken in the Confederacy."[39] In Columbia, Harriott Middleton, the daughter of a wealthy planter, described how her elderly father was turned out of his house by Captain Pierce of the
157th New York Volunteers, who told him, "You damn old rebel
you, get out your house this minute. I mean to burn it down and
set you afloat in the world."[40]

Sherman's soldiers often expressed a particularly republican
contempt for the pretensions of the Southern aristocracy, but they
were not necessarily any more enamored of poor whites, whom
Thomas Osborn described as "lower than the negro in every respect, not excepting general intelligence, culture and morality"
and "not fit to be kept in the same sty with a well to do farmer's
hogs in New England." The tempo of destruction was sometimes
fueled by anger at the sight of Confederate POW camps, where
captured soldiers lived—and often died—in horrific conditions.
At Camp Lawton, near Millen, Georgia, soldiers found the
corpses of Union prisoners still lying in holes they had dug with
their bare hands—a sight that moved many of them to take re-
venge on Millen. At the infamous Andersonville prison camp in
Georgia, thirteen thousand men died in little more than a year
due to lack of food, sanitation, and medical care. Seven thousand died in the summer of 1864 alone, mostly of scurvy. John
McElroy, a former prisoner at Andersonville, subsequently observed that this outcome could have been avoided by "a few wagon
loads of roasting ears and sweet potatoes," which were readily
available in the state, and condemned the failure to do so "in the
midst of an agricultural region filled with all manner of green
vegetation" as something that "must forever remain impossible of
explanation."[41]

Many of Sherman's soldiers were mystified and outraged by the condition of Georgia's prisoners. During the Thanksgiving Day celebrations held by Sherman's troops at Milledgeville, the appearance of emaciated prisoners from Andersonville "sickened and infuriated the men who thought of them starving in the midst of plenty," according to one officer, and intensified the level of destruction in the surrounding area as a consequence. A similar reaction followed the Union liberation of Camp Sorghum, near Columbia. "The doom of Columbia was sealed at Camp Sorghum," wrote Pepper, "and neither General Sherman nor any other man could have saved it from severe treatment, even had no other circumstances occurred."[42]

Some of Sherman's soldiers clearly reveled in their power, such as the soldier who watched his comrades set fire to the burning Ursuline convent in Columbia and asked the evacuated nuns and their charges, "What do you think of God now? Is not Sherman greater?" Some soldiers took an almost aesthetic pleasure in the strange and often beautiful landscapes of destruction that they created. One soldier was awed by the sight of the burning pine forests of North Carolina "as big as a mountain and roaring like a bursting volcano." Watching a forest fire near Saluda, George Nichols found a "terrible sublimity in the scene that I shall never forget" as frightened animals and men with smoke-blackened faces fled the "flames, galloping over the ground like a frightened steed."[43] At Columbia, Thomas Osborn described the "magnificent splendor of this burning city" as "an advantage to the cause and just punishment for the state of South Carolina."[44]

Sherman's army was not an army of brutalized insensate avengers, however. At the battle of Griswoldville, soldiers expressed sympathy for the old men and boys they killed and wounded. "The scenes of death, pain, and desolation seen on the field will never be erased from the memory of those who witnessed it," wrote one Iowa soldier. "I could not help but pity them as they lay on the ground pleading for help but we could not help them as we were scarce of transportation."[45]

Many soldiers were similarly sympathetic to the civilians they encountered. On entering Columbia, one Union soldier saw a young girl playing with a puppy on a porch and promptly brained the dog with his rifle, leaving her crying. Another soldier soothed her by converting a cigar box into a tiny coffin before burying the dog. In Georgia two homeless orphaned girls were cleaned up and fed by soldiers and brought to Savannah, where they were taken back to the Union by a wounded lieutenant and adopted. In North Carolina, the Ohio infantryman S.A. McNeil recalled how "a little girl of perhaps ten years came from a house wringing her little hands and crying 'Soldiers, our house is burning,'" whereupon "at least a hundred" soldiers rushed to the house and put the fire out.[46]

The presence of children often induced soldiers to spare their homes or leave enough food for them to eat, and there were also cases in which soldiers gave children their own rations. On Christmas Day, 1864, a Union captain near Savannah ordered ninety men to load wagons with food, which was then distributed to the needy in an area stripped by both Federals and Confederates, with branches tied to the heads of mules to make them look like reindeer. Many soldiers were appalled by the behavior of their army. "You never can imagine a pillaged house, never—unless an army passes right through your town," wrote Charles Brown, a clerk with the Twenty-First Michigan, of the destruction in South Carolina, "and if this thing had been [in the] North I would bushwhack until every man was either dead or I was." Major James A. Connolly declared himself "perfectly sickened by the frightful devastation our army was spreading on every hand" in South Carolina. Of the destruction inflicted on Louisville, Georgia, on November 27, an Illinoisan soldier wrote, "I never can sanction such proceeding, believing that no man who ever was a gentleman could enter a private house & disgrace our uniform and the service as many of our men did today."

Even Sherman often felt pangs of conscience at the reality of the policy that he had adopted. Hitchcock records a campfire conversation in which Sherman recounted that he had refused a request from an old woman for a guard for her house and told his officers, "I'll have to harden my heart to these things. That poor woman today—how could I help her? There's no help for it. The soldiers will take all she has." Such regrets, in typical Sherman fashion, were rationalized on the basis that "Jeff Davis is responsible for this."[47]

Many soldiers justified their actions in the same way, not because they reveled in cruelty—though some certainly did—but because they believed that the South had brought such treatment on itself and that their actions would bring the war to a swifter conclusion. Some argued that such destruction was necessary to preserve the Union and insisted even to those on the receiving end that it was ultimately for their own good. "Is this the way to make us love them and their Union?" asked Dolly Lunt Burge. "Let the poor people answer whom they have deprived of every mouthful of meat and of their livestock to make any!" One Columbia resident sarcastically compared Sherman's soldiers to "crusaders": with "'this glorious Union' constantly on their lips, they wanted to re-establish the Union even if by doing so they annihilated the present population."

Most of Sherman's soldiers were interested in subjugating rather than annihilating the South, and some regarded what they were doing as less destructive than the battles they'd taken part in and a preferable alternative to them. "It is terrible to consume and destroy the sustenance of thousands of people, and most sad and distressing in itself to see and hear the terror and grief of these women and children," observed Henry Hitchcock. "But personally they are protected and their dwellings are not destroyed. . . . It is mercy in the end."[48]

Many Northerners took the same view. On May 24, 1865, the Armies of the Potomac and the James paraded down Pennsylvania Avenue in Washington on the first day of the Grand Review of the Armies. The following day, tens of thousands of Northerners turned out to watch Sherman's ragtag army parade through the capital. Unlike the Eastern armies, Sherman's army made no attempt to spruce itself up for the occasion. The soldiers, many still barefoot, proudly sported the motley uniforms they had assembled during the march along with their faded battle flags. They brought with them turkeys, raccoons, hogs, and chickens from Southern homes, as well as some of the freed slaves who had followed their march, all of which impressed the cheering crowds who watched them pass throughout the day. "The acclamation given Sherman was without precedent . . . greater than the day before," wrote a reporter from the *New York World*.

It is doubtful whether these cheering crowds cared very much whether the actions of Sherman's citizen army were in accordance with the usages of war or the morality of making war on civilians. To most of those present, victory negated the need for such questions, and to many it seemed that Sherman had saved the Union by defeating its enemies, not with a battle but with a march.

5

"More Perfect Peace"

There is no doubt that Sherman's campaign was a formidable military achievement, in terms of its logistics, organization, leadership, and the determination and collective willpower that made it possible. In six months, an army of sixty thousand marched through some seven hundred miles of hostile territory, wading through or building pontoon bridges across innumerable streams, swamps, and flooded major rivers, corduroying muddy roads and tracks with a relentless efficiency that astounded its opponents. For much of that time, Sherman's army was entirely cut off from its line of supply and dependent for its survival on what it could take from the land and people along the route. Throughout these campaigns, its lines produced few stragglers and never lost their shape or coherence, despite marching in two separate wings for most of the time. The Confederates were powerless to stop its progress.

The strategic impact of these campaigns is more debatable. In a valedictory speech to the Army of the Tennessee on September 30, 1875, Sherman told his listeners, "The consequences of this march were felt all over the country. All acknowledged that when Savannah should be taken the road to Richmond was clear, and that the war was at an end. . . . Certain it is that this march was great in its conception and in its execution grand—that the blow was struck at the right moment and in the right direction."[1] This blow, Sherman explained, exposed the Confederacy as a "hollow shell" and demonstrated to Southerners and the wider world that its adherents were a defeated people with nothing left to fight for.

Others have similarly hailed the symbolic and psychological impact of Sherman's campaigns. "The moral effect of this march . . . [through Georgia] was greater than would have been the most decided victory," declared the Confederate general Edward Porter Alexander.[2] For *The Times* of London, Sherman's march proved that the Confederacy was "an egg, hard only on its shell or circumference, and utterly insubstantial within." In 1876, Sherman's pugnacious cavalry commander General Hugh Kilpatrick agreed: "The very fact that Sherman reached the sea, demonstrating the fact that a well-organized army, ably led, could raid the South at pleasure; there was not a man in all the land but knew the war was virtually over, and the rebellion ended."[3] Still others have pointed to Sherman's destruction of Confederate war matériel, confiscation of foodstuffs, and disruption of transportation links, depriving the Army of Northern Virginia of much-needed food and supplies. For Ulysses Grant, the march destroyed the Confederate strategic reserve and left the rebellion "nothing to stand upon."

These claims have not gone uncontested. The historian Alfred Castel, a stringent critic of Sherman's generalship, has argued that his marches were strategically irrelevant and that the war might have ended even sooner if he had marched his army directly to Virginia instead of taking the longer route via Savannah.[4] In his memoir *Forty-Six Years in the Army*, published in 1897, Hood's nemesis at Franklin General John M. Schofield insisted that Sherman's main objective had always been Lee's army in Virginia, and that his intention was always to get his army to Richmond rather than to give a "manifestation of the power of the nation by destroying Southern property."[5]

The latter strategy, Schofield suggested somewhat damningly, was emphasized retrospectively by Sherman only because his army failed to reach Richmond in time to assist Grant's campaign. Given the intentions that Sherman outlined to Grant and his own subordinates before and during his campaigns, Schofield's arguments do not seem entirely plausible. There is no doubt that Sherman ultimately intended to reach Virginia and help Grant "get Lee," but his letters and telegrams consistently emphasize the damage that his army would inflict on Georgia and the Carolinas as sufficient justification for his campaigns in itself, whether the aim was destruction of war resources, reduction of civilian morale, or simply a just punishment for rebellion. "I regard my two moves from Atlanta to Savannah and Savannah to Goldsboro as great moves as if we had fought a dozen successful battles," he told his wife on March 26, 1865.[6]

There is some anecdotal evidence to suggest that the morale of the Confederate army in Virginia was affected by Sherman's marches. On February 15, 1865, the governor of North Carolina, Zebulon B. Vance, observed that "thousands and thousands" of Confederate soldiers were absent without leave, while "hundreds of thousands of bushels of grain now rot at various depots of the South for want of transportation"—a development that was at least partly due to Sherman's destruction of the Georgia railroad network.[7] That same month, Robert E. Lee wrote to Vance from Richmond: "Desertions are becoming very frequent and there is good reason to believe that they are occasioned to a considerable extent by letters written to the soldiers by their friends at home."

Lee also commented on the absence of "the boldness and decision which formerly characterized" the defenders of Richmond—a development that he attributed to "the communication received from the men from their homes urging their return and abandonment of the field."[8] But desertions and demoralization were already evident in the Confederate armies long before Sherman's armies entered Georgia, and it is difficult to establish a direct correlation between Sherman's campaigns and the rate of desertions during the winter and spring of 1864–65. Coupled with Sheridan's scorched-earth campaign in the Shenandoah Valley, Sherman's campaigns certainly deprived the Army of Northern Virginia of food and munitions, at least temporarily, but Lee's army was still being fed—admittedly on drastically reduced rations—when he surrendered to Grant at Appomattox.

It is also true that the presence of Sherman's army in North Carolina blocked any possibility of a southern escape route for Lee's army when Grant broke his line at Petersburg. The Confederacy conceivably might have dissolved its conventional forces and organized a campaign of guerrilla warfare in the spring of 1865, but this would have required a willingness to fight on, which was conspicuously absent. Sherman's contribution to this demoralization is also open to question. The fact that so few Georgians responded to the exhortations from Confederate generals and politicians to wage a Russian-style partisan war suggests that the appetite for resistance was already minimal. Even before the army left Atlanta, the state governor, Joseph Brown, was in negotiations with Sherman about the possibility of withdrawing the state from the rebellion, and the ease with which Sherman's forces sliced through Georgia and captured Savannah certainly did not encourage resistance in the Carolinas.

Sherman's reference to the timing is significant. After nearly four years of brutal warfare, his campaign clearly had an impact very different from the one it might have had if such a strategy had been carried out earlier. Ultimately the extent to which his campaigns actually contributed to the military collapse of the Confederacy must remain something of an open question. However, the stature of Sherman's campaigns as an iconic episode in American military history is due not only to what they actually achieved, but also to what they were believed to have achieved—and even more to the persuasive idea they gave rise to, that in certain circumstances, civilian society could be legitimately targeted and punished in order to achieve both military and broader psychological and political effects. These campaigns cannot be understood or assessed only in terms of their contribution to the end of the war. For Sherman, destruction was always a calibrated and pragmatic measure that could be intensified or reduced in order to achieve strategic objectives that were not limited to the war itself, but were also concerned with what came afterward.

The Peacemaker

In 1903 Sherman was honored with an equestrian statue created by the sculptor Augustus Saint-Gaudens at Fifth Avenue and Fifty-Ninth Street in New York, which bears its subject's observation that THE LEGITIMATE OBJECT OF WAR IS A MORE PERFECT PEACE. Visiting the monument soon afterward, the novelist Henry James was unimpressed, considering it a "perversity" and "ambiguity" that failed to capture the "Sherman of the terrible march" and the "misery, the ruin, and vengeance of his track."[9] But the destruction that Sherman left in his track was by no means incompatible with his commitment to a "more perfect peace."

Sherman often qualified even his most extreme threats and pronouncements with the proviso that the South could avoid such consequences by abandoning the rebellion, and he was always prepared to show magnanimity once his objectives had been achieved. This pragmatism was already evident in 1862, when he became military governor of Memphis. Though he was prepared to visit harsh collective punishment on the population in order to eliminate guerrilla activity, he also followed the model established by the Duke of Wellington in the post-Napoleonic occupation of France by allowing the city to run its own affairs as long as it didn't interfere with Union military operations. On arrival in the city on July 21, he found "the place dead; no business doing, the stores closed, churches, schools, and every thing shut up. The people were all more or less in sympathy with our enemies, and there was a strong prospect that the whole civil population would become a dead weight on our hands."[10]

These institutions were quickly reopened, and the day-to-day management of the city was handed over to the civil authorities, so that "very soon Memphis resumed its appearance of an active, busy, prosperous place." Sherman also ordered his quartermasters to distribute food from army stores to eight hundred destitute women and children and to provide food and medicines for the local asylum and hospitals, "as a pure charity to prevent suffering just as we would to Indians on the frontier or to shipwrecked people." He adopted a similarly light touch at Savannah. No sooner had his army entered the city than he ordered its shops, churches, and schools reopened and ensured that food supplies were shipped from the North and distributed to the city's inhabitants. As in Memphis, the mayor and city council were allowed to exercise their functions, and the population was allowed to choose whether to remain in the city or be transported behind Confederate lines. Though newspapers were "held to the strictest accountability" and threatened with severe punishment "for any libelous publication, mischievous matter, premature news, exaggerated statement," they were allowed to publish.

Some two hundred people left the city for Charleston or Augusta, but the majority remained and, in Sherman's own judgment, "generally behaved with propriety, and good social relations at once arose between them and the army." Sherman also placed his army under strict orders of good behavior. In addition to ensuring security in the city, his soldiers entertained the local population with "guard-mountings and parades, as well as the greater reviews," which "became the daily resorts of the ladies, to hear the music of our excellent bands." In this way, normality was quickly restored to the point when Rear Admiral J.A. Dahlgren, commander of the South Atlantic Blockading Squadron, visited Savannah at the beginning of January 1865, he reported to the secretary of the navy, Gideon Welles, "I have walked about the city several times, and can affirm that its tranquility is undisturbed. The Union soldiers who are stationed within its limits are as orderly as if they were in New York or Boston."[11]

Such discipline was conspicuously absent in South Carolina but reinforced in North Carolina when Sherman's army occupied Raleigh and Chapel Hill. "Now that the war is over, I am as willing to risk my person and reputation as heretofore to heal the wounds made by the past war, and I think my feeling is shared by the whole army," he wrote to Joe Johnston, following Lee's surrender at Appomattox. Such declarations reflected Lincoln's own policy of "malice toward none, with charity for all" as a basis for postwar reconciliation. But Sherman went further than his political masters during the surrender negotiations with his great adversary at Daniel Bennett's farmhouse. Without consultation with Washington, Sherman presented a set of "general propositions" to Johnston and his co-negotiator John Breckinridge, which guaranteed Southerners who signed loyalty oaths "their political rights and franchises, as well as their rights of person and property" and the reconstitution of state governments.

Sherman later claimed that this agreement was in keeping with Lincoln's own intentions, but its de facto guarantee of the right of slavery shocked many members of his administration, particularly Secretary of War Edwin Stanton, who assumed temporary control of the government following Lincoln's assassination. To Sherman's Republican critics, his agreement with Johnston constituted an illegitimate intervention into politics by a military commander, which reflected his own pro-Southern sentiments. Though Stanton and some Northern newspapers suggested that Sherman harbored dictatorial ambitions, the most likely explanation for his political largesse was his desire to end the war without provoking his defeated opponents into a guerrilla campaign, coupled with an overweening self-confidence that made him believe he was able to do anything he wanted.

Whatever Sherman's motives, there is some irony in the fact that the man suspected of treason by Northerners would later be more despised by Southerners than any other Union general. Even his staunch friend Grant believed that Sherman had gone beyond his authority, and on April 24 he traveled to Raleigh and ordered him to reopen negotiations. Two days later, Sherman and Johnston met again at Bennett Place, and Johnston agreed to a strictly military surrender without the previous political guarantees.

This agreement satisfied Sherman, who told his wife, "The mass of the people south will never trouble us again. They have suffered terrifically, and I now feel disposed to befriend them—of course not the leaders and lawyers, but the armies who have fought and manifested their sincerity though misled by risking their persons."[12] But Sherman was bitter and angry at his treatment in Washington, which confirmed his loathing of politicians, and he was dismayed by the vengeful mood that he detected there. "I confess, without shame, that I am sick and tired of fighting—its glory is all moonshine," he wrote to a friend in May, "even success the most brilliant is over dead and mangled bodies, with the anguish and lamentations of distant families, appealing to me for sons, husbands, and fathers . . . as far as I know, all the fighting men of our army want peace; and it is only those who have never heard a shot, never heard the shriek and groans of the wounded and lacerated (friend or foe), that cry aloud for more blood, more vengeance, more desolation. I *know* the rebels are whipped to death."[13]

Sherman's error of judgment, if such it was, was soon forgotten, and his status as a national hero remained undiminished by it. For the North, the end of the war unleashed pent-up energies that found an outlet in completion of the transcontinental railroad, settlement of the West, and the rapid industrial and urban expansions that brought on America's Gilded Age. In the South, however, the end of the war brought poverty and economic collapse, whose consequences were often particularly dramatic in the states that Sherman's armies had passed through.

Aftermath

In 1866, the English baronet and future Conservative politician Sir John Kennaway (1837–1919) visited Georgia and South Carolina with a party of Oxbridge students as part of an educational tour to observe the effects of the Civil War. Traveling by train from Chattanooga to Atlanta, Kennaway observed "stations destroyed or gutted all along the line and charred ruins met the gaze wherever human habitations had been."[14] In Marietta, formerly "one of the prettiest and most rising towns in Cherokee Georgia," he said, "Little now remained of it but blank walls and skeleton houses." In Atlanta, all five railroad lines destroyed by Sherman's army were back in operation, and new wooden workhouses were springing up on the sites of demolished foundries, yet lawlessness and robbery were so common that Kennaway and his companions were obliged to observe a ten o'clock curfew, with military patrols on the streets to enforce it.

Traveling in a windowless train through central Georgia, Kennaway concluded through conversations with fellow passengers and his own observations of the postwar devastation still visible along the route of the railroad that the state was a shadow of its prewar prosperity, whose "country is devastated, its stock destroyed, its currency worthless. Labor is scarce and crops scanty; and above all, a moral depression hangs over the soil, and seems for a time to forbid exertion." South Carolina presented a similar picture of desolation. On June 1, 1865, Mary Chestnut wrote of "three days of travel, over a road that had been laid bare by Sherman's torches. Nothing but smoking ruins was left in Sherman's track. That I saw with my own eyes. No living thing was left, no house for man or beast." Returning to her home in Charleston from Greenville at the end of 1865, the novelist Caroline Howard Gilman wrote of "Sherman's Desolation," in which "Scarcely a farm house, not an elegant and hospitable plantation residence on the way, all ruin, ruin; and in Columbia the last rays of twilight were on the ruins."[15]

Much of this destruction was restricted to a limited geographical area, and most of Georgia and the Carolinas remained untouched.[16] Despite the destruction and confiscation of food supplies and livestock, there was no evidence of famine or starvation. The abundant Georgia crop of 1864 that fed Sherman's armies also kept the population alive, even during the tough winter of 1864–65. Some civilians survived by living on scraps from abandoned Union camps, while others were helped by friends and relatives. "Every one we meet gives us painful accounts of the desolation caused by the enemy. Each one has to tell us his or her own experience, and fellow-suffering makes us all equal and makes us all feel interested in one another," wrote Dolly Lunt Burge.

Georgians and Carolinians were also fed by Union soldiers, who sometimes distributed rations to the same communities they had so recently wrecked. In May 1865, Brigadier General E.F. Winslow estimated that 25,000 to 50,000 destitute people had been fed by his soldiers in and around Atlanta, some of whom walked forty miles to get food. Between January and April 1866, the newly created Freedmen's Bureau distributed food to destitute blacks and whites in Georgia and South Carolina. Although the population did not starve, there was nevertheless considerable distress and hardship in both states. One Savannah landowner claimed that it would be easier "to go into the wild wilderness and clear the forest than attempt the reclamation of my lands." In May 1865, the Episcopal *Diocesan Records* at Orangeburg reported that "most of the few who were well off among his parishioners are now poor; that widows and orphans, who had saved a little from the wreck of their property in the low country, are stripped of that little, and that defenseless females were living on the scraps left by those who had taken from them their supplies for domestic use." Writing in March 1866, the poet Henry Timrod (1828–67), who lost his source of income when the newspaper office of the *South Carolinian* was destroyed during Sherman's capture of Columbia, told a friend, "You ask me to tell you my story for the last year. I can embody it all in a few words: *beggary, starvation, death, bitter grief, utter want of hope!*"[17]

Poverty was often particularly difficult to bear for wealthy Southerners who had lost their slaves and servants and sometimes had to work for the first time in their lives. In July 1865, Grace Elmore complained that she and the other women of her household were no longer "ladies of leisure" and were "left without means, forced to work without hope for country, and only to obtain bread."[18] On September 13, the *New York Times* estimated that out of $400 million of property in South Carolina at the beginning of the war, "only something like fifty millions now remained in shape."[19] This list of property that had been "destroyed or swept away" during the war included household furniture, farming implements, animals, slaves, and plantation houses. Some of this destruction was due to Sherman's armies, but there is no evidence that Sherman's campaigns crippled the economic development of Georgia or the Carolinas in the long term.

John Kennaway's descriptions of his train journeys make it clear that the destruction of the railroad system was less systematic than Sherman himself believed. Atlanta was soon repopulated, and the city continued to grow exponentially, attracting some eight hundred thousand visitors to the Cotton States and International

Exposition in 1895. Columbia was also rebuilt and generated a small construction boom in the immediate postwar years. But economic recovery did not mean that the South was pacified or that Southerners had reconciled themselves to the new order. Within a few years of Sherman's marches, both Georgia and the Carolinas were caught up in a new struggle between the former slave states and the federal government, in which Southern whites sought to reestablish their former dominance over the freed slaves using their own strategies of terror.

Reconstruction

In *The Art of War*, Antoine de Jomini warned that wars involving "the occupation or conquest of a country whose people are all in arms" rarely produce positive outcomes. Such occupations require an army to "make a display of a mass of troops proportional to the obstacles and resistance likely to be encountered, calm the popular passions in every possible way, exhaust them by time and patience, display courtesy, gentleness, and severity united, and particularly, deal justly."[20] The most successful American military occupations have generally been carried out in accordance with these principles, from Winfield Scott's brief occupation of Mexico in 1847 to the more ambitious postwar social transformations and reconstruction programs overseen by the U.S. military in Germany and Japan after World War II.

In the aftermath of the Civil War, much of the South was placed under military occupation, but the rapid demobilization of the Union Army soon reduced the overall military presence in the former Confederate states to only six thousand soldiers, which soon proved singularly inadequate in dealing with a turbulent and often openly seditious white population that was determined to reassert its dominance over the freed blacks. Responsibility for

defending black lives and property and managing the incorpora-
tion of some 4 million former slaves into the new political and
economic order fell primarily to the newly formed Freedmen's
Bureau, under the direction of Sherman's former subordinate General Oliver Otis Howard. Inadequately staffed and funded and
with little support from Lincoln's successor, President Andrew
Johnson, Howard's organization struggled to cope with the complex challenges of enforcing black civil rights as reconstructed
state governments sought to reimpose the prewar racist order in a
new form. No sooner had the war ended than many Southern
states imposed stringent vagrancy laws and black codes in an attempt to force freed slaves to remain on the plantations.[21]

These efforts were accompanied by official and unofficial acts of
violence and punishment that included lynchings, floggings, imprisonment, chain gangs, and random murders of "insolent"
blacks or black soldiers. In Georgia, John Kennaway heard frequent stories of attacks on freedmen in remote country districts
and wrote of "murders, whippings, tying up by the thumbs" in
South Carolina. Such acts were rarely punished, and violence became more systematic and organized as white Democrats sought to
deprive freed slaves of the rights that accompanied national citizen-
ship and to intimidate Republican politicians, Northern carpet-
baggers, and Southern scalawags.

In the immediate postwar period, the federal government was
either passive or complicit in this process. In September 1865,
President Johnson rescinded Sherman's "forty acres and a mule"
policy, and the abolitionist Howard was given the bitter task of in-
forming its beneficiaries in South Carolina that their lands were
to be returned to their former white owners. Johnson's reversal
was a concession to an emerging counterrevolution in the South
that increasingly resembled a covert insurgency. In a report to
President Johnson from South Carolina that year, Major General
Carl Schurz described a level of "aversion and resentment" toward

the army and the North throughout the South that resulted from "the animosities inflamed by a four years' war, and its distressing incidents." Schurz also cited a report from one of his officers at Winnsboro, South Carolina, on July 19, which noted, "The spirit of the people, especially in those districts not subject to the salutary influence of General Sherman's army, is that of concealed and, in some instances, of open hostility. . . . A spirit of bitterness and persecution manifests itself toward the negroes. They are shot and abused outside the immediate protection of our forces by men who announce their determination to take the law into their own hands, in defiance of our authority."[22]

At first sight, this observation suggests that Sherman's campaign of destruction had succeeded in dissuading some sections of the population from war and sedition, but the "spirit of bitterness and persecution" was soon so generalized throughout the South that it is difficult to reach such conclusions. When Radical Republicans in Congress challenged Johnson's lenient hands-off policy in the South and pushed the government to take a more proactive position on black civil and political rights, Southern whites unleashed what Eric Foner calls a "wave of counterrevolutionary terror" aimed at the disenfranchisement of the black population and the destruction of the Republican party apparatus in the South. Between 1868 and 1871, the Ku Klux Klan, White Liners, Red Shirts, and other paramilitary groups assassinated black and white politicians and carried out full-scale military-style assaults on government buildings and black schools and churches in a campaign of murder, assassination, and torture that exceeded anything carried out by Sherman's armies in terms of its casualties and its level of cruelty and sadism. Black and white Republican politicians, white teachers who taught in black schools, and ordinary black men and women were shot in their homes, kidnapped and mutilated, drowned, raped, and beaten with almost complete impunity throughout the Deep South.

In Georgia, the Freedmen's Bureau reported 336 cases of murder or attempted murder of freedmen between January 1 and November 15, 1868. In October 1870, a mob of 2,500 armed whites drove 150 blacks from their homes in Laurens County, South Carolina, killing nine Republicans. Torchlight parades, the white cassocks of the Ku Klux Klan, drums and military displays, and exemplary public killings were all part of the pageantry of terror that white "Redeemers" imposed on the South. In South Carolina, Sherman's former adversary Wade Hampton commanded a Red Shirt militia with some thirty thousand armed members, many of whose units were led by former Confederate officers. In 1871 Ulysses Grant declared a number of districts in South Carolina to be in a "state of rebellion" and enacted the Third Enforcement Act, known as the Ku Klux Klan Act, which empowered the army to carry out mass arrests of Klan members.

The subsequent trials succeeded in curbing Klan activity temporarily in some parts of the state. In 1877, however, the last occupying troops left the South, a triumph for the racist order that would keep Southern blacks disenfranchised for nearly a century. In 1919, the British journalist and World War I veteran Stephen Graham followed the route of Sherman's march through Georgia, where he found former slaves living in conditions that were "poorer and barer than the average you would see in Russia."[23] In effect, the South did "trouble" the North again and regained much of what it had lost during the war in a different form, thus rendering America's first attempt at postwar social transformation a spectacular failure.

The Indian Fighter

Sherman had little involvement with these developments. Though he did not favor a permanent army of occupation in the South and was personally opposed to giving voting rights to blacks, his attention was mostly focused elsewhere. In 1865 he was appointed commander of the newly created Military Division of the Missouri, with a much reduced force of six thousand soldiers tasked with protecting settlers from "hostile" Indians on the Western frontier and overseeing the completion of the transcontinental railroad network. Sherman had once described the Civil War as a "big Indian war," and his new command coincided with a period of renewed resistance to white settlement from the Indian tribes on the Great Plains and a new federal policy of forced assimilation.

The destroyer of Southern railroads took a keen personal interest in the Union Pacific Railroad, personally reconnoitering routes through the Rocky Mountains and assigning troops to protect its workers, many of whom included veterans from his campaigns in the Deep South. Sherman's attitudes toward Native Americans were infused with a strong streak of racial Darwinism. Though he respected their bravery and recognized that they had legitimate grievances regarding their treatment by the government and white society, he regarded them as primitives and an impediment to progress and civilization. "The more I see of these Indians the more convinced I am that they all have to be killed or maintained as a species of paupers," Sherman wrote to his brother in 1868. "Their attempts at civilization are simply ridiculous."[24]

Sherman's proclivity for extremist statements was often present in his observations on the "Indian troubles." When a detachment of eighty soldiers was wiped out by a combined force of Sioux, Cheyenne, and Arapaho warriors near Fort Phil Kearny, Wyoming, on December 21, 1866, Sherman told Grant, "We must act with vindictive earnestness against the Sioux, even to their extermination, men, women, and children."[25] These prescriptions were not put into practice, but Sherman's response to Indian resistance drew heavily on the methods he had first observed in the Seminole War. Traditionally, the Plains Indians fought during the summer and withdrew to settled camps during the winter. Sherman ordered his troops to attack these camps outside the fighting season, when their war ponies were weak and the loss of their food supplies meant starvation or surrender.

As was often the case with Sherman, this strategy had a dual military and political purpose. With few troops at his disposal and faced with small bands of mounted warriors who specialized in rapid hit-and-run raids in a vast territory with limitless possibilities for escape, winter campaigning was a cost-effective alternative to allowing "fifty hostile Indians to checkmate three thousand soldiers." At the same time, the destruction of their food supplies would target the whole population and facilitate the government's assimilationist policy by driving Indians back into reservations. Sherman's indispensable lieutenant during these campaigns was the bulldoggish Philip Sheridan, who commanded the Department of the Platte.

In the winter of 1868, U.S. Cavalry units attacked the Southern Cheyenne, the Kiowa, the Arapaho, and the Comanche in northern Texas and Oklahoma, burning their camps and destroying or seizing their ponies and food supplies. One of their commanders was the Civil War hero Lieutenant Colonel George Armstrong Custer, who was ordered by Sherman to attack hostile tribes along the Washita River in order to "destroy their villages and ponies, to kill or hang all warriors, and bring back all women and children." On November 26, Custer led 720 men from the Seventh Cavalry in a dawn attack on the snowbound camp of fifty-eight lodges led by the friendly Cheyenne chieftain Black Kettle on the Washita River. In a battle that quickly turned into a rout, Custer's men killed over a hundred Indians, including Black Kettle and his wife. The majority of the dead were not armed warriors, but women and young children, most of whom, according to the writer and anthropologist George Bird Grinnell, a student of the Cheyenne, "were shot while hiding in the brush or trying to run away through it."[26]

Custer's raid against a widely respected Cheyenne chief received some criticism in the East, but Sheridan condemned such critics as "good and pious ecclesiastics . . . aiders and abetters of savages who murdered, without mercy, men, women and children." Sherman declared himself "well satisfied" with Custer's attack. In 1869 Philip Sheridan was appointed commander of the Military District of the Missouri, following Sherman's promotion to commander in chief of the U.S. Army. Between 1869 and 1883, Sheridan's forces fought 619 separate engagements with the Plains tribes, using a combination of offensive raids and winter campaigns that made little distinction between fighters and noncombatants. Writing to Sherman in 1873, Sheridan justified his methods in the following terms: "If a village is attacked and women and children killed, the responsibility is not with the soldiers but with the people whose crimes necessitated the attack. During the war did one hesitate to attack a village or town occupied by the enemy because women or children were within its limits? Did we cease to throw shells at Vicksburg or Atlanta because women or children were there?"[27]

During the Red River War of 1874–75, Cheyenne, Kiowa, and Comanche were starved into reservations along the southern plains as Sheridan's commanders pursued them relentlessly, destroying their camps and deporting their leaders. Sheridan also attacked the material basis of Plains Indian society. In 1871, the hunting of buffalo herds by white hunters reached new heights following the discovery of a new way of making leather from buffalo hide. Between 1872 and 1874, an estimated 3,700,000 buffalo were slaughtered in the West, of which only 150,000 were killed by Indians. In 1875 Sheridan opposed an attempt by the Texas legislature to conserve the remaining buffalo, and praised the hunters "who have done more in the last two years, and will do more in the next years, to settle the vexed Indian question, than the entire regular army has done in the last thirty years. . . . They are destroying the Indians' commissary, and it is a well-known fact that an army losing its base of supplies is placed at a great disadvantage."[28] For Sheridan, the extermination of the buffalo was "the only way to bring lasting peace and allow civilization to advance."

By 1875, most of the tribes on the southern Plains had been forced onto reservations, and the focus of the "Indian question" shifted to the powerful Lakota Sioux in southern Dakota. When the Sioux rejected an offer from a government commission to buy the Black Hills, where gold had been discovered the previous year, Sherman authorized Sheridan to begin military operations against them, thus unleashing a chain of events that culminated in Custer's defeat at the Battle of the Little Big Horn on June 25, 1876. A furious Sherman now declared that "forbearance has ceased to be a virtue toward these Indians, and only a severe and persistent chastisement will bring them to a sense of submission." All reservations in Sioux country were now placed under military control and their inhabitants treated as prisoners of war. Indians outside these reservations were regarded as "hostiles" and hunted down remorselessly.

Throughout the winter of 1876–77, cavalry columns systematically pursued a policy of starvation against the Sioux and Cheyenne, burning their camps and seizing their supplies of dried buffalo meat, their ponies, and their buffalo robes, leaving their destitute inhabitants exposed in the mountains in below-zero temperatures. By May 1877, most of the Indians had come into the reservations. Despite sporadic resistance to white settlement over the coming years, the defeat of the Sioux effectively marked the end of America's long conquest of the Native American population.

Sherman regarded his contribution to the settlement of the West as one of his greatest achievements. "I have been travelling, in three months, in beautiful cars abundantly provided with every comfort, over an extent of more than ten thousand miles of country, every mile of which is free from the danger of the savage and is being occupied by industrious families," he wrote to his wife in 1883, during his last official trip to the West. "Every day I am reminded of little things done, or words spoken which have borne fruit. I honestly believe in this way I have done more good for our country and for the human race than I did in the Civil War."[29] Asked by a *Denver Times* interviewer for his views on the Indian question, he replied, "I do not see what is to prevent them from gradually becoming an extinct race, but in any event I don't think they will ever again become a factor in the general policy of this country; the railroads have settled that."[30]

In his memoirs, he attributed the completion of the Union Pacific Railroad to the Civil War, which "trained the men who built that national highway" and provided soldiers who were willing to "fight the marauding Indians just as they had learned to fight the rebels down at Atlanta." For Sherman, both marauding Indians and rebels were obstacles to the advancement of an American civilization that he considered destined for international greatness. Yet he always remained wary of the fragility of this civilization and continued to rail at the "demagogues, dynamite fiends, fools, hypocrites and mischief-makers" whom he regarded as a threat to American stability during the Gilded Age. In 1877 he criticized a decision by Congress not to use federal troops to suppress "labor riots." Ten years later, he warned, "I am not afraid of the red flag, if any disturbing element comes from abroad or within, we will squelch it quicker than we did the civil war."[31]

Despite his reactionary political views, Sherman was never tempted to follow Grant and run for presidential office. Following his retirement in 1883, he spent much of his time attending army reunions and traveling back and forth across the country as a sought-after speaker and national celebrity. His appearance was invariably greeted by the strains of "Marching Through Georgia"—a song that he came to detest. He also traveled widely abroad, visiting London, Paris, Germany, Russia, and Cuba, where he told his wife that the Cubans praised "El Grande Marcha" (*sic*) and compared him to Hannibal and Julius Caesar.

On February 14, 1891, just after his seventy-first birthday, Sherman collapsed in his rocking chair while rereading *Great Expectations* and died shortly afterward. More than thirty thousand soldiers and veterans accompanied his coffin to the train in New York that took it to Saint Louis. There another twelve thousand veterans, soldiers, and local dignitaries accompanied his body on a seven-mile procession from the station to the Calvary Cemetery, where his son Tom read the funeral oration. In this way, America said farewell to the soldier who, in the words of the poet and Civil War veteran Richard Watson Gilder, "fought for freedom, not glory; made war that war might cease."[32]

PART II

Legacies

6

Soldiers

The memory of the Civil War looms large in the American wars of the twentieth century. Generations of officers absorbed tactics and strategies during "staff rides" to Civil War battlefields and studied Stonewall Jackson's Valley Campaign, Grant's turning movement at Vicksburg, and Lee's audacious division of his army during the Seven Days Battles. The great Civil War commanders provided moral, tactical, and strategic inspiration to a succession of generals from Pershing, Patton, and MacArthur to "Stormin' Norman" Schwarzkopf and Tommy Franks.

During the First Gulf War, General Schwarzkopf made Grant's memoirs his bedside reading and placed on his desk a Sherman quotation: "War is the remedy our enemies have chosen, and I say let's give them all they want." General Wesley Clark, the commander of NATO forces during the Kosovo War, has praised Sherman as "a man who used his skill and insight not only to blaze a trail of destruction across the American South but also to create a new form of maneuver, a 'strategy of the indirect,'" because of which "future generations of military leaders would ask themselves if there wasn't a way of avoiding the big battles, of breaking the enemy through indirect maneuver. And they looked back, always, to Sherman to find the answer."[1]

Politicians have also drawn lessons from Sherman's campaigns. In the closing months of World War I, the Republican Party senator Henry Cabot Lodge urged the U.S. government and its allies to force Germany's complete surrender and march "on to Berlin," declaring that "the Republican Party stands for unconditional surrender and complete victory, just as Grant stood." Cabot Lodge argued that invasion and occupation would confirm Germany's defeat and justified this view on the basis of his youthful memories of the Civil War, when he had followed "with deepest interests Sherman's march to the sea."[2]

Cabot Lodge's political adversary President Woodrow Wilson also referred to Sherman's campaigns in these debates, but as an argument *against* imposing a harsh punitive peace on Germany. "The thing that holds me back is the aftermath of war," he told his cabinet secretary. "I come from the South and I know what war is, for I have seen its wreckage and terrible ruin."[3] As an eight-year-old boy, Wilson had watched Confederate soldiers preparing to defend Augusta against Sherman's advancing army. He told his cabinet of his memories of relatives in Columbia describing "the outrageous deeds of Sherman's troops." Wilson also cited Reconstruction as an argument against the occupation of Germany; he remembered it as a "dark chapter of history" and a period of "fear, demoralization, disgust, and social revolution."

These very different interpretations suggest that Sherman's influence on American warfare was not as one-dimensional as his critics have sometimes claimed. Some associated Sherman with the "terrible ruin" and cruelty of war and the extension of military destruction beyond the battlefield, but there were also those who regarded his campaigns in the Deep South as a tactical and strategic model for *minimizing* military destruction. Neither of these interpretations was obvious in the immediate aftermath of the Civil War. Apart from some recommendations regarding the formation and supply of armies on the march, Sherman himself did not include his most famous campaigns in a section on military lessons of the war in his memoirs, which was mostly concerned with suggestions for the reorganization of the U.S. Army and the professionalization of its officer class. In 1906 the Leaven-worth Infantry and Cavalry School in Kansas, which was founded at Sherman's instigation, began the practice of visiting Civil War battlefields to provide officers with insights into the "face of battle." On these so-called staff rides or tactical rides, officers consulted handbooks on particular Civil War battles published by the newly established Army War College and replayed the struggle on game boards based on topographical maps of the battle-grounds like the Germans, whose *Kriegsspiel* (war-gaming) would later become standard practice in the U.S. military.[4]

Sherman's name is conspicuously absent from these writings, and his campaigns in Georgia and the Carolinas barely feature at all. This absence is partly due to the fact that the post–Civil War army did not expect to be fighting wars in which such methods would be necessary, and also to the U.S. Army's own ambivalence toward his policy of devastation. In *The Principles of Strategy, Illustrated Mainly from American Campaigns* (1894), the influential military intellectual Captain John Bigelow cited Sherman and Sheridan's destructive campaigns as examples of a "political strategy" that "carried the war home to the enemy's people" by targeting the civilian population and its government. Though Bigelow recognized that such political strategy might be useful in wars in which "the people of a republic are a more decisive objective than those of a despotism or absolute monarchy," he remained doubtful whether "the idea of dispiriting a people may be advantageously carried" and speculated that "the infliction of suffering on a people who can stand all that can be inflicted only makes the military problem more difficult by embittering them."[5]

In 1895, the Massachusetts military historian John Codman Ropes similarly suggested that Sherman had "conducted war on obsolete and barbarous principles" and that his campaigns had "violated one of the fundamental canons of modern warfare" in destroying "property which was not needed for the supply of his army or of the enemy's army."[6] One of Sherman's own former subordinates, Major General John M. Schofield, made not dissimilar criticisms in his 1897 memoirs. These less-than-ringing official endorsements did not mean that Sherman's campaigns were forgotten or ignored, however, and within a decade of his death the "psychological" strategy of destruction that he developed in Georgia and the Carolinas was implemented to devastating effect in the first of America's foreign wars that followed the Civil War.

Benevolent Destruction

More than any of America's wars, the Philippine War of 1898–1902 bore the direct imprint of Sherman's campaigns in terms of both strategy and personnel. The war was an inadvertent and mostly unexpected consequence of the Spanish-American War. On May 1, 1898, the U.S. Navy's Asiatic Squadron under Commodore George Dewey destroyed the Spanish fleet in Manila harbor and found itself in joint control of the Philippine capital with three or four thousand members of Emilio Aguinaldo's Army of Liberation, which had previously been a de facto ally of the United States. In December 1898, the United States bought the Philippines from Spain during the negotiations in Paris that ended the Spanish-American War, and President McKinley adopted a policy of "benevolent assimilation" toward the islands. As a consequence, the U.S. Army's Eighth Corps in the Philippines was ordered to suppress Aguinaldo's Army of Liberation and "win the confidence, respect, and affection of the inhabitants of the Philippines."

This mission turned out to be much more difficult than anticipated. Though Aguinaldo's poorly armed *insurrectos* were no match for the better-equipped U.S. troops in conventional battles, they were able to inflict significant casualties with ambushes, snipers, booby traps, and attacks on lone soldiers or stragglers in the

Conquerors: American soldiers displaying enemy skulls after unknown battle, between 1899 and 1913. Courtesy of the Library of Congress.

tropical landscape of swamps, rice paddies, inaccessible mountains, and muddy roads that did not favor pursuit operations. In response the Americans frequently made no distinction between fighters, suspects, and sympathizers. Civilians and captured *insurrectos* were often subjected to various forms of torture, including the "water cure," in which suspects were pumped full of water and stomped or suspended headfirst into wells and buckets of water to extract information, after which they were often killed.

In the spring of 1899, General Loyd Wheaton, a Civil War hero who had served under Sherman, ordered his men to burn every village within a twelve-mile radius along the Pasig River in response to a guerrilla ambush. One of Wheaton's soldiers later described the scene: "A long black column of smoke sprang up . . . cascoes [flatboats] were dragged up to the fires and burned and the entire district so destroyed so that it would seem necessary not only for a bird but even a Filipino to carry his rations while crossing it."[7]

Aguinaldo's forces also destroyed crops and property in an attempt to slow down the U.S. advance or terrorize the population into supporting them, but the punitive measures adopted by the army were based on the realization that the Filipino desire for independence was more popular and deep-rooted than the McKinley administration had predicted. In May 1900, the dull and unimaginative American commander General Elwell Otis was replaced by the fifty-four-year-old Civil War hero Arthur MacArthur Jr., the former military governor of northern Luzon, who extended a general amnesty to rebels who declared their loyalty to the United States. Very few Filipinos took advantage of this offer, and MacArthur's commanders increasingly called for more aggressive measures that recalled the Lincoln administration's hard-war policy during the Civil War.

In February 1901, a battalion of Seventh Infantry and five companies from the Forty-Eighth U.S. Volunteer Infantry conducted a scorched-earth campaign in the guerrilla stronghold of Abra Province in northern Luzon; villages, crops, and storehouses were systematically ruined and burned, till commanding officer Major William C. Bowen reported that "the entire province was as devoid of food products as was the valley of the Shenandoah after Sheridan's raid during the Civil War."[8]

Food-denial operations were sometimes coupled with a tactic that had been vociferously condemned by the American press when employed by Spanish forces in Cuba—civilian populations were forced into stockaded "zones of protection" or "colonies," while the army devastated the evacuated areas so that the guerrillas could not find subsistence in them.

On September 28, 1901, a group of armed *insurrectos* under the command of General Vicente Lukbán carried out a surprise attack on the recently established base of Company C of the Ninth

Infantry Regiment at the town of Balangiga, on the island of Samar, in which fifty-nine soldiers were killed and twenty-three wounded, many of them horribly mutilated. In response the American commander General Adna R. Chaffee appointed Brigadier General Jacob H. Smith as commander of the Sixth Separate Brigade, with orders to take control of the pacification of Samar and Leyte. Known as Hell Roaring Jake because of his stentorian voice, Smith told Major Littleton W.T. "Tony" Waller, the commander of three hundred marines sent to assist these operations in October: "I want no prisoners. I wish you to kill and burn, the more you kill and burn the better it will please me."

When Waller asked for clarification of these orders, he was told to kill every male on the island above the age of ten. For the next three months, Smith's troops did their best to fulfill his instructions to turn Samar into a "howling wilderness," in a chaotic, brutal, and badly organized campaign that wreaked havoc on the island's 250,000 inhabitants. While U.S. Navy gunboats patrolled the coastline and rivers to prevent the guerrillas from being resupplied, columns of soldiers trekked through swamps and jungle, burning villages, hamlets, and farms and destroying or confiscating livestock and food supplies.

These operations soon reduced much of the population to starvation, till some of Smith's own commanders pleaded with him to allow food supplies to be brought from outside the island to prevent famine. Subsequent estimates of the death toll from these operations have ranged from 2,500 to 50,000, and they were widely criticized in the United States despite their effectiveness against Lukbán's guerrillas. Smith's radical orders were revealed when Major Waller was court-martialed for the executions of eleven prisoners during a disastrous thirty-five-mile march into the interior of Samar. Summoned as a witness, Smith affirmed that "treachery must be punished, that war must be prosecuted vigorously; that war was hell; that great General Sherman had said that 'war is hell,' and that the quicker the war was ended the less cruelty," but nevertheless denied that he had ordered Waller to carry out indiscriminate killings.[9]

As a result of this trial, Smith was also court-martialed and was found guilty of "conduct to the prejudice of good order and military discipline." Smith received considerable support from many of his fellow officers, and he was quietly retired rather than punished, while Waller was acquitted. The pacification of Samar coincided with an equally destructive but far more effective campaign under General James Franklin Bell, commander of the Third Separate Brigade in the provinces of Batangas, Laguna, and Tayabas. A West Point graduate and a lawyer and professor of military science and tactics, Bell was cut from very different cloth than the hard-drinking and manically ferocious Smith. In December 1901, Bell prepared for the coming campaign by issuing a series of telegraphic circulars to his post commanders and the population, carefully outlining his orders.[10] As in Samar, all civilians were to be removed to "zones of protection" with their possessions, and anyone remaining outside them would be considered hostile and their property subject to confiscation or destruction. In the event of any attacks on American soldiers or collaborators, Filipino prisoners would be selected at random and shot. Officers were ordered to burn the nearest homes and villages whenever telegraph wires were cut or bridges were destroyed by insurgents.

Bell justified these measures in very Sherman-like terms. In his third telegram, he declared, "Military necessity frequently precludes the possibility of making just discriminations, but it should be borne in mind that the greatest good to the greatest number can best be brought about by putting a prompt end to insurrection. A short and severe war creates in the aggregate less loss and suffering than benevolent war indefinitely prolonged." Like Sherman, Bell also saw his campaign as an instrument of long-term pacification. In a letter to his immediate superior, Major General

Wheaton, on December 26, he stated: "A peace brought about by peace commissioners prior to the suffering by these people of the real hardships of war would almost certainly be followed by another insurrection within the next five years. These people need a thrashing to teach them some good common sense, and they should have it for the good of all concerned."

As on Samar, these methods were brutally effective. On April 16, 1902, the revolutionary commander Miguel Malvar y Carpio surrendered, and 2,973 *insurrectos* soon followed his example. Exactly one month later, Bell issued his final circular, number 38, which declared an end to these special war measures in order to "re-establish a feeling of security and tranquility among the people as rapidly as possible." On June 23, martial law was suspended and Batangas was handed over to a civil government made up of conservative members of the local Filipino elite acting under the auspices of the U.S. Bureau of Insular Affairs. By this time, hundreds of villages in the province had been destroyed, large areas of farmland had been devastated, and some 75 to 90 percent of the cattle had been slaughtered. Many of the people were still in concentration camps, where malnourishment and cramped and unsanitary conditions bred cholera, measles, and other diseases that killed thousands. The U.S. Army itself estimated that the population of Batangas fell by more than 90,000 between 1896 and 1902, and others have suggested that as many as 100,000 Filipinos died from hunger, fighting, or disease in the province as a direct consequence of Bell's operations.[11] The Batangas campaign was the last major operation of a war that cost 4,200 American lives and the lives of 16,000 to 20,000 *insurrectos*. The death toll among Filipino civilians has been variously estimated from 200,000 to a million, either as a direct result of military operations or from war-related hunger and disease—an outcome that the Civil War historian Michael Fellman has attributed to the "American terrorist war practices" adopted by Bell, Smith, and other U.S. commanders.[12]

At the Lodge Committee hearings on the conduct of the war in 1902, Bell's methods were defended by U.S. Army public relations officer Arthur Lockwood Wagner, the most influential military intellectual in the first decade of the twentieth century, who compared the burning of towns and villages to Sherman's destruction of Atlanta, which he called a "cruel measure, but it was a measure of military necessity."[13] In a letter to the Senate on May 7 that same year, Secretary of War Elihu Root declared that Bell's operations had been carried out with the approval of the War Department and described them as "the most effective and the most humane which could possibly be followed." Such approval ensured that Bell, unlike Smith, was not court-martialed or censured. Whereas Smith's career ended in disgrace, Bell went on to head the Command and General Staff School at Fort Leavenworth and subsequently become chief of the Army General Staff. Today, more than a century later, his telegrams are still cited at the U.S. Army's Combat Studies Institute (CSI) at Fort Leavenworth as a "masterpiece of counterguerrilla warfare" and a valuable source of "insights" into counterinsurgency campaigns in Iraq and Afghanistan.

Sherman in Vietnam

Many of the methods adopted in the Philippines also formed part of the more "scientific" pacification campaigns of the Vietnam War. In his memoirs, Colin Powell recalls his youthful participation in operations against Vietcong guerrillas in the A Shau Valley: "We burned down the thatched huts, starting the blaze with Ronson and Zippo lighters. . . . Why were we torching houses and destroying crops? Ho Chi Minh had said the people were like the sea in which his guerrillas swam. . . . We tried to solve the problem by making the whole sea uninhabitable. In the hard logic of war, what difference did it make if you shot your enemy or starved him to death?"[14]

Philip Sheridan had once espoused a similar "hard logic" when he ordered the burning and destruction of barns and food storehouses in the Shenandoah Valley and Indian camps during winter campaigns on the Great Plains. In Vietnam, Vietnamese villages suspected of containing persons with Vietcong sympathies were routinely destroyed to deny food and sanctuary to guerrillas or as an act of collective punishment. In many cases, the Vietnamese homes—or "hootches" to U.S. soldiers—were demolished by dynamite and plowed under by specially adapted bulldozers known as Rome plows or set on fire by "Zippo squads" wielding cigarette lighters. Other villages were bombed from the air together with their surrounding crops. During Operation Pipestone Canyon in May 1969, four marine battalions and units of the Army of the Republic of Vietnam (ARVN, the South Vietnamese Army) and the South Korean Army attacked Go Noi Island, a delta area approximately five miles long and two miles wide in Quang Nam Province. At least 750,000 tons of bombs were dropped on the island before the population was removed and their villages demolished and plowed under, thereby transforming "a densely populated, heavily wooded area into a barren wasteland, a plowed field," as the after-action report approvingly recorded.[15]

As in the Philippines, Sherman was often cited in connection with these campaigns. In 1969 the army journalist Jay Roberts described the actions of Captain Ernest Medina's C company at My Lai as "an old tactic and a good one. Sherman's march to the sea. You've just got to. We saw soldiers drag a body from hut and throw it in a well to destroy the water supply."[16] During Medina's 1971 court-martial in Atlanta, Mary McCarthy described the March to the Sea as an "earlier war crime" comparable to My Lai.[17] In 1974, a Georgia judge justified his decision to release Second Lieutenant William Calley, the only U.S. soldier found guilty of the massacre, from house arrest at Fort Benning in Columbus, Georgia, with an exposition of Sherman's philosophy of war in which he concluded, "The point is that Sherman is absolutely right: not in what he did, but about the nature of war: war *is* hell."[18]

The particular hellishness of the Vietnam War owed more to the more recent innovations in U.S. counterinsurgency strategy than it did to Sherman's campaigns. Under the U.S. commander General William Westmoreland, the primary metric of military achievement was a weekly body count of enemy casualties. The U.S. Army sent out reconnaissance patrols as bait, drawing out enemy forces so that they could be annihilated by artillery or tactical air strikes. This search-and-destroy strategy was intended to produce a "crossover point" where the enemy would conclude that fighting was no longer in its own rational interest. In practice it degenerated into a program of incentivized killing and massive destruction that made little distinction between armed fighters, Vietcong sympathizers, and Vietnamese civilians.[19]

Between December 1968 and May 1969, the Ninth U.S. Infantry Division carried out a round-the-clock "surprise and shock" campaign known as Operation Speedy Express in the Vietcong stronghold of the Upper Mekong Delta, in an attempt to bring the area under the control of the Saigon government before the upcoming Paris peace negotiations. For six months, the division conducted this offensive, supported by ARVN units, naval and aerial bombardments, and helicopter gunships, under the direction of its notoriously gung-ho commander, General Julian J. Ewell, and his chief of staff, Colonel Ira Hunt.

Ewell and Hunt were obsessed with increasing their kill statistics; one of their officers later recalled that "commanders were under constant pressure to produce body count as a measure of their own effectiveness." At the beginning of Speedy Express, Ewell's division had an average body count of eight enemy dead for each dead American soldier. Within a month of the operation, the ratio had risen to 21:1. In April the following year, it reached an extraordinary 134:1. By the end of the operation, the Ninth Infantry claimed to have killed 10,899 Vietcong, yet only 748 weapons were recovered. In their after-action report, Ewell and Hunt described these operations as a means of "un-brutalizing" the war through a combination of combat operations and psychological warfare directed at the "destruction of the enemy's will to fight and the winning of the confidence of the civilian populace." Raids on villages were followed by civic action teams who held raffles with chickens and ducks as prizes, handed out free T-shirts with the colors of the South Vietnamese government, provided medical care, distributed food, and entertained the populace with military bands and country music ("a big hit with the Vietnamese").[20]

This very American combination of destruction and civic action was an essential and often incongruous component of the Vietnam War. As in the Philippines and the Indian wars, Vietnamese peasants were removed en masse at gunpoint from their destroyed villages to fortified "strategic hamlets" in order to drain the "sea" in which the Vietcong guerrillas swam. In some cases, U.S. combat units arrived with trucks and helicopters and forcibly removed the people *before* razing their villages, poisoning their wells, and destroying their rice paddies to prevent them from returning. In the summer of 1967, the 101st Airborne's Tiger Force, a forty-five-man "kick-ass" reconnaissance unit formed by Colonel David Hackworth to "out-guerrilla the guerrillas," carved a legendary trail of atrocities through the Song Ve Valley in Quang Ngai Province as part of Westmoreland's Task Force Oregon operations in the Central Highlands. After wrecking rice paddies and driving seven thousand peasants with their cattle and water buffalo out of the valley, Tiger Force embarked on a spree of rape and murder. Its soldiers shot farmers on sight, killed civilians and mutilated their bodies, and threw hand grenades into bunkers containing men, women, and children.

At the end of the summer, *New Yorker* correspondent Jonathan Schell flew over Song Ve and found that "all the houses there had been destroyed."[21] Schell also observed fields and crops turned uniformly brown as a result of the U.S. Army's Operation Ranch Hand defoliation program, authorized by John F. Kennedy and continued by his successor, Lyndon B. Johnson. Between 1961 and 1971, the U.S. military and the South Vietnamese Army defoliated some 5 million acres of forest and jungle with Agent Orange and other herbicides in an attempt to expose the supply trails and hiding places used by the Vietcong and the North Vietnamese Army, in what a historian of Operation Ranch Hand, David Zierler, has called "a scale of chemical warfare unseen since World War I."

Like Sherman, American strategists of the Vietnam War saw destruction as an instrument of sociopolitical engineering. As James William Gibson has pointed out in his forensic analysis of the U.S. techno-war in Vietnam, some technocrats regarded the evacuation of the rural population as a form of "development."[22] In the aftermath of the 1968 Tet Offensive, the political scientist Samuel Huntington suggested that the application of U.S. military power on a "massive scale" could promote a "massive migration from countryside to city," in which rural villagers would become exposed to the benefits of an "American-sponsored urban revolution" that would undercut "the Maoist-inspired rural revolution."[23]

These aspirations were never realized. Unable or unwilling to understand the powerful nationalist impulse in Vietnamese history, often remarkably oblivious to the bitterness and anger that its bombing and counterinsurgency campaigns engendered among the population that it aspired to "save," the U.S. government remained committed to the zero-sum domino theory of international relations that presented every Third World leftist or nationalist movement as the product of an international Communist conspiracy. Such representations were particularly anomalous and inappropriate in Vietnam, where the Eisenhower administration was told by the CIA as early as 1956 that Ho Chi Minh would have won 80 percent of the vote had scheduled elections taken place across the whole of Vietnam. Unwilling to accept this outcome, successive U.S. administrations committed the army to uphold a government in South Vietnam that too many Vietnamese did not want, and never had wanted, and fight a war without a viable political strategy, ending in a humiliating withdrawal that has haunted the U.S. military ever since.

The Indirect Approach

The rural pacification campaigns of the Philippines and Vietnam belong to a tradition of American counterinsurgency warfare that developed from Sherman's Southern campaigns and the Indian wars in that they made little distinction between armed fighters and civilians and their political, military, and psychological goals overlapped. But Sherman's strategies and philosophy of war also embody certain assumptions and practices that were intrinsic to America's conventional wars in the twentieth century. In an analysis of World War I in the early 1920s, Lieutenant Commander Holloway Halstead Frost of the U.S. Navy argued that "when great nations are at war with approximately equal military forces it will seldom be possible to win a purely military decision" and that future wars should follow the Civil War campaigns of Sherman and Sheridan and take the form of "direct attacks on the enemy economic forces."[24]

For Frost and for many military strategists in the interwar years, attacks on economic targets not only offered a potential solution to the strategic deadlock of industrialized warfare, but also pointed the way toward a less destructive form of war than the bloody stalemate of World War I. One of the most influential exponents of this view was the British military strategist Basil Henry Liddell Hart. A captain in the British army during World War I, Liddell Hart was the foremost British military intellectual of the interwar period. His theories on mobile warfare, maneuver, and the role of mechanized forces were heavily influenced by his disgust with the meat-grinding carnage that he witnessed in France. In a series of books and articles written in the 1920s, Liddell Hart promulgated a war of movement—the "indirect approach"—as an alternative to the static battlegrounds of World War I.

In *The Strategy of Indirect Approach* (1929), Liddell Hart argued that battles between heavily armed industrialized armies had become so costly as to make them militarily unviable and that future armies should seek to avoid such confrontations by targeting the adversary's rearguard command-and-communications structure. These proposals were not entirely new, and Liddell Hart offered numerous historical precedents dating back to the Greek-Persian Wars to show how the indirect approach had been put into practice. He suggested, "It is . . . more potent, as well as more economical, to disarm the enemy than to attempt his destruction by hard fighting. . . . A strategist should think in terms of paralyzing, not of killing." This advice had particular resonance in the aftermath of World War I.[25]

For Liddell Hart, William Tecumseh Sherman was the first modern general to have fully grasped and implemented these principles. In his biography *Sherman: Soldier, Realist, American* (1929), he hailed Sherman's "economy of force by manoeuvre" in Georgia and the Carolinas as a more intelligent form of war than Grant's "direct strategy" in Virginia. He argued that Sherman's strategies and tactics were more suited to the "psychology of a democracy" and the new demands of mechanized warfare, with their emphasis on speed, mobility, and territorial gains rather than the bludgeoning destruction of the enemy's armed forces that Grant favored. In Liddell Hart's view, the "indirect" dimensions of Sherman's campaigns manifested in rapidity of movement coupled with a tactical flexibility that enabled Sherman to place his opponents "on the horns of a dilemma" regarding his intentions. Rather than attack enemy strong points, Sherman had gone between and around them. Instead of seeking battle, he had exerted a form of "moral pressure" on Southern civilians that precluded the need for "serious physical pressure" on the Confederate Army.

These components of Sherman's campaigns, Liddell Hart insisted, were particularly relevant at a time when the invention of the internal combustion engine and the caterpillar track and the development of airpower offered new instruments for eliminating the "deadly ground"—the space between an advancing and defending army—and targeting the enemy rear guard. Long before World War II, Liddell Hart argued that tanks and mechanized forces could be used for "deep strategic penetration," in much the same way that Sherman had used horses, wagons, and infantry columns. These ideas were echoed by Liddell Hart's British contemporary the military historian and journalist General J.F.C. Fuller. A tank commander during World War I, Fuller was not an admirer of Sherman, but his views on mechanized warfare and the "rebirth of mobility" were not that far removed from Liddell Hart's formulations. In a May 1918 memorandum, Fuller argued that the British army should switch from the destruction of German soldiers, or "body warfare," to "brain warfare" aimed at the destruction of Germany's command and supply structures, through "a sudden eruption of squadrons of fast-moving tanks, which unheralded would proceed to the various enemy headquarters, and either round them up or scatter them."[26]

Such ideas were part of a more general "rebirth of mobility" in the aftermath of World War I that was shared by most of the armies that had taken part in it. In 1918, the American Expeditionary Force under General John J. Pershing suffered huge losses in Grant-like massed assaults on German defensive positions, and in the interwar years U.S. military strategists increasingly concluded that such confrontations were insufficient in themselves to produce military decision and began to adapt the new era of mechanization to older traditions of American war making.

Raiders

Like many Union commanders, Sherman had great respect for the destructive raids carried out by the Confederate cavalryman Nathan Bedford Forrest, but he tended to use cavalry for screening, reconnaissance, and feints, leaving the work of destruction to fast-moving infantry units. In a 1928 memorandum, "A Mechanized Unit," Major General Adna R. Chaffee Jr. (1884–1941), the son of the former military governor of the Philippines, called for the replacement of the U.S. horse cavalry by mechanized forces. A former cavalry officer himself, Chaffee proposed that these new units would emulate the "army-sized raids through Georgia, Alabama and the Carolinas" carried out by Sherman and the destructive 525-mile cavalry rampage carried out by James Harrison Wilson in the aftermath of Sherman's marches, penetrating deep into the enemy rear guard, targeting command, control, and logistical networks in a strategy that echoed Liddell Hart's "indirect" formulations.[27]

In 1940 Chaffee became commander of First Armored Corps, the U.S. Army's first armored force. In his first address to his officers, he declared that its purpose was "to attack through hostile weakness. It creates surprise ... by the sustained celerity and power of tactical movement. It uses its mobility to choose the most favorable direction for attack to reach vital enemy rear areas." The "father of the U.S. armored force" did not live long enough to put these ideas into practice, but his emphasis on "celerity and power" was shared by his contemporary and another former cavalry officer General George S. Patton Jr. Patton was a member of the American Tank Corps and commander of the U.S. tank school in France during World War I, and his views on mechanized warfare were strongly influenced by German interwar texts, which advocated a dynamic war of movement combining detachments of motorized infantry with tanks and armored units. As commander of the U.S. Seventh Army in North Africa and Sicily, Patton acquired a reputation for slashing, fast-moving, and somewhat reckless offensives using motorized infantry and armor. His most famous campaign took place in France, following the D-day landings, when he was given command of the U.S. Third Army during the Allied breakout from the Normandy lodgment area. Patton arrived in France more than a month after the initial landings and found the Allied armies bogged down in the "hedgerow war" of the Normandy *bocage* that recalled the cramped battlefields of the Civil War.

Faced with the looming prospect of a static World War I–style front line, General Omar Bradley launched his First Army in a combined aerial bombing and infantry offensive called Operation Cobra on July 25, piercing the German defensive lines and opening the way for what Russell Weigley called a "virtual road march" that appealed "to the passion for moving that is so much a part of the American character and heritage." This "passion for moving" was the cornerstone of Patton's concept of war, just as it had once been of Sherman's. On August 1, the Third Army advanced into Brittany with the objective of capturing Brest and other German-held Breton ports. In a speech to his staff officers, Patton outlined the kind of campaign he wanted with characteristic bluntness and disregard for military convention: "Flanks are something for the enemy to worry about, not us. . . . We are advancing constantly and are not interested in holding anything, except the enemy. . . . Our basic plan of operation is to advance and keep on advancing regardless of whether we have to go over, under, or through the enemy."[28]

Sherman's thrust into central Georgia was based on a very similar principle of constant motion. If Liddell Hart is to be believed, Patton may have been partly inspired by this campaign. In a meeting in England shortly before departing for France, Patton told Liddell Hart that he had once spent some weeks studying Sherman's Atlanta campaign with his biography in hand as a "very good guide"—a combination, Liddell Hart suggested, that influenced Patton's decision to carry out a Sherman-style campaign in Normandy.[29] The Third Army's movements certainly followed the broad outlines of Liddell Hart's indirect approach. Patton's campaign was directed toward the destruction of German armies rather than the devastation of civilian property. But like Sherman, Patton emphasized speed and mobility to punch through weak points in the German defensive lines or bypass them altogether, using armored columns and mechanized infantry to penetrate deep into the enemy rear guard, disrupting lines of communication and giving his opponents no time to redeploy or reorganize their defenses.

Patton also followed Liddell Hart's concept of "selling the dummy" and placing his opponents "on the horns of a dilemma" regarding his line of attack and his ultimate destination, by allowing his divisional commanders to exploit "breaks" and gaps and vary the route of their advance in order to maintain their forward momentum. In the era of radio and telephone communications and aerial reconnaissance, Patton's motorized divisions could not "vanish" as Sherman's army had after leaving Atlanta, and they received a constant flow of intelligence information from aircraft, the Forces Françaises de l'Intérieur, and a thirty-man mobile reconnaissance team known as Patton's Household Cavalry, which moved ahead of them.

Nevertheless, the speed of the Third Army's advance often meant that radio contact with headquarters was temporarily broken, and Patton's commanders were expected to show the same capacity for improvisation that Sherman had once expected from his corps commanders and make decisions in accordance with Patton's general guidelines. To move as quickly as possible, Patton's troops were expected to travel lightly, and the Third Army's rapid progress was a prodigious feat of teamwork, administration, and logistical organization, in which supplies of food, ammunition, and gasoline were brought forward from Normandy in trucks and sometimes dropped from the air. One of Patton's commanders described the supply trucks following the advancing columns "like a band of stage-coaches making a run through Indian country. We got used to keeping the wheels going, disregarding the snipers, and hoping we wouldn't get lost or hit."

Using these methods, Third Army advanced four hundred miles and fought on two fronts, five hundred miles apart, in the first three weeks of August, liberating 47,829 square miles of French territory and taking thousands of prisoners. Between August 1 and September 24, Patton's "flying columns," as Eisenhower called them, drove the Germans toward Brest before turning eastward toward the Loire Valley, bypassing Paris, and heading toward Reims, Verdun, Commercy, and the Moselle River with such speed that soldiers often rode on tanks, trailers, and jeeps as well as in trucks, in a campaign whose "brilliant rapidity" was subsequently praised by the Allied supreme commander as "perhaps the most spectacular ever seen in modern warfare."[30]

By the end of September, the Third Army was within eighty miles of Hitler's West Wall, the defenses along the Rhine known as the Siegfried Line, when its gasoline finally ran out, after supplies were diverted to the British Second Army. That autumn the entire Allied advance on Germany ran out of steam as a result of supply shortages. The speed and verve of Patton's "American blitzkrieg" had nevertheless captured the imagination of the American public. When Patton's great rival General Bernard Montgomery pressed Eisenhower to place the Third Army in a more static flank-protection role while the Second British and First American armies advanced toward the Ruhr, the supreme commander replied,

"The American public would never stand for stopping Patton in full cry, and public opinion wins war." In December Montgomery once again recommended that the Third Army fall back into a defensive position in order to allow the British to take the lead in the coming offensive against Germany. Patton's section chiefs produced a seven-point memorandum rejecting this proposal, arguing that "the American (soldier and public) psychology must be considered. . . . Third Army troops know and understand the attack. They do not know or understand the retreat or general withdrawal."[31]

Sherman's decision to abandon Atlanta had once been based on very similar considerations. In the event, these debates were made irrelevant by Field Marshal Gerd von Rundstedt's desperate and initially successful counteroffensive in the Ardennes forest. Moving with the same breakneck speed and fighting in freezing conditions, Patton's forces relieved the beleaguered First Army at Bastogne. Following the Allied victory in the Battle of the Bulge, the Third Army joined the broad-front offensive on Germany, breaching the Siegfried Line and crossing the Rhine on March 22. By the time the Third Army made contact with the Red Army on May 8, it had captured twelve thousand cities, towns, and villages in six different countries, killed, wounded, or taken prisoner nearly 3 million German soldiers, overrun military bases and installations, liberated concentration camps, and destroyed two major armies, while its own casualties amounted to 21,441 battlefield dead and 99,224 wounded, in one of the most devastating and celebrated campaigns in American military history.

Leapfrogging

Like the March to the Sea, the popularity of Patton's campaigns was due not just to their speed and seeming irresistibility, but also to their relatively low cost in American lives. In the Pacific campaign, General Douglas MacArthur adopted a variant of the indirect approach in even more challenging conditions during the Allied invasion of the Pacific. In France and Germany, Patton's divisions hurtled down roads that were visible on any tourist map. In the Pacific, Allied soldiers faced some 668,000 tenacious Japanese troops in swamps, mountains, and deep jungle that often lacked roads or even paths, conducting complex land, air, and naval operations with supply lines that reached across thousands of miles of land and sea and included coral reefs, atolls, and innumerable islands. When MacArthur was appointed supreme commander of the Southwest Pacific Area (SWPA) on April 18, 1942, following his defeat in the Philippines, the Allied strategic plan in the Pacific was to mount a two-pronged step-by-step offensive, with MacArthur's forces moving through Papua New Guinea and the southwest Pacific in conjunction with amphibious landings through the Marshall and Gilbert Islands in the central Pacific under the direction of Admiral Chester Nimitz (1885–1966), commander in chief of the Pacific Ocean Area.

These efforts required a complex and grueling combination of air, land, and amphibious operations whose ultimate goal was the conquest of Rabaul, the capital of New Britain and the bastion of Japanese military power in the Pacific. On August 7, the First Marine Division landed on the islands of Guadalcanal and Tulagi, beginning a bloody to-and-fro naval and land campaign that finally ended in an American victory in February the following year. Between November 22, 1942, and January 22, 1943, Australian and American troops destroyed the Japanese garrison at Buna-Gona, New Guinea, in a bloody confrontation that cost the lives 8,500 Allied soldiers. Faced with a potentially endless series of costly "storm landings" against well-entrenched Japanese positions, in August 1943 the Allied chiefs of staff abandoned the attempt to capture Rabaul and opted to neutralize it instead. In

September MacArthur outlined his strategy in the Western Pacific islands: "Key points must of course be taken, but a wise choice of each will obviate the need for storming the mass of islands now in enemy possession. 'Island hopping' with extravagant losses and slow progress . . . is not my idea of how to end the war as soon and as quickly as possible."[32]

In December 1943, American fliers bombed Rabaul's airfields and naval bases, and in February and March the following year MacArthur ordered an amphibious assault on the more weakly defended island of Los Negros in the Admiralty Islands to the west of New Britain. With its supply line cut, Rabaul's garrison of a hundred thousand was left stranded until the war ended. Other Japanese-held islands were similarly neutralized. MacArthur also applied his leapfrogging strategy to the conquest of New Guinea. Between April and July 1944, Allied forces conducted a series of amphibious landings on the northern coast of New Guinea from Finschhafen to Sansapor in the Vogelkop Peninsula, beginning with a naval assault on the Japanese airbase of Hollandia in the Humboldt Bay area of Dutch New Guinea. The real objective of this operation was the coastal town of Wewak, four hundred miles farther east, where twenty thousand crack troops from the Japanese Eighteenth Army under the command of General Hatazō Adachi were braced for an Allied assault.

Instead of attacking Wewak, MacArthur's air force bombed the three weakly defended Japanese air bases at Hollandia and Ataipe, which was roughly halfway between Humboldt Bay and Wewak. In this way, Adachi's Eighteenth Army was cut adrift as the Allied armies gained 750 miles without fighting a major battle. In July, Adachi attempted to reverse these gains with a counterattack from Wewak. Weakened by malaria and an exhausting 400-mile jungle trek, his troops suffered massive casualties. After the war, a senior Japanese intelligence officer praised MacArthur's strategy, which "with minimum losses, attacked and seized a relatively weak area, constructed airfields and then proceeded to cut the supply lines to [our] troops in that area. . . . Our strongpoints were gradually starved out."

MacArthur's policy of "hitting 'em where they ain't" was partly a response to the strategic geography of the Pacific, and like Patton's campaign in Normandy it evoked a lost "romantic" form of warfare won by guile, intelligence, and dash rather than brute force. These campaigns did not preclude physical destruction. Patton's reliance on tactical air support and artillery bombardments reduced German-defended villages into rubble-strewn "Third Army memorials." MacArthur's territorial leaps were made possible by the extension of the "bomber line," the distance from which the air force could attack Japanese positions from airfields or aircraft carriers.

In the Pacific, amphibious assaults on fortified positions could not always be avoided and were often preceded by "softening-up" bombardments and followed by a savage struggle that wreaked havoc on soldiers and civilians alike. Between April and June 1945, nearly half of Okinawa's three hundred thousand inhabitants died during the three-month battle for the island. In February 1945, MacArthur ordered an assault on Manila; in it 70 percent of the city was destroyed and a hundred thousand Filipinos were killed. Most of the civilian dead were massacred by the vengeful Japanese, but the destruction of the city was also due to the American use of tanks and artillery in street fighting characterized by what the Thirty-Seventh Infantry's After-Action Report described as "literal destruction of a building in advance of the area of friendly troops."[33]

Allied artillery and aerial bombings in Normandy and Germany left a similar trail of wrecked military vehicles, of roadsides choked with the corpses of soldiers, animals, and civilians, of ruined towns and roofless villages, and of rubble-choked streets that had to be cleared by bulldozers to allow the Allied armies to get through them. From June 6 to 8, Royal Air Force (RAF) and U.S. Eighth Air Force planes pulverized the city of Caen in an attempt to prevent German reinforcements from bolstering their defenses. Though these raids had little military impact, they killed some 600 civilians and reduced much of the city to rubble. The advance of the Third and Seventh armies into the Saar-Palatinate was accompanied by similar scenes of devastation. "It is difficult to describe the destruction," wrote one Seventh Army divisional commander during pursuit of German motorized units through the Pfälzerwald, the Palatine Forest. "Scarcely a man-made thing exists in our wake; it is even difficult to find buildings suitable for CP's: this is the scorched earth." In the town of Zweibrücken, the advance American units found some 5,000 people, out of a population of 37,000, living in cellars and caves while fires burned uncontrollably above them.[34]

As in the Philippines, some of this destruction was a consequence of airpower and artillery directed against military positions rather than civilian targets, even if the distinction was often irrelevant in practical terms. In two separate raids, in January and April 1945, American and British bombers bombed the German-held Gironde Estuary near Bordeaux with explosives, the standard thermite- or phosphorus-based incendiaries, and a new invention, "jellied gasoline," or napalm; the raid destroyed the former vacation town of Royan, killing more than a thousand civilians.[35] The civilian death toll was a by-product of airpower aimed at German defensive positions. However, many of the devastated towns and cities that the Third and Seventh armies encountered in Germany had been destroyed long before their arrival—by another variant of the "indirect strategy," which was aimed not at soldiers but against the German people.

Wings of Victory

Once again, Sherman's campaigns have often been cited in connection with these developments. "Once proportionality and discrimination were subverted by Sherman, it is arguable that they made the severities of modern American war making at least conceptually possible, from the saturation bombing of World War II, to Hiroshima and Nagasaki, to the Christmas bombing of Hanoi and Haiphong in 1972," argues James Reston Jr. in his indictment/investigation of Sherman's campaigns.[36] Those who make such claims tend to imagine a direct causal link that is by no means obvious. Nevertheless, these parallels are not outlandish. In *Paris; or, The Future of War* (1925), Liddell Hart himself wrote that "aircraft enables us to *jump over* the army which shields the enemy government, industry, and people and *so strike direct and immediately at the seat of the opposing will and policy.*" Liddell Hart did not explicitly advocate the bombing of civilians, and he later rejected the policy of bombing German civilians during World War II. But the prophets of airpower who emerged after World War I had no such reservations. In August 1917, the British government appointed General Jan S. Smuts to head a commission to examine the use of airpower in response to the raids by German Gotha bombers on London that summer. The subsequent report concluded that "the day may not be far off when aerial operations with their devastation of enemy lands and destruction of industrial and populous centres on a vast scale may become the principal operations of war."[37]

In *The Command of the Air* (1921), Giulio Douhet (1869–1930), the former commander of the Italian aviation battalion at Turin, predicted that future wars would be decided by massive bombing raids on cities and civilian population centers, using explosives and chemical and bacteriological weapons. Subjected to this "merciless pounding from the air," he predicted, "the time would soon come when, to put an end to the horror and suffering, the peoples themselves, driven by an instinct of self-preservation, would rise up and demand an end to the war."[38] Similar ideas percolated through the strategic debates on the use of airpower in the United

States in the same period. In *Air Warfare* (1926), Major William C. Sherman (no relation), an Air Corps pilot and instructor in air tactics at Fort Leavenworth, stated, "A decision is reached not by the actual physical destruction of an armed force, but by the destruction of its believe [*sic*] in ultimate victory and its will to win," maintaining that airpower could play a role in achieving this objective.[39] The most influential advocate of airpower in the interwar period was Major William "Billy" Mitchell, a pilot in Pershing's army during World War I, who borrowed heavily from Douhet's concept of aerial bombing against the enemy's "vital centers."

In Walt Disney's 1943 celebration of his ideas and theories, *Victory Through Air Power*, Mitchell described airpower as the "dominant feature of military operations. Airpower can fly directly to the vital centers of an opposing state and neutralize them. It can destroy the cities and wreck the aqueducts. It can knock out the lines of communications. It can destroy the food supply. It can make the people helpless to resist." In the same film, Mitchell's disciple Major Alexander de Seversky predicted that airpower would soon "transform the entire surface of our planet into a battlefield. The distinctions between soldiers and civilians will be erased." Mitchell's vision of airpower was initially out of step with U.S. military thinking in the interwar years. Though the Tactical Air Corps accepted in principle the notion that airpower could be used to target the morale, the will to win, of the civilian population, air force debates tended to focus on precision bombing of economic and military targets rather than wholesale terrorizing of civilians.[40]

These priorities changed when America entered World War II in 1941. At the beginning of the war, President Roosevelt explicitly rejected the indiscriminate bombing of civilians, and even when the U.S. Air Force joined the bombing of Germany, it remained committed to precision bombing in daylight bombing raids on German industrial, economic, transportation, and communications targets rather than indiscriminate strategic or wide-area bombing of German cities by night favored by the Royal Air Force. The daylight raids initially targeted shipyards, submarine bases, ball-bearing factories, and railway and road networks, but the distinction between precision bombing aimed at military or economic targets and strategic attacks on entire cities was not always easy to maintain in bombing raids on the water, sewage, and electrical systems and other elements of the infrastructure that enabled German cities to function.

As de Seversky noted, "The kind of large-scale demolition which would be looked upon as horrifying vandalism when undertaken by soldiers on the ground can be passed off as a technical preparation or 'softening' when carried out by aerial bombing," and such destruction inevitably produces a broader psychological and physical impact on the surviving population. For John Steinbeck, aerial bombing was a new form of frontier warfare, in which "the American boy simply changes the nature of his game. Instead of raiding Sioux or Apache, instead of buffalo or antelope, he lays his sights on Zero or Heinkel, on Stuka or Messerschmitt."[41]

Bombing raids exacted a high cost in British and American air crews and downed planes, and daylight raiders were especially vulnerable to antiaircraft fire and attacks from German fighter planes as a result of their greater visibility. It was partly in an attempt to reduce these costs that American bombing strategies moved closer to the British model of saturation bombing and strategic devastation by night in the last year of the war. But American war planners also explicitly embraced the strategies advocated by their British allies. In 1943 the Air Corps commander General Henry "Hap" Arnold declared, "War has become vertical. . . . Strategic air power is a war-winning weapon in its own right, and is capable of striking decisive blows far behind the battle line, thereby destroying the enemy's capacity to wage war."[42] Though Arnold publicly condemned the "terror bombing" of civilians, he privately confided to his subordinates that "this is a brutal war and . . . the way to stop the killing of civilians is to cause so much damage and destruction and death that the civilians will demand that their government cease fighting."[43]

Sherman once justified his own campaigns with very similar arguments. He had set out to project the power of the U.S. government into the "innermost recesses" of the South. U.S. air war planners built mock cities at the Dugway Proving Ground in Utah, with replicas of Berlin tenements and Japanese residential neighborhoods, where scientists, academics, and technicians from Standard Oil and other companies studied the impact of various incendiaries and bombs on houses equipped with curtains, cots,

". . . in their innermost recesses." Mock German village with observation bunker, Dugway Proving Ground. Courtesy of the Library of Congress.

furniture, and children's toys to test their flammability and maximize the destruction.

In late July 1943, the Eighth Air Force carried out a joint attack with the RAF on Hamburg, in which explosives and incendiaries generated a firestorm that burned, crushed, and suffocated between 60,000 and 100,000 people and gutted much of the city. On February 3, 1945, more than nine hundred B-17 bombers took part in a night raid on Berlin with the RAF called "Operation Thunderclap," which was specifically intended to deal a knockout blow to civilian morale; it killed 3,000 people. On February 13–15, 1945, the Allies carried out an even more destructive raid on Dresden, which killed at least 35,000 people and transformed the city into what one British pilot called "a sea of fire covering in my estimation some 50 square miles."

In all, some 305,000 German civilians were killed and 780,000 wounded in raids that destroyed or partially destroyed fifty cities and made 7.5 million German civilians homeless. Civilian casualties were often obscured by euphemistic bureaucratic language in which the success of such operations was measured by lists of factories or bridges destroyed or numbers of workers who had been "dehoused." The impact on German morale was more difficult to measure. The U.S. Strategic Bombing Survey that followed the Allied invasion of Germany found that the population "showed surprising resistance to the terror and hardships of repeated air attack, to the destruction of their homes and belongings, and to the conditions under which they were reduced to live. . . . The power of a police state over its people cannot be underestimated."[44]

Paper Cities

Both the legitimacy and the effectiveness of bombing German cities have continued to be debated by historians. Regardless of whether or not it "worked" on its own terms, the strategy of bombing German civilians in order to crush their will to fight or support their government did not meet with universal favor, even within the U.S. military. Patton considered the bombing of German cities to be "barbaric, useless and sadistic." In a memorandum to General Carl A. Spaatz, commander of U.S. Strategic Air Forces in Europe, a staff officer declared it "contrary to [American] ideals to wage war on civilians."[45] However, although American air-war planners had some reservations about bombing German civilians, they had a very different attitude toward the Japanese. During the 1930s, Mitchell and other American airpower advocates identified flammable Japanese "paper cities" and "teeming bamboo ant heaps" as natural targets in the event of war. These recommendations were realized to terrible effect during the massive B-29 raids on Japanese cities in 1945 that followed the promotion of General Curtis LeMay (1906–90) to lead the Twentieth Bomber Command in the Mariana Islands in December 1944. In February 1945, LeMay was ordered to experiment with incendiary bombings of selected Japanese urban centers. On February 20, his forces carried out their first incendiary raid, on the city of Kobe.

This was followed by the massive raid on Tokyo on the night of March 9–10, in which 334 bombers flew as low as 4,900 feet and created an inferno without historical precedent. At least 83,000 people were burned, boiled, or suffocated to death in a conflagration that transformed much of the city into a wasteland. LeMay considered this raid a resounding success and vowed to continue to "bomb and burn them till they quit." Throughout the summer, Japan's largest cities were relentlessly bombed, and operations analysts began preparing for a bombing campaign against "all urban areas with a population greater than 30,000 peoples" that would have included 180 towns in total, and involved spraying rice paddies with oil, defoliants, and biological agents in order to starve the population.

As in Germany, operations analysts talked of "man-hours lost" and "dehoused" workers in ostensibly targeting Japan's factories and wartime cottage industries, but the broader intentions behind LeMay's campaigns were summed up approvingly by an editor of the *Atlanta Constitution*, despite the city's history of wartime destruction, who observed that it was "shocking to think of the thousands who must be burned to death" in such attacks but nevertheless concluded, "If it is necessary, however, that the cities of Japan are, one by one, burned to black ashes, that we can, and will, do." Such approval was fueled by racist depictions of the Japanese as a bestial and subhuman enemy and also by the belief that the bombing of Japanese cities would "save lives"—meaning the lives of American soldiers. At least 806,000 Japanese civilians were killed or wounded in nine months—more than all the Japanese soldiers killed during the whole war—in a campaign that one of MacArthur's key aides described in a confidential memorandum as "one of the most ruthless and barbaric killings of civilians or non-combatants in history."[46]

If the scale of destruction exceeded anything in the history of American warfare, it was not always carried out within clear strategic parameters. "It was not necessary for us to burn every city, to destroy every factory, to shoot down every airplane or sink every ship, and starve the people. It was enough to demonstrate that we were capable of doing all this," observed the writers of the Strategic Bombing Survey after the war.[47] In an account of the Tokyo raid in the *New Yorker*, LeMay's public-relations officer compared LeMay's actions to "a decision like Grant's when he let Sherman try to march through Georgia."[48] In an interview after the war, LeMay defended his actions, saying, "There are no innocent civilians. It is their government and you are fighting a people, you are not trying to fight an armed force anymore. So it doesn't bother me so much to be killing the so-called innocent bystanders." Asked about the morality of such methods, LeMay replied, "Actually I think it's more immoral to use *less* force than necessary, than it is to use *more*. If you use less force, you kill off more of humanity in the long run because you are merely protracting the struggle."[49]

In Errol Morris's documentary *The Fog of War*, Robert McNamara, who worked as a statistical analyst with LeMay's Bomber Command, explained that his role was to make LeMay's operations "more efficient, i.e., not more efficient in the sense of killing more, but more efficient in weakening the adversary. I remember reading that General Sherman in the Civil War . . . the mayor of Atlanta pleaded with him to save the city. And Sherman essentially said to the mayor just before he torched it and burned it down: 'War is cruel. War is cruelty.' That was the way LeMay felt."[50]

LeMay's cruelty was like Sherman's "statesmanship" in its attempt to demonstrate the futility of further resistance by attacking people in their homes and neighborhoods. These intentions were often made explicit in leaflets dropped on cities that were about to be bombed, and warning their inhabitants to flee and also blithely advising them to overthrow their government, regardless of whether or not it was possible for them to do so.

On August 6, 1945, the United States ushered in a new era of military destruction when the *Enola Gay* dropped an atomic bomb on Hiroshima, killing and wounding 150,000 people; three days later, another nuclear attack, on Nagasaki, killed or injured 80,000. There is no space here to consider the historical debate regarding whether the atomic bomb was really necessary to make Japan surrender or the degree to which its use was determined by wider geopolitical objectives regarding the Soviet Union.[51]

These attacks demonstrated that America had won what President Harry Truman called "the battle of the laboratories," and the justifications for their use offered by Truman and American officials were essentially the same as those used to justify the even more destructive firebombings that preceded them. On various occasions, Truman argued that the bomb was a cruel but ultimately humane necessity, which hastened the end of the war and precluded the need for an invasion and the resultant loss of life on both sides. But the bombing of Hiroshima and Nagasaki was also a "strategic" act of political and military coercion, designed to force the Japanese government to surrender by demonstrating that U.S. leaders had the will and the ability to kill civilians in even greater numbers if necessary. From the American perspective, the radio announcement by Emperor Hirohito on August 15 announcing Japan's surrender provided the most conclusive proof that this message had been received.

Bomb-o-grams

By the end of World War II, America's bomber fleets had become a confirmation of American military technological supremacy, and airpower was firmly embedded in the nation's conventional and unconventional war strategies. Airpower played a major role in the massive destruction inflicted on both North and South Korea during the Korean War (1950–53). UN (almost entirely American) air forces flew 1,040 sorties and dropped 698,000 tons of bombs and rockets on North and South Korea filled with white phosphorus, thermite, napalm, nerve gas, defoliant chemicals, or clusters of bomblets filled with metal balls and fiberglass fléchettes to maximize injuries to people. In September 1950, the British journalist Reginald Thompson described the impact of American firepower on Seoul and its surrounding villages as "a new technique of machine warfare" in which "the slightest resistance brought down a deluge of destruction, blotting out the area. Dive bombers, tanks and artillery blasted strong points, large or small, in town and hamlet, while the troops waited at the roadside as spectators until the way was cleared for them. Few people can have suffered so terrible a liberation."[52]

Airpower was also used for "strategic" attacks on civilian population centers, particularly after the Chinese intervention in November 1950, when UN troops were driven back across the 38th parallel. Between November 1950 and February 1951, American bombing raids killed 67,000 North Korean civilians, in a campaign intended by the commander of the Far East Air Force (FEAF), General George E. Stratemeyer, to "destroy every means of communication and every installation, factory, city, and village" in North Korea. Air force pilots complained that there were not enough targets left to bomb.[53]

Traveling through North Korea in 1951, the Hungarian correspondent Tibor Méray found "a complete devastation between the Yalu River and the capital" that he compared to "travelling on the moon . . . every city was a collection of chimneys." General William Dean, a POW during the war, reported that most towns and cities in the North had become "unoccupied shells" reduced to "rubble or snowy open spaces" by 1952, and that their inhabitants either were living underground or had been relocated to canyons to escape the bombers. The official U.S. military history of the war admitted that "we killed civilians, friendly civilians, and bombed their homes: fired whole villages with the occupants—women and children and ten times as many hidden Communist soldiers—under showers of napalm"—an outcome that its authors insisted was necessary in response to an enemy whose "savagery towards the people" was comparable to the Nazi treatment of Poland and Ukraine.[54]

Following the Chinese intervention, American civilian and military leaders also flirted with the possibility of using atomic weapons. In March 1951, MacArthur called for a "D Day atomic capability" to use against the incoming Chinese armies and China itself, and subsequently wrote of his desire to drop "between 30 and 50 atomic bombs . . . strung out across the neck of Manchuria" to form a "belt of radioactive cobalt" that would prevent a land invasion from the North. In April that year, MacArthur was replaced by Eighth Army commander General Matthew Ridgway. Though the military continued to discuss the possibility of using tactical nuclear weapons, its bombing strategy increasingly became an extension of diplomacy, which was not aimed at unconditional surrender, as in Japan, but at forcing North Korea and the Chinese government to accept an armistice on U.S. terms.

In April 1952, the FEAF outlined a new policy of "maximum selected destruction" directed toward "targets of military significance so situated that their destruction will have a deleterious effect upon the morale of the civilian population engaged in the logistic support of enemy forces."[55] In addition to renewed attacks on towns and cities, the target list was expanded to include dams and hydroelectric plants. In the summer of 1953, U.S. pilots bombed three dams, which supplied 75 percent of the North's food production, in an attempt to prevent the harvesting of 250,000 tons of rice. The massive Toksan Dam was breached by fifty-nine F-84 Thunderjets in May, flooding twenty-seven miles of river valley and parts of Pyongyang. These efforts were regarded by the military as instrumental in inducing North Korea and China to sign the armistice agreement at Panmunjom on July 27, 1953, according to one U.S. field officer, who claimed, "Our around-the-clock air operations brought to all North Korea the full impact of war. The material destruction wrought, the panic and civil disorder created, and the mounting casualties in civilian and military populations alike became the most compelling factors in enemy accession to an armistice."

American bombing campaigns in Vietnam were intended to generate the same "compelling factors." In January 1967 alone,

U.S. planes dropped 63,000 tons of ordnance on South Vietnam, two and half times the peak month in Korea. Between 1964 and 1973, Laos was bombed an average of every eight minutes and achieved the unwelcome distinction of being the most heavily bombed country per capita in world history. Between 1965 and 1968, an average of 32 tons of bombs was dropped on North Vietnam every hour. In total, some 400,000 tons of napalm bombs were unloaded on Indochina, compared with 14,000 tons in World War II and 32,557 tons in Korea.

Unlike World War II or Korea, the bombing of North Vietnam was not intended to inflict massive destruction and loss of life. Though some military officers urged the Johnson administration to conduct an all-out bombing campaign in the North, civilian leaders were anxious that such a campaign might lead to war with China and the Soviet Union. In 1964 the U.S. ambassador to South Vietnam, Henry Cabot Lodge, rejected a bombing campaign that would "lay the whole country to waste" on the grounds that "there will be nobody left in North Vietnam on whom to put pressure. . . . What we are interested in here is not destroying Ho Chi Minh . . . but getting him to change his behavior."[56] Such aspirations resulted in the "measured and limited air action" known as Rolling Thunder, which began in April 1965 and continued on and off for the next two years.

In two years, American pilots flew 148,000 sorties and bombed an array of targets that included towns, cities, factories, bridges, churches, schools, pagodas, a convent, and private homes. U.S. pilots often complained about the restrictions placed on their operations that were designed to avoid large-scale civilian casualties and the negative political consequences that came with them, but if these raids did not result in the massive urban devastation of the Korean War, they nevertheless inflicted widespread physical destruction on a largely agricultural society. In December 1966, Harrison Salisbury, the deputy editor of the *New York Times*, visited the town of Nam Định, forty miles southwest of Hanoi, which had been repeatedly bombed for more than a year, leaving "block after block of utter desolation." Salisbury insisted that Nam Định had no military significance, but the distinctions among military, economic, and political targets were irrelevant in a bombing campaign intended to break the will of the North Vietnamese government by terrorizing its people.

In December 1966 the scientific advisory group JASON concluded that this stop-start bombing campaign had had no measurable impact on North Vietnamese support for the rebels in the South or on the "determination of Hanoi and its people" to continue the war, and that this failure represented a more general failure "to appreciate the fact . . . that a direct, frontal attack on a society tends to strengthen the social fabric of the nation, to increase popular support of the existing government, to improve the determination of the leadership and its people to fight back."[57]

Though some U.S. military commanders regarded such reports as an incentive to escalate the bombing, the negative publicity caused by these raids and the lack results led the Johnson government to bring Rolling Thunder to a halt. Coercive bombing returned in 1972 after the North Vietnamese invasion of the South. On several of his secret White House tapes from that year, President Richard Nixon can be heard in conversation with his secretary of state, Henry Kissinger, drunkenly threatening to bomb North Vietnam's harbors and its dike system. In practice Nixon limited himself to the six-month Linebacker I bombing campaign between May and October 1972, followed by Linebacker II, or the Christmas Bombing, of Hanoi and Haiphong in December.[58]

These campaigns were partly aimed at the North Vietnamese Army in the South, which may have lost as many as 100,000 soldiers as a result of the October raids. But the bombings were also intended to pressure the government in Hanoi to accept American terms at the stalled peace negotiations in Paris. In total 2,200

North Vietnamese civilians were killed and 1,600 were wounded in these raids, whose impact might have been much greater had it not been for the evacuation of much of the population from the targeted areas. From Nixon's point of view, these operations were a success. On the night of December 27–28, North Vietnam officials sent a note agreeing to return to the Paris peace negotiations, and on January 23, 1973, a peace agreement was signed.

The extent to which these raids contributed to this outcome is debatable, because the North did not alter its negotiating position and was able to keep its army in the South; the chief North Vietnamese negotiator, Hà Văn Lâu, even called the bombing campaign an "aerial equivalent to Dien Bien Phu." The Linebacker raids nevertheless demonstrated once again the willingness of American leaders to use airpower as a bludgeon of political coercion and intimidation and to extend the "hard hand of war" to civilians in ways that made the burned plantations and Chimneyvilles of the Civil War appear almost quaintly reserved by comparison.

7

Civilians

The century between the end of the Civil War and the escalation of the Vietnam War in 1965 was marked by a striking paradox. On the one hand, more international laws, treaties, and conventions regulating the conduct of warfare were drawn up and signed by more countries than during any other period in human history. The Hague Conventions on Land War of 1899 and 1907, the International Law Association's 1938 Amsterdam Draft, which declared that "the civilian population shall not form the object of war," and the Fourth Geneva Convention on the Protection of Civilian Persons in Time of War were all part of a new international attempt to humanize or "refine" war, as Sherman disparagingly put it, which mandated armies to avoid unnecessary suffering and the deliberate targeting of civilians or other "protected persons."

Yet these developments coincided with—and to some extent were a product of—a period of unprecedented global violence in which these rules and regulations were systematically violated or disregarded. At the beginning of the twentieth century, civilian deaths constituted between 10 and 15 percent of wartime deaths. By the end of the century, some 75 percent of wartime dead were civilians and noncombatants. In 1948 the Southern historian John Bennett Walters Jr. published an article, "General Sherman and Total War," based on his PhD thesis, in the *Journal of Southern History* and subsequently expanded it into the book *Merchant of Terror: General Sherman and Total War* (1973). In it Walters accused Sherman of having initiated his army into "the savage art of destruction and the disregard for human rights which the rules of war had sought to mitigate," thereby establishing a "record for systematic torture, pillage, and vandalism unequalled in American history."[1]

As the title suggests, Walters also linked Sherman to the conduct of war in the twentieth century. Various historians have challenged and rejected these claims, and Walters's melodramatic and exaggerated depiction of Sherman's campaigns makes them relatively easy to refute. These associations have nevertheless endured. In 1992 Sherman's biographer Charles Edmund Vetter claimed that his "justification of economic, psychological and sociological warfare opened the door to its [total war's] fullest development in the form of dropping atomic bombs on the noncombatant cities of Japan."[2] Today American high school textbooks and the popular press still routinely refer to Sherman as the spiritual father of total war, and these claims are worth revisiting in order to understand the similarities—and the differences—between Sherman's concept of war and some of the tributaries of violence that followed.

Total War

Total war means war waged without moral restraint. The term can also refer to the maximization and reorganization of the economic, social, and industrial resources of a society to achieve military objectives. For the historian David Bell, some of these tendencies were already evident in the French Revolutionary Wars, especially the war of extermination waged by the revolutionary armies against royalist rebels in the Vendée region between 1793 and 1796, which he described as "a kind of warfare

whose scale had little or no precedent, whether in the mobilization of population and resources, the ambitious and ill-defined
war aims, the demonization of enemy populations."[3] Other historians have found precedents in the horrendous destruction inflicted on Portugal by French and British armies during the
Napoleonic Wars or, even further back, in the Thirty Years War.

The term *total war* was coined by Giulio Douhet in his exposition of airpower in 1921 to describe war waged against the civilian population and resources of the opposing state as well as its
uniformed armies. In 1924, the German infantry and General
Staff officer Joachim von Stülpnagel outlined a theory of *Volkskrieg*
(people's war), predicting that the coming wars would be waged
without clearly defined theaters of operations or any distinctions
between the front and the rear guard. In these wars, von Stülpnagel predicted, armies would no longer be bound by moral constraints
in their treatment of civilians. "We can show no consideration for
the population if the outcome of the war depends on it. In the war
of the future, death behind the front has to be viewed like death
at the front."[4] In his 1935 tract *Der totale Krieg*, the former German commander in World War I Erich Ludendorff likewise
outlined a grim vision of "totalitarian warfare" based on the complete mobilization of the whole nation and its resources in wars
"not only aimed against the armed forces, but also directly against
the people."[5]

At first glance, there is little connection between these ideas
and Sherman's philosophy of war. Sherman certainly shared the
belief that modern wars were fought between societies as well as
armies and that civilians could be legitimately intimidated in order to achieve political and military outcomes, but there were
always limits to the violence that he was prepared to inflict in order to achieve them. Even though he talked of "exterminating"
Southerners in his more irate moments, he did not attempt to
put these ideas into practice. He was too suspicious of American

society's potential for "anarchy" to welcome the notion of the "complete mobilization of the whole nation," and preferred a well-trained professional army to volunteers, whom he regarded with contempt at the beginning of the war.

Nevertheless, there are some peripheral historical connections between his campaigns in the South and some of the wars that followed. In 1865 Sherman's aide-de-camp Major George Ward Nichols claimed, "History . . . will search in vain for a parallel to the scathing and destructive effects of the Invasion of the Carolinas. The immediate disasters to the Rebel cause, the cities captured, arsenals and munitions of war destroyed, the communications severed, will be appreciated by the military mind in Europe, as well as by our own army and people."[6] Such appreciation was not nearly as general as Nichols predicted, but neither was it entirely absent.

One of the justifications for the Spanish-American War in 1898 was American outrage at the "reconcentration" policy enforced in Cuba by the Spanish general Valeriano Weyler y Nicolau (1838–1930). While serving in Cuba and Santo Domingo during the American Civil War, Weyler was sent to Washington as a military attaché, and he was a great admirer of Sherman, whom he met. Weyler was particularly impressed by his tactics in Georgia and the Carolinas. In February 1896, he was appointed captain-general of Spanish forces in Cuba, with the task of suppressing a powerful anti-Spanish rebellion in the countryside. In response Weyler introduced a series of draconian measures. Guerrilla prisoners were summarily shot, and villages and houses of known or suspected sympathizers were burned and their food supplies confiscated or destroyed.

Sent by President McKinley to investigate conditions in Cuba in 1897, former congressman William J. Calhoun described a journey from Havana to Matanzas by train: "The countryside outside of the military posts was practically depopulated. Every house had been burned, banana trees cut down, cane fields swept by fire, and everything in the shape of food destroyed. . . . I did not see a house, man, woman or child, a horse, mule, or cow, nor even a dog. . . . The country was wrapped in the stillness of death and the silence of desolation."[7]

This devastation was not due only to the actions of Spanish troops or Weyler's specially constituted battalion of Spaniards and pro-Spanish Cubans known as the Cazadores (Hunters) de Valmaseda, named after Weyler's former commander the Conde de Valmaseda. The Cuban Liberation Army also burned farms and plantations and lynched landowners.

In 1897, however, Weyler introduced a new policy of forcibly evacuating civilians from the countryside and "reconcentrating" them in fortified stockades in order to break the links between the people and the guerrillas. Between 155,000 and 170,000 civilians died of hunger and disease in these camps, according to the more recent scholarly estimates. In the American press, these policies earned Weyler a nickname, the Butcher, and made his name a byword for Spanish cruelty in Cuba. Weyler consistently rejected allegations that his methods were uniquely barbaric, and he and his government excused them by saying that they were no different from those used by the American government during the Civil War. When the American consul in Cuba, Fitzhugh Lee, nephew of Robert E. Lee, asked Weyler about civilian suffering in the concentration camps, he received the very Sherman-like reply that "everything is fair in war."[8]

In a self-justifying memoir, Weyler quotes a letter from the Spanish minister of state to his counterpart in Washington in 1897, which provides an exhaustive list of comparable actions carried out during the War of Secession, from the forced "reconcentration" of civilians and prohibitions on trade and commerce to "the burning of entire cities, the ruin and devastation of immense and most fertile regions, to the annihilation of all goods of the adversary." The letter also cites Hunter's and Sheridan's campaigns in the Shenandoah Valley and the forced depopulation of Atlanta by the "illustrious and respected General Sherman" as precedents. The minister reminded the American government of the "supreme motivation for such actions by the victorious Sherman" in his memoirs and his letter to Mayor Calhoun in Atlanta, and praised his arguments as "upright and illustrious concepts that the Spanish government will not hesitate to make its own, applying them to Cuba."[9]

Given the U.S. Army's civilian concentration camps in the Philippines and Vietnam, there is some irony in the probability that "Butcher" Weyler was inspired by the U.S. Army. Sherman's campaigns also had some influence on the British army, through the writings of Sir Garnet Wolseley, the field marshal and commander in chief of the British Armed Forces from 1895 to 1901. In 1861 Wolseley visited the disunited States as a Civil War observer. Though he was a strong Confederate sympathizer, like many British army officers, Wolseley was also a great admirer of Sherman, whom he wrote about in a number of articles in British military journals.

Wolseley also cited the methods used by the Union Army for destroying Southern railroads in his bestselling textbook, *The Soldier's Pocket-Book for Field Service* (1869), which contained detailed instructions on how to destroy and reconstruct railroad lines, modeled on the techniques developed by Union engineers during "the American war." Borrowing methods almost exactly from Sherman's chief of engineers, Orlando Poe, and the head of the War Department's railroad bureau, Herman Haupt, Wolseley recommended that track should be uprooted by squads of soldiers using U-shaped metal tools, after which the sleepers were to be burned in order to soften the rails until they could be "bent into the shape of a U, or round a tree or telegraph pole."

In a section on protection of railways, Wolseley recommended that saboteurs should be dissuaded by proclamations warning that anyone caught damaging railways or telegraph lines would be "hanged without mercy," just as Union generals had done in Missouri and parts of the South. Where these warnings failed to achieve their objectives, he suggested, "It may be possible to make the inhabitants living along it responsible for its preservation, and it may sometimes be necessary to make severe examples by burning the houses near the spot where any injury was done to it."

Wolseley himself made some "severe examples" during the Third Anglo-Ashanti War in the Akan interior of the Gold Coast in modern-day Ghana of 1873–74, when he followed the British victory at the Battle of Amoaful on January 31, 1974, by marching on the Ashanti capital, Kumasi. After ordering his troops to carry reduced rations in order to increase their mobility, Wolseley entered the abandoned Ashanti capital four days later and summoned the Ashanti king to negotiate a peace agreement. When the king refused to appear, Wolseley's troops blew up the royal palace, then burned the city and all the villages they passed through during their retreat because, he later wrote, "In my heart I believed that the absolute destruction of Koomassee, with its great palace, the wonder of West Africa, would be a much more striking and effective end to the war than any peace treaty."[10]

Sherman also impressed one of Wolseley's protégés, Colonel G.F.R. Henderson, the head of the Cadet School of the Royal Military Academy at Sandhurst and the author of a number of studies of Civil War strategies and battles, including an important study of Stonewall Jackson. Henderson also praised Ulysses Grant as "the first to perceive that in a comparatively fertile country it was possible to subsist an army without magazines" during his Vicksburg campaign, and described both Sherman's campaigns and James Harrison Wilson's "mounted infantry" raids in the South as the most comprehensive realization of the Union raiding strategies, describing them as "extraordinary enterprises which did so much [damage] to the enemy's communications."[11]

The closest British parallel to Sherman's campaigns took place during the Second Anglo-Boer War, 1899–1902, in South Africa, when the British commander General Frederick Roberts and his chief of staff, Major General Horatio Herbert Kitchener, put a scorched-earth policy into effect in western Orange Free State in June 1900 in response to successful guerrilla tactics of the Boer armies under General Christiaan de Wet. Ordered to "destroy or remove everything which may help the enemy or his horses or his oxen to move," British troops destroyed some twenty thousand farms, leaving the families homeless and much of the veld littered with slaughtered animals, some of whose carcasses were thrown into wells and dams to poison the water supply.

Food denial was only one objective of these operations. Unable to locate and capture de Wet's elusive guerrillas, Kitchener and Roberts adopted a strategy of indirect psychological pressure that was primarily directed against women, children, and the elderly—the easiest targets. These objectives were made explicit by General Thomas Kelly-Kenny, who told one detachment to "burn all farmhouses—explain reason (for so doing) as they have harboured enemy and not reported to British authorities as required. The question of how to treat women and children and what amount of food and transport will arise, as to the first part they have forfeited all right to consideration and must now suffer for their persistently ignoring warnings against harbouring and assisting our enemy."

Not surprisingly, this "strategic" destruction frequently became merely a license for looting. Letters from British soldiers are filled with descriptions that recall Sherman's campaigns in the South in the violent intrusions into female domestic space and the vindictive destruction of pianos, furniture, and other property of no military but great sentimental value.[12] "I go into all the rooms and turn everything upside down, cut the mattresses of the beds open to look for rifles," wrote one soldier. "If I am sent to a farm to see what is in it and to get the women out I never hesitate to burn the place before I leave, and only give the people five minutes to pack up and get into the wagon. I have no pity on them no matter how they weep."[13] Another soldier told his mother, "We were only there a few minutes but we did do a little damage in a short time. I put the butt of my rifle through a large looking glass over the mantelpiece and put my foot through a sideboard with glass doors. One of the others smashed up a piano and an organ. The women didn't half scream."[14]

Many British soldiers regarded Boer women in much the same way as Sherman's soldiers had regarded the women of the South, as active and defiant participants in the war who deserved destitution and humiliation. Others were more ambivalent. Thomas Henderson Thomson, an Australian in the Bushmen's Corps, described his participation in the operations: "We burnt hundreds of homes [in the] pouring rain & had to turn the women & children out in the wet with only a few clothes & very little food. It is a job I can't stand & I hope we can get away from it soon. We came over to fight men, not women and children."[15]

In December 1900, Kitchener adopted the policy of "concentrations" enacted by Weyler in Cuba and Bell in the Philippines, ordering the removal of Boers and black Africans into "camps of refuge" surrounded by barbed wire and guards to prevent any contact between the prisoners and the guerrillas. Isolated on the veld in overcrowded tent cities, without sufficient food, medical attention, or blankets, some 28,000 Afrikaners and 20,000 black Africans died in the course of the war, most of them women and children. These camps scandalized British and world opinion and were later cited by the Nazis to refute claims that their concentration-camp system was anomalous or especially cruel.

Civilian deaths during the British "burn and capture" campaign were often due to poor sanitary conditions and mismanagement rather than the result of deliberate policy, but they were often accepted by the British military establishment as a tragic but inevitable necessity in order to bring the war to an end. Many officers shared the outlook expressed in a December 1901 letter to *The Times* of London, whose author justified programs of slaughter by neglect in prison camps with a quotation from none other than Philip Sheridan: "The proper strategy consists in inflicting as telling blows as possible on the enemy's army, and then in causing the inhabitants so much suffering that they must long for peace, and force the government to demand it. The people must be left with nothing but their eyes to weep with over the war."[16]

Sheridan reportedly made these recommendations during the Franco-Prussian War of 1870–71, which he witnessed as an observer with the Prussian General Staff after he was asked by the German chancellor, Otto von Bismarck, how his army should respond to attacks on German troops from *Francs tireurs* and other irregulars. At first glance, this encounter, between one of the most ruthless Union exponents of hard war and an army that was associated more than any other with the concept of total war, seems to bear out the thesis of a direct line of descent between the Civil War and its more destructive successors. But the German response to French resistance drew on a panoply of possible reprisals that were already well established among nineteenth-century European armies, even if it was magnified by Prussian outrage at continued resistance away from the battlefield, which Karl Marx mocked.[17]

From the Prussian army's perspective, such resistance was a violation of the rules of war and a threat to the security of its troops. To suppress it, combatants without "distinguishing marks" were shot or hanged on the spot or sentenced to ten years' penal servitude in Germany. The army also took French public officials as hostages to deter acts of sabotage, and in some cases placed them on the front of trains to deter attacks. In addition, towns that refused to provide food or requisitions to the German army were fined, bombed, and burned. French politicians and jurists denounced these acts of barbarism as particularly Prussian and a violation of the rules of war, but similar measures were adopted by many nineteenth-century armies in the same period.[18]

Severities

The behavior of the Prussian army in France pales beside the *Vernichtungsbefehl* (extermination order) issued by General Lothar von Trotha in response to the Herero and Nama Rebellions in German South West Africa, in which men, women, and children were driven out into the desert and denied food and water or imprisoned in forced-labor camps—a policy that reduced the Herero population from 80,000 to 15,000 and the Nama by half by 1911. In 1905 the German army waged an even more destructive campaign to suppress the Maji Maji Rebellion in German East Africa (later Tanganyika), when three columns under the command of the German governor Count Adolf von Gotzen burned villages and crops throughout the southern part of the country in a deliberate famine strategy that, according to the historian Thomas Pakenham, resulted in 250,000 to 300,000 deaths.[19]

At first glance, these colonial campaigns present far more compelling precedents for the barbarism of total war than the American Civil War—a conflict that the Prussian chief of staff Helmuth von Moltke was reported to have described as "two armed mobs . . . from which nothing can be learned." But the Civil War did not go entirely unnoticed by the German army. In 1868 Major Ferdinand von Meerheimb presented a paper on Sherman's campaign in Georgia to the Militärische Gesellschaft in Berlin, which compared the devastation of the state to that of the Thirty Years War while claiming that "Sherman used these harshest measures with a heavy heart" because "they alone would bring a quick and sure peace."

The manual *Kriegsbrauch im Landkriege* (*Usages of War on Land*), issued by the German General Staff to its soldiers during World War I, expressed a philosophy very similar to the Lieber Code, asserting, "Certain severities are indispensable in war, nay more, the only true humanity very often lies in a ruthless application of them."[20] The German army resorted to numerous "severities" in Belgium and on the Eastern Front during World War I. In August 1914, invading German troops entered the ancient city of Louvain, near Brussels, and responded to sniper attacks by destroying more than a thousand homes and the university library with explosives and firebombs. There followed a looting spree in which soldiers took everything from musical instruments to food, wine, and lingerie. The procedure was repeated in other towns and cities as German troops responded to real or imagined incidents of *Franktireurkrieg*, "sharpshooter war," with violent reprisals against Belgian civilians.[21]

Terrified of *Francs tireurs* and convinced—not without reason—that civilians were helping them, the German army frequently exacted the most extreme reprisals and countermeasures from the nineteenth-century military tradition, according to the principle that "the innocent must suffer with the guilty." Some of these measures were justified by German commanders by an admittedly broad interpretation of "military necessity" and thus were excused as permissible under the Hague conventions.[22]

But the German military administration also imposed crippling requisitions and financial contributions on Belgian cities that went well beyond what was allowed under the conventions, forcibly deporting 120,000 Belgian workers to Germany and France and draining the country's resources to the point that much of the Belgian population was saved from starvation only by a special dispensation permitting food relief from the American-run Commission for Relief for Belgium. From the point of view of the German army and government, the subjugation of the Belgian people and economy to the war effort was a wartime expedient that was as *militarily* necessary as the "severities" adopted in response to *Francs tireurs*. Despite the widespread Allied condemnation of the Belgian occupation, Germany was by no means unique in its willingness to regard the civilian population as a military resource or an object of war.

As early as 1863, the Cambridge University political economist Henry Fawcett in his *Manual of Political Economy* criticized the "feeling of false humanity" that had "attempted to make the rights of private property respected in war."[23] Fawcett denounced what he regarded as a hypocritical form of war: "Life may be sacrificed with as much prodigality as ever. The foremost mechanical genius of this mechanical age is devoted to the production of weapons of death; but civilization, it is said, demands that there be no wanton destruction of property." For Fawcett, any attempt to "palliate the material disaster of war" was counterproductive, because "war will be rendered less frequent, if a whole nation is made to feel its horrible consequences, instead of concentrating all the horrors in the sacrifice of thousands of helpless victims who may be marshaled at the caprice of a despot." In 1914, the British navy imposed a blockade on food shipments to Germany and the Central Powers whose explicit purpose, according to the high lord of the Admiralty, Winston Churchill, was to "starve the whole population—men, women, and children, old and young, wounded and sound, into submission."[24] The success of these efforts was soon reflected in reports of famished women in Berlin breadlines, rising civilian mortality rates, and a dramatic increase in child malnutrition—all of which were intensified by American entry into the war in 1917, making the blockade all but impenetrable. By the end of the war, millions of people in Germany, Austria, and the Balkans were on the brink of starvation, and British soldiers in the Rhineland in 1919 were horrified by the sight of "hordes of skinny and bloated children pawing over the offal" from their camps.[25]

Estimates of German deaths caused by malnutrition and disease have ranged from 424,000 to 763,000. The Allied blockade was another indication of the changing parameters of modern warfare, in which civilians as well as armies could be seen even by democratic states as legitimate targets. Attacks on economic resources and morale appeared to be a solution to the problem of meat-grinder stalemates between powerful industrial states, just as they had once seemed to Sherman. Ideology, racism, and hypernationalist "othering" of the enemy have contributed to the extreme violence of twentieth-century warfare, but again and again armies and governments have invoked military necessity as a justification for actions that would normally be considered abhorrent and shameful. Though some armies have been more willing to do this than others, even democratic states that nominally accept moral and legal constraints in wartime have been prepared to dispense with or suspend such limits, just as Lincoln once did, in order to win.

In a memorandum to the British Cabinet in October 1917, Winston Churchill, munitions minister and former high lord of the Admiralty, rejected the idea of a bombing campaign against Germany in retaliation for the Gotha raids on London, arguing, "It is improbable that any terrorization of the civil population which could be achieved by air attack could compel the Government of a great nation to surrender."[26] However, Churchill was not averse to bombing Iraqi rebels with poison gas in the immediate postwar period. Then as prime minister during World War II, he embraced the same strategy he had once rejected when he endorsed what he himself called the "terror" bombing of German cities. On August 25, 1940, the RAF carried out its first bombing raid on Berlin in retaliation for a German raid on London. On September 3, 1940, Churchill claimed that "the Bombers alone provide the means to victory. We must therefore develop the power to carry an ever-increasing volume of explosives to Germany, so as to pulverise the entire industry and scientific structure on which the war effort and the economic life of the enemy depends."[27]

The British bombing campaign gained new momentum in 1942, when RAF Bomber Command began attacking residential neighborhoods and other built-up areas in order to target "the morale of enemy civil population, in particular industrial workers." On May 30, the RAF conducted its first thousand-plane raid, on Cologne, using a combination of explosives and incendiaries designed to kill people in the largest possible numbers. For the next three years, the RAF pulverized German cities relentlessly and remorselessly. This strategy was partly a consequence of British strategic weakness. With their country isolated and vulnerable, and with little possibility of waging a conventional war in Nazi-occupied Europe, Britain's leaders had clearly reached a very different understanding of what was militarily necessary—and morally acceptable—than their predecessors had during World War I. Other countries likewise embraced the terror bombing of civilians as a military necessity. The gassing of Ethiopian villages by the Italian air force; the Japanese bombing of Nanking and other Chinese cities; the Fascist and Nazi bombings of Guernica, Madrid, and Warsaw—all these events were a testament to the lowering of the moral threshold by twentieth-century armies that was made possible by the advent of airpower, enabling a few people to kill many thousands without ever having to observe the consequences of their actions firsthand.

Scorching the Earth

The barbarism of twentieth-century warfare and the blurring of the boundaries between armies and civilians were not limited to wars between states. By the mid-twentieth century, irregular and guerrilla conflicts had become a ubiquitous feature of modern warfare, from the resistance to German and Japanese occupations during World War II to the wars of decolonization that followed. On May 13, 1941, the Wehrmacht adopted a special dispensation for the forthcoming invasion of the Soviet Union known as the *Kriegsgerichtsbarkeitserlass* (War Jurisdiction Decree), which authorized its officers to carry out collective reprisals against civilians in response to any acts of partisan resistance. During the Nazi advance on Moscow, German infantry units burned villages, executed hostages, and destroyed property, crops, and livestock in "mopping up" operations behind the lines, and the reliance on destruction, devastation, and massacre became ever more pronounced as resistance continued to grow and the German advance was halted.

In the Ukraine, Field Marshal Walther von Reichenau, commander of the Sixth Army, adopted a policy of burning houses, confiscating food, and shooting or hanging hostages in operations against partisans, whom he regarded as "murderous animals." On December 16, 1942, the German supreme commander of the armed forces, Field Marshal Wilhelm Keitel, authorized German troops throughout Europe "to take any measures without restriction and even against women and children if these are necessary for success" in a struggle against "bandit warfare" and "communist-trained fighters," which Keitel insisted "has nothing to do with a soldier's chivalry nor with the decisions of the Geneva Conventions."[28]

Antipartisan operations in the "Wild East" often overlapped with massacres of Jews and Slavic racial inferiors that had nothing to do with pacification or counterinsurgency. In other respects, however, the Nazi response to partisan warfare, or *klein Kindergarten Krieg* ("little kindergarten war"), echoed the atrocities in Cuba, the Transvaal, and the Philippines. Before the invasion, the Twelfth Infantry Division was issued "Guidelines for the Conduct of Troops in Russia," which authorized soldiers to shoot or hang any member of a "Partisan-Battalion" not wearing a uniform or mark of identity. Other forms of "ruthless action" included the burning of houses suspected of harboring partisans ("The fire forces the partisans to jump and makes shooting easy") and the destruction of "suspect" villages and the forced removal of their inhabitants.[29] Antipartisan operations took the form of large-scale *Kessel* ("cauldron") offensives in which suspected guerrilla areas were first surrounded and cordoned off before German troops turned inward, driving out or killing the inhabitants, burning their villages, destroying crops, and seizing animals in order to create "desert zones."

Such operations contributed to a civilian death toll that reached well into the millions, and increased popular support for the partisans. Though some German commanders recognized that brutality was counterproductive and advocated more sophisticated and moderate methods, including the recruitment of local militias, extreme violence remained an essential component of Nazi antipartisan warfare as the war turned against Germany, and was often accompanied by the massive and indiscriminate destruction of crops, livestock, food, and industrial machinery. Retreating from a Soviet counteroffensive toward the Dnieper River in September 1943, one member of the Grossdeutschland Division wrote in his diary that "we were ordered to destroy all villages, as well as to take to the rear all the cattle. I cannot judge whether this measure was absolutely necessary, but it caused deprivation and misery to the population left behind."[30]

Similar policies were adopted elsewhere in Occupied Europe. In Greece, more than a thousand villages were razed, twenty thousand civilians were shot, and a million Greeks lost their homes as a result of the total war waged by Wehrmacht and Waffen-SS units in 1943. In France some of the worst Nazi atrocities took place after the Normandy invasion, when local commanders and the SS responded to any act of resistance with wholesale reprisals as part of a deliberate policy to terrorize the people in an effort to prevent them from supporting the Allied armies.

Nazi counterinsurgency tactics also influenced the Japanese Imperial Army in its response to Communist and Nationalist guerrillas in China and Southeast Asia. Between 1933 and 1937, the Japanese Kwantung Army successfully eliminated anti-Japanese resistance in Japan's puppet state Manchukuo, using a range of methods that included the forcible relocation of some 5.5 million Chinese civilians into ten thousand "collective hamlets" on the same model used in Cuba, the Philippines, the Boer War—and later in Vietnam. As in these wars, towns and villages that lay outside these camps were destroyed to deny food to the guerrillas, and these campaigns had a devastating impact on the civilian population as well.

In May 1940 General Okamura Yasuji, commander of the North China Area Army, implemented a policy ordered by his superiors known as Sankō Sakusen, the Three Alls Strategy (kill all, burn all, loot all), also known as Jinmetsu Sakusen, the Burn to Ash Strategy, against Communist guerrillas in northern China. According to historian Chalmers Johnson, the method was "to surround a given area, to kill everyone in it, and to destroy everything possible so that the area would be uninhabitable in the future."[31] In one such operation, 800 people from the village of Peihuan died when poison gas was pumped into the tunnels where they were hiding. In a three-month operation in the Chin-Ch'a-Chi border region, 4,500 Chinese were killed, 17,500 deported, and 150,000 houses destroyed. As many as 2 million people may have died by violence or starvation, as the North China Area Army practiced what the historian Lincoln Li has called "a scorched earth policy in reverse."[32] Like Weyler's *cazadores* in Cuba and the Union armies in the South, German and Japanese commanders regarded the distinction between civilians and armed combatants as either nonexistent or irrelevant and found that it was easier to target the fighters by attacking their supporters. Okamura's ravaging troops in northern China moved without a supply line, taking their food from the local population, and used a body count metric of success like their counterparts in the Vietnam War.

German and Japanese commanders justified violence and terror on the grounds of military necessity, and these arguments were sometimes accepted by their victorious enemies. In October 1944, General Lothar von Rendulic, the German commander in Finland and Norway, ordered his troops to burn Finnish villages during a scorched-earth retreat from Lapland. At the Nuremberg trials, Rendulic was found not guilty of unlawfully destroying civilian property on the grounds that "urgent military necessity warranted the decision made." He received a twenty-year sentence for other offenses; it was commuted to ten, and he was freed after three years. This successful defense became known as the Rendulic rule, and its general acceptance was such that it was still referred to in the U.S. Army's rules of engagement in the 2003 invasion of Iraq.[33]

Following World War II, most Western armies adopted more "scientific" and "political" methods of counterinsurgency and antisubversive warfare that eschewed the kinds of massive destruction carried out by Nazi and Japanese armies. But armies continued to use military force as an instrument of punishment and/or political coercion against civilians and noncombatants, whether it was the French army dropping napalm on peasant villages during the Algerian war, the Israeli bombing of towns and villages in south Lebanon in response to Palestinian cross-border attacks, or the massive destruction inflicted on the anti-apartheid "frontline states" as a result of the "total strategy" waged by South Africa and its allies in the 1980s. In Afghanistan in the same period, the Red Army conducted a brutal war against the Afghan mujahideen in which rural villages were bombed, and their crops, wells, and water supply poisoned or destroyed as a policy of food denial to the guerrillas that was collective punishment of the entire population.

Guerrillas, terrorists, and other "non-state agents" have often adopted their own small-scale forms of total war that make no distinction between combatants and noncombatants or even deliberately target civilians. All these developments contributed to the lowered threshold of twentieth-century war and moved the notion of combat far beyond the battlefield.

To suggest, as John Bennett Walters and others have done, that Sherman was somehow responsible for these streams of twentieth-century barbarism fails to account for the relative restraint of his campaigns in comparison with their successors and ignores equally barbaric acts of military violence that preceded the Civil War and could be cited as precedents for his campaigns. Classical historians' gleeful descriptions of Roman soldiers slaughtering "barbarian" women, children, and old people in the aftermath of battle; the massacres carried out by crusaders in the Holy Land; the razing of cities by the armies of Ghengis Khan; the destruction of the Aztec capital Tenochtitlán by Cortés's invading army—all these premodern episodes belong to a grim tradition of military violence against civilians that long precedes the modern concept of "total" warfare. Sherman's decision to wage war on Southern civilians certainly belongs to this tradition, but the limited and calibrated destruction that his army visited on the South was also a departure from it, reflecting the modern drift toward rule-based warfare exemplified by the Lieber Code. The allegation made by Walters, J.F.C. Fuller, and others that his methods *caused* a "moral regression" in warfare tend to exaggerate both the destruction that he inflicted and the extent to which "civilized" warfare was really civilized in practice. Such accusations also tend to ignore the extent to which Sherman's strategies, tactics, and philosophy of war were the products of a broader understanding of how wars could be fought and won that was shared by many of his contemporaries and then became more consensual and widespread as the wars of the twentieth century revealed the impossibility and irrelevance of Napoleonic notions of "the decisive battle" as the crucial ingredient of warfare.

Blitzkrieg

Something similar can be said of Sherman's alleged influence on the more conventional military strategies and tactics that also fall under the rubric of total war. If Basil Liddell Hart is to be believed, Sherman's campaigns had a decisive impact on twentieth-century warfare through adoption of his "indirect approach" by many armies and generals, including not only Patton's Third Army, but also the German pioneer of tank warfare Heinz Guderian and the "desert fox" Erwin Rommel, both of whom were cited by Liddell Hart as his "disciples." Liddell Hart's inclusion of the British Eighth Army's North African desert campaigns and the Israeli army during the Six-Day War as practitioners of his indirect method appears to extend Sherman's influence even further.

In a discussion of the German blitzkrieg campaigns of World War II in his memoirs, Liddell Hart claimed, "The development of the theory owed much to the study I made, in reflection on the entrenched deadlock of 1914–18, of ways and means by which an earlier case of deadlock had been overcome in the American Civil War, particularly by Sherman in the western theatre."[34] Liddell

Hart declared that his biography of Sherman led the War Office to carry out a "Sherman march" maneuver at its training camp in Aldershot, and that the Aga Khan arranged a meeting with General Werner von Blomberg, the head of the German military delegation at the disarmament conference in Geneva in 1932. According to Liddell Hart, von Blomberg "had been very impressed by the deductions I had drawn from Sherman's campaigns for modern application, and had been applying them in the training of the troops for East Prussia" and told him that he and Chief of Staff von Reichenau were producing a special translation of Liddell Hart's book for private circulation to their officers rather than wait for a German edition.[35]

These claims have been disputed by historians, who have accused Liddell Hart of deliberately exaggerating his influence.[36] In his study of the German military in the interwar years, James Corum maintains that "a careful examination of pre-war German books, documents, and articles yields no evidence that Liddell Hart was widely known in the German army or that he had any influence whatsoever upon German tactical thinking"—a claim that also seems to negate Sherman's purported influence. Corum traces the origins of the blitzkrieg strategy not to Liddell Hart or Sherman but to the era of Hans von Seeckt, the general chief of staff from 1919 to 1920 and army commander from 1920 to 1926, whose analysis of German military failure in World War I concluded that "the universal levy in mass, this gigantic parade of armies" was no longer the essential instrument of war.

In a report to the army high command on February 8, 1919, von Seeckt argued, "The whole future of warfare appears to me to lie in the employment of mobile armies, relatively small but of high quality and rendered distinctly more effective by the addition of aircraft, and in simultaneous mobilization of the whole defense force, be it to feed the attack or for home defense."[37]

Other German generals reached similar conclusions. In his interwar bestseller *Achtung-Panzer!* Heinz Guderian briefly cites Liddell Hart, Fuller, and the British tank warfare campaigns of World War I as influences in outlining his strategic proposals for rapidly moving mechanized tank/infantry units. But his ideas also drew on the "deep battle" theories advanced by Soviet commanders of the same period, and the Nazi blitzkrieg strategy—a term Guderian didn't use himself—that defeated France was one product of a common search for alternatives to the static battles of World War I in which all the great military powers were engaged.[38]

Patton and other American generals modeled their campaigns in Normandy and France on Guderian's blitzkrieg strategy, but German officers also studied America's early experiments with mechanized warfare during interwar visits to the First Cavalry base at Fort Knox and to Fort Leavenworth. These interactions suggest a common process of cross-fertilization rather than the influence of Liddell Hart or Sherman. However, they resulted in the tactics that were implemented to such devastating effect by the Wehrmacht in Poland, France, and the Soviet Union, and it is certainly possible to see Shermanlike features in these campaigns. In the summer of 1941, German infantrymen marched up to twenty-seven miles a day behind the advancing Panzer columns heading toward Moscow, sometimes sleeping only two hours a night or not at all. Like Sherman's army, the advancing armies were ordered to live off the land. Three days before the invasion began, the Eighteenth Panzer Division was ordered to carry only essential supplies and rely on "full exploitation of the land."

Despite the formation of "booty-registration units" to list economic assets in the conquered territories, these expeditions frequently descended into looting and pillaging a population regarded by many German soldiers as primitive, subhuman, and "Asiatic." These "wild requisitions" overlapped with more systematic campaigns of scorched earth and devastation as the advancing Nazi armies destroyed and confiscated food and livestock. Such operations contributed to the deaths of millions of Russians from starvation, cold, and disease, and whatever their superficial similarities to Sherman's campaigns in the South, these operations owed more to the ideological and racial fixations of Nazism and its absolute disregard for even the most elementary laws of war than they did to Liddell Hart and his biography of a Civil War general.[39]

America's Army

It was against this background that the American way of war acquired its distinctive features by the end of the Vietnam War. In conventional warfare, the U.S. military relied heavily on its technological supremacy, particularly its fleets of bombers and fighters, to destroy its enemies' armed forces and achieve rapid military decision. Though not averse to Grant-style campaigns of attrition, sieges, and assaults, the U.S. military and the American public favored slashing cavalry-style offensives, using mobility, speed, and maneuver to make deep territorial gains and target command-and-control structures and lines of communication. As the armed enforcer of the world's premier industrial power and the essential guardian of the global capitalist economy, the U.S. military has always demonstrated a special aptitude for logistics that was already evident in the Civil War and was subsequently honed into a unique ability to organize and transport large numbers of men and materials across the most extended and attenuated international supply lines.

When Woodrow Wilson declared war on Germany on April 16, 1917, the German military predicted that the war would be over before America was able to enter it. Instead the U.S. Army was able to mobilize 4,800,000 men in less than a year. By the time American troops first went into action at the Saint-Mihiel salient on September 12, 1918, the military had refitted French ports to receive its cargo ships, shipped 7.5 million tons of supplies to France, and built more than a thousand miles of railroad track in French territory. During World War II, these logistical skills overcame the extraordinary challenges of the Pacific and supplied Patton's army for most of its headlong charge through France, and they have remained essential to the projection of American military power ever since.

America's desire to obliterate its enemies at a distance with its technological superiority has been shaped by a public aversion to prolonged wars and a determination to preserve the lives of its soldiers. As a result, foreign civilians have sometimes been merely an expendable consequence of the reliance on overwhelming firepower and limitless ordnance that British journalist Reginald Thompson observed in Korea, but at other times deliberate targets. "The Yank style of fighting was to wait for the artillery and let the big guns blast the enemy positions as barren of all life as possible. It saved many American lives but it took longer," recalled Lieutenant General Robert L. Eichelberger, commander of the U.S. Eighth Army in the Pacific in 1944 and 1945.[40] In the words of General Frederick C. Weyand, the last American field commander in Vietnam, "War is death and destruction. The American way of war is particularly violent, deadly and dreadful. We believe in using 'things'—artillery, bombs, massive firepower—in order to conserve our soldiers' lives."[41]

American wars, unlike those fought by Nazi Germany and Japan during World War II, have been "democratic" wars in the sense that there has been a high degree of civilian participation at the strategic level. In theory these wars were subject to some degree of public scrutiny and generally conducted in accordance with the rules and conventions of war, at least at an official level.

Unlike the Wehrmacht or the Imperial Japanese Army, the U.S. military did not generally sanction the deliberate killing of civilians, even when it carried out operations in which mass deaths of civilians were inevitable. "I never had an order, 'Go out and kill civilians,'" declared a witness to the Dellums Committee Hearings on War Crimes in Vietnam. "Orders were 'get a big body count, search and destroy; if you are in a free fire zone, you can shoot anything that moves.'"[42]

In all its wars, the U.S. military demonstrated a remarkable ability to transform men from an array of backgrounds very quickly into courageous, resilient, and skillful soldiers who were able to fight in the most difficult conditions, whether in the swamps of South Carolina, in tropical Pacific islands, in freezing foxholes in the Hürtgen Forest and the Ardennes, or in the jungles of Vietnam. As members of a democratic army that fought "moral" wars, America's citizen soldiers were expected to adhere to the highest standards of military honor and the laws and conventions of war, but these expectations were not always realized, in either "good" or "bad" wars. "What kind of war do civilians suppose we fought, anyway? "asked Edgar L. Jones, a former ambulance driver and a war correspondent during World War II, in an article in the *Atlantic Monthly* in 1946. "We shot prisoners in cold blood, wiped out hospitals, strafed lifeboats, killed or mistreated enemy civilians, finished off the enemy wounded, tossed the dying into a hole with the dead, and in the Pacific boiled the flesh of enemy skulls to make table ornaments for sweethearts, or carved their bones into letter openers."[43]

In the aftermath of the Normandy landings, the mayor of Le Havre was bombarded with letters from angry residents complaining of drunkenness, jeep accidents, and sexual assaults on French women by American and other Allied troops in what one of his respondents called "a regime of terror . . . imposed by bandits in uniform." In Germany the U.S. Army's judge advocate general (JAG) reported a "tremendous increase in the numbers of rapes . . . when our troops arrived on German soil." The sexual assaults were "sometimes . . . accomplished through the application of direct force, at other times by submission resulting from the occupants' fear of their lives."[44] American soldiers were often larcenous. In Normandy and Germany, American and other Allied troops broke into the houses of civilians to steal food, alcohol, and personal possessions as souvenirs or for profit. At Quedlinburg in Thuringia, American soldiers stole precious medieval Bible manuscripts and other objects, and a Captain Robinson stole five paintings from the Städel Museum in Frankfurt. Two officers from the Women's Army Corps stole $1.5 million worth of jewelry from Princess Mary of Hesse.[45]

Similar acts had taken place in the Philippines in 1898, where American soldiers looted the homes of Filipinos, their nominal allies. In Korea, Reginald Thompson watched GIs stealing from the South Korean peasants who were supposed to be their allies, as well as from North Korean civilians. Thompson attributed such behavior to the American dehumanization of all Koreans as "Gooks," a tendency that he regarded as a psychological defense mechanism. Without it "these essentially kind and generous Americans would not have been able to kill them indiscriminately or smash up their homes and poor belongings. By calling them 'Gooks' they were robbed of humanity."[46] The racial dehumanization of enemy fighters and the civilian population was also a feature of American wars in the Philippines, Vietnam, and, more recently, Iraq, but the racism seems to intensify when combined with gleeful celebrations of the military's destructive power. In Korea, both soldiers and the American press reveled in the effects of napalm "hell bombs" on Communist troops—and towns and villages. In Vietnam off-duty soldiers and civilian advisers sang, "Bomb the schools and churches. / Bomb the rice fields, too. / Show the children in the courtyards / What napalm can do."[47]

The dehumanization of the enemy has also been matched by the dehumanization of the soldiers themselves, many of whom have returned from America's wars brutalized and psychologically traumatized, incapable of readjusting to a society that has little comprehension of the wars they fought in. The impact of American warfare on civilians has been due to far more than the failings of its soldiers. In James Franklin Bell's scorched-earth operations in the Philippines, in the bombing campaigns of World War II, in Korea and Vietnam, and in the export of U.S. counter-insurgency doctrines during the Cold War, America's political and military leaders shared the belief held by many twentieth-century governments regardless of their political ideology that civilians were no longer to be considered neutral bystanders in war but rather part of the enemy nation's warmaking capacity, and that it was therefore legitimate to use varying degrees of physical force against them. This recognition did not mean that unlimited violence against civilians was accepted as a general principle. The same U.S. Air Force that once firebombed Japanese, German, and Korean cities officially rejects the notion of military necessity as a license for unrestricted destruction: "Complementing the principle of necessity and implicitly contained within it is the principle of humanity which forbids the infliction of suffering, injury, or destruction not actually necessary for the accomplishment of legitimate purposes."[48]

This principle has sometimes been disavowed in practice, but it has not been permanently abandoned. And the planners of even the most violent expressions of strategic terror and destruction against civilians in World War II, Korea, and Vietnam invariably exuded the special moral fervor that often accompanies American warfare. "Whenever we engage in a war or move in on some other country, it is always to liberate somebody," observed Edmund Wilson in his literary study of the Civil War.[49]

In *The Soul of Battle* (1999), Victor David Hanson placed Sherman and Patton in the same tradition as the Theban general Epaminondas, whose army invaded the Spartan region of Laconia in 370–69 B.C.E. and freed two hundred thousand helots. For Hanson, Sherman's and Patton's armies were a product of a liberating impulse that he regarded as the essence of "democratic warfare," whether freeing Spartan helots, Georgian slaves, or the prisoners of German concentration camps. This impulse, he argued, gave all these wars the elevated "soul" that was intrinsic to moral crusades against tyranny and evil. That American armies have overthrown or played a part in the overthrow of some of the worst regimes in history is indisputable, but Hanson's grand moral narrative too readily conflates the consequences of these wars with their intentions and ignores the frequent use of American military power to install or uphold an assortment of tyrants for geopolitical convenience.

Sherman did not regard either the Confederacy or slavery as evil and would certainly have accepted the latter were it not for the disobedience of the former. Patton was shocked at the sight of the survivors of the concentration camps liberated by his troops, but his government did not enter the war to save Jews. MacArthur "liberated" a South Korea created as an American anticommunist bulwark so as to hand it back to the Syngman Rhee dictatorship that was no less brutal and oppressive than its North Korean enemy. U.S. support for the South Vietnamese strongman Ngô Đình Diệm, the shah of Iran, and (initially) Saddam Hussein was based on very similar calculations. This does not mean that the liberating impulse in American war making is entirely fictitious. But even the most fervently "moral" of America's wars invariably involve more sordid economic and geopolitical objectives that are rarely made clear to the public or ordinary soldiers. Looking back on his thirty-three years of military service, the decorated former Marine Corps general Smedley D. Butler described himself as "a high class muscle man for Big Business, for Wall Street and the bankers. In short, I was a racketeer, a gangster for capitalism."[50]

Yet even when America's wars and military interventions have been driven by much the same economic and geostrategic self-interest that motivates other nations' wars, these goals were generally pursued—when possible—through the installation or preservation of pro-American democratic governments that would secure open markets and guarantee essential resources. In situations where democracy has not produced governments compatible with American interests, U.S. leaders have had no compunctions about using American military power overtly or covertly to overthrow democratic governments and install or support dictatorships, whether in Nicaragua, Guatemala, Iran, or Indonesia. Yet even when American military power was used to suppress a popular movement for independence, as it was in the Philippines, it was presented as an altruistic act of liberation—"bringing civilization" or "spreading democracy." The moralistic facade of America's wars has often justified ruthless, indiscriminate violence, but, like Sherman, the U.S. military has also combined this capacity for destruction with a very American approach to military occupation, in which self-interest and pragmatism have sometimes produced surprisingly positive outcomes.

Waging Peace

In April 1914, President Woodrow Wilson dispatched a naval force with six thousand marines to the Gulf of Mexico to bring pressure to bear on the Mexican strongman General Victoriano Huerta. When Huerta refused an order from the U.S. Navy to apologize for the temporary detention of U.S. Marines who had gone ashore at Vera Cruz by firing a twenty-one-gun salute in honor of the U.S. flag, Wilson ordered marines to occupy the port facilities and seize the Customs House, which was one of the Mexican government's main sources of income. Though Rear Admiral Frank F. Fletcher refused to carry out a "wholesale bombardment" of the city to avoid civilian casualties, this incursion turned into a full-fledged battle between the marines and Mexican soldiers and cadets from the Vera Cruz Naval Academy, supported by armed civilians. The conflict spread from the port into the city.

"Opposed by an enemy they could not see, in the streets of a strange city where every house was an ambush and every church tower had a fighting top," in the words of war correspondent Richard Harding Davis, marines and navy "bluejackets" engaged in what was then the most intense urban combat in U.S. history, fighting house to house and sometimes floor by floor, killing several hundred Mexicans—both armed and unarmed—and losing 130 Americans.[51] Having shot up a city in a country with which the United States was not at war—over a macho question of honor—Wilson placed Vera Cruz under military rule in the command of Major General Frederick Funston, an officer who had forcefully defended harsh methods against "unruly savages" in the Philippines.

In Mexico Funston adopted a very different policy and conducted a remarkably progressive—if puritanical—seven-month occupation that began to reform the city's finances and local government, reopened its schools and recruited new teachers, built new roads and banned gambling, marijuana, cocaine, and cockfighting, and vaccinated much of the population against smallpox before it was abruptly brought to an end. This little-known episode embodied the same combination of "coercion and attraction" employed during the Philippine-American War that has become as much a part of the American way of war as blowing things up

Raising the flag, Vera Cruz, April 27, 1914. Courtesy of the Library of Congress.

and killing people. In *Military Government* (1920), Colonel Harry A. Smith argued against "a military occupation marked by harshness, injustice, or oppression" because it would generate "lasting resentment against the occupying power in the hearts of the people of the occupied territory"; he described the ideal form of military government as one based on "just, considerate, and mild treatment of the governed by the occupying army" that would "convert enemies into friends."[52]

This idea shaped subsequent American occupations in Latin America and the Caribbean in the interwar years and especially the occupation of Japan and Germany after World War II. In both their aims and their practices, American military occupations have generally been radically different from the predatory "belligerent occupations" conducted by Japan in Manchuria or Nazi Germany in the Soviet Union. At its best, U.S. occupation policy followed the prescription in the U.S. Army's World War II–era Field Manual 27-5, that military government should be "just, humane, and as mild as practicable."[53]

In Germany and Japan, U.S. occupying armies oversaw a complex and extraordinarily difficult process of postwar reconstruction and social and political transformation that was largely successful in both countries, even though some of the objectives were compromised or suspended in the interests of short-term stability and the priorities of the Cold War. In Japan, the U.S. military administration directed by Douglas MacArthur—an intelligence officer during Funston's occupation of Vera Cruz—oversaw a remarkably progressive occupation in the country that he had so recently devastated; it destroyed the institutional foundations of Japanese militarism and paved the way for a parliamentary democracy that eventually embraced a pacifist foreign policy with such fervor that it resisted American attempts to rearm Japan during the Cold War.

American occupation regimes were not always so benign, however. In 1915 Woodrow Wilson dispatched 330 U.S. Marines to Haiti to restore order and protect American business interests following the assassination of the Haitian president. This expedition turned into a nineteen-year occupation in which marines and an American-created gendarmerie supported a series of weak and venal Haitian presidents. In 1919–20 the introduction of a corvée labor system by the new government prompted a peasant uprising known as the Cacos Revolt. In response, marines and gendarmes conducted a campaign of rural pacification in which at least three thousand Haitians were killed in operations that made little distinction between armed combatants and sympathetic or even neutral civilians.

In October 1919, the U.S. high commissioner for Haiti Colonel John S. Russell condemned the fact that "troops in the field have declared and carried on what is commonly known as an 'open season' where care is not taken to determine whether the natives are bandits or 'good citizens' and where houses have been ruthlessly burned merely because they were unoccupied and native property otherwise destroyed."[54] As in the Philippines, punitive antiguerrilla hunts were accompanied by the construction of new roads, built by unpaid peasant corvée labor largely to facilitate the penetration of the country by foreign corporations, but also by the construction of bridges, hospitals, irrigation channels, and telephone systems under marine supervision, before the occupation ended in 1934.

All these episodes provided the U.S. military with the common sense and expertise in the conduct of occupations that would later be so conspicuously absent in its disastrous management of the Iraq War. By the end of the Vietnam War, however, there was little indication that the U.S. military would draw upon this legacy in the future, as the army began a process of readjustment, reorganization, and retrenchment, beginning with the abolition of the draft in 1973 and the establishment of the All Volunteer Force (AVF) that Sherman had regarded as the military ideal. As a result of the huge rearmament programs of the Reagan era, the military began to reacquire some of the prestige it had lost in Vietnam and got a new generation of weapons and technologies intended to produce a smaller, leaner army for conventional and unconventional war. Apart from the "covert" wars and "rollback" campaigns of supplying anti-Soviet guerrillas such as the mujahideen, conventional military strategy in the Reagan years was still largely geared toward waging a deep-strike counteroffensive against a putative Soviet invasion of Western Europe on the Patton model. In war-gaming scenarios and training exercises, the military endlessly rehearsed a mechanized war of maneuver based on close air support, which would drive the Soviets out of Europe by penetrating deep behind their advancing formations. But in the last decade of the century, the age of superpower confrontation came to an abrupt and unexpected end, and the U.S. military entered a new period in its history, in which the old assumptions of "total" and "limited" war were no longer valid. The change called into question the very purpose of the military's vast destructive powers.

8

The New American Way of War

At the end of the Cold War, the United States became the world's only military superpower, with a global reach unprecedented in world history. In addition to more than seven hundred military bases and installations in twenty-nine countries throughout the world, its fleet of warships, submarines, and aircraft carriers patrolling the world's oceans had long since transformed Alfred Thayer Mahan's sea-power ambitions into a permanent reality. Since the end of the Vietnam War, it had bolstered its arsenal of intercontinental ballistic missiles, bomber fleets, fighter planes, and attack helicopters with a new generation of high-tech weapons that included radar-invisible stealth fighters, AC-130 gunships, laser-guided missiles, and laser-guided smart bombs. Following the abolition of the draft, a smaller and more streamlined professional army had taken full advantage of the technological revolution and laid the foundations for a digitalized battlefield command system that no other military in the world could match.

All these developments gave the military a unique ability to fight any enemy anywhere in the world, while making the United States impregnable. Yet hardly had the euphoria of the West's "victory" begun to wear off than a pessimistic school of thought within the American political and military establishment predicted that the United States faced a new era of "persistent conflict" from an unpredictable array of natural and artificial enemies that include terrorists, rogue states, drug cartels and other mafias, and dictators armed with weapons of mass destruction, and that the maintenance of America's global military presence was essential for national security and also for the stability of the international system.

In the same period, the military, its analysts and strategists, and key institutions, such as the Army War College and the Joint Readiness Training Center, increasingly stressed the importance of "military operations other than war" and "full dimensional operations," in which the military was expected to prepare for a range of activities, from peacekeeping, "stability operations," humanitarian assistance, emergency disaster relief, and "conflict termination."

According to the concept of "three-block war" elaborated by U.S. Marine General Charles Krulak in the late 1990s, soldiers might be obliged to engage in combat, humanitarian, and stability operations simultaneously within the contiguous space of three city blocks. The idea that war could have humanitarian and altruistic objectives was often reinforced by the notion that new high-tech weaponry and more accurate targeting systems and sensors would make it possible to restrict "collateral damage"—civilian casualties and property destruction—to an acceptable minimum.

In 1996 the Joint Chiefs of Staff's *Joint Vision 2010* claimed that precision targeting had made it possible to "achieve the necessary destruction or suppression of enemy forces with fewer systems" and deploy the "necessary concentration of combat power at the decisive time and place—with less need to mass forces physically than in the past." New capabilities would also "relieve our Service men and women of the need to be physically present at the decisive points in battle or in other operations, or to be exposed to conditions of great danger and hardship."[1]

The idea that the U.S. Army might be able to win wars without the need for its soldiers to be "physically present" on the battlefields was to some extent a product of a new sense of technological supremacy. But technology also made it possible, at least in theory, to limit the extent of wartime destruction at a time when it was becoming increasingly difficult to find a viable rationale for the use of military power as an instrument of American foreign policy and when interstate conflict was increasingly regarded as a historical anachronism. After more than a century in which American warfare had been based on annihilation of enemy forces and sometimes enemy civilians as well, a new era now beckoned in which the military would seek to become "preeminent in any form of conflict" without risking the lives of its own soldiers and while causing minimal destruction.

Operation Just Cause

These expectations shaped a range of armed conflicts in which America became involved in the aftermath of the Cold War, including three major wars, an on/off air war with Iraq, naval skirmishes with Iran, peacekeeping missions and occupations in the Balkans and Somalia, and the occupation of Haiti. In December 1989, these new doctrines were tested for the first time when the United States invaded Panama in order to topple and arrest the CIA protégé and narco-dictator General Manuel Noriega. Ostensibly intended to safeguard American lives and "defend democracy" in response to Noriega's brutal crackdown on political opposition, the invasion was actually also motivated by the imminent implementation of the 1977 Carter-Torrijos Panama Canal Treaty, which was due to restore full sovereignty over the Canal Zone to Panama by the end of the century.

For the military, the invasion was an opportunity to dispel "Vietnam syndrome"—the humiliation of the world's foremost industrial power being beaten by a Third World agricultural society despite its overwhelming firepower and the moral collapse of the U.S. Army and the loss of domestic prestige that accompanied that defeat. Panama also provided an opportunity to demonstrate America's new technological weaponry and its tactical and operational prowess. In October 1989, General Carl Stiner, the commander of the U.S. Army's Southern Command, presented to the Bush administration an invasion plan that called for simultaneous attacks against twenty-seven targets from land, air, and sea to rapidly destroy Noriega's command-and-control structure. This plan became the basis for Operation Just Cause, which began at 12:30 a.m. on December 20, when a combined task force of 27,000 infantry, sailors, paratroopers, and special forces attacked some 14,000 Panama Defense Forces (PDF) personnel, police, national guard, and paramilitaries. Subjected to simultaneous naval, ground, and aerial attacks involving paratroopers, special forces, and regular infantry in addition to a stunning display of firepower from Apache and Cobra attack helicopters, Sheridan light assault vehicles, AC-130 gunships, and the new F-117 Nighthawk stealth fighters, Noriega's forces were rapidly overwhelmed and effectively defeated by the time the sun came up.

Stiner's strategic plan combined well-established American principles of speed, mobility, and overwhelming force with seamlessly integrated joint operations and the new technological weaponry at the U.S. Army's disposal, but it was also subject to stricter rules of engagement than any previous American wars. Indiscriminate artillery and aerial bombardments and attacks on military targets close to "critical public facilities" were prohibited, and soldiers were obliged to show maximum restraint when firing at the enemy, even to the point of shooting at defended buildings rather than directly at their defenders in order to make them surrender.

These rules appear to have been mostly observed. When a stealth fighter attacked the main PDF barracks, it dropped a bomb fifty yards away in order to stun its defenders rather than destroy the building. Psychological operations teams equipped with loud-speakers played an important role in reducing the level of destruction by exhorting PDF forces to surrender or by simply calling telephones in defended buildings to persuade their defenders to give up—the "Ma Bell approach." Twenty-four radio programs and leaflet distributions disseminated the same message of the futility of resistance.

The military's concern with keeping civilian casualties and physical damage to a minimum was partly influenced by the close proximity of some forty thousand Americans in the Panama Canal Zone and also by the desire to leave as much of the country's infrastructure intact as possible. These efforts also reflected the Pentagon's new emphasis on media presentation as an important factor in shaping military outcomes and preventing a repetition of the "living-room war" in Vietnam, where militarists have often cited the impact of television coverage of civilian deaths on international and domestic public opinion as a decisive factor in the U.S. defeat. Media coverage of the Panama invasion was therefore carefully managed in the U.S. Army's first use of the media pool system, and its specially selected correspondents saw little or nothing of the combat until it was over.

These efforts would not have surprised Sherman, who was famously hostile to the Union press and frequently banned Northern reporters from accompanying his armies. On one occasion, Sherman court-martialed the reporter Thomas Knox, who wrote a critical article on his failed offensive at Chickasaw Bayou, for making "sundry and false allegations and accusations" against the army "to the great detriment of the interest of the National Government and comfort of our enemies."[2] These charges were rejected at the court-martial, but Knox was banned from associating with Sherman's army. Pentagon efforts to control media coverage of the Panama War were more subtle but no less effective. Reporters found themselves forced to watch CNN reports or official briefings in windowless rooms.

As a result, few journalists saw the controversial series of events that followed the U.S. attack on the PDF military headquarters in the heart of El Chorrillo, one of Panama City's working-class districts, in the first hour of the invasion. Most of El Chorrillo's fifteen thousand residents were asleep when the attack took place, and they woke to find that their neighborhood had become a battle zone, as helicopters blasted the *comandancia* building and U.S. soldiers and Noriega loyalists fought running gun battles in the surrounding streets. Fires quickly spread throughout El Chorrillo, forcing most of its people to flee their homes. Pentagon spokesmen accused Noriega's paramilitaries of setting the fires, but residents insisted that they were spread by tracer bullets and artillery and some alleged that U.S. soldiers had intentionally burned down individual houses with incendiaries.

The Spanish journalist Maruja Torres watched what she later recalled as a bombardment—"a genuine, authentic, super-technical and modern bombardment by the most powerful army in the world, of one of the poorest neighborhoods in the capital" from her room at a Marriott Hotel.[3] By morning fifteen blocks of El Chorrillo had been burned to the ground, and most of its fifteen thousand inhabitants were homeless. Both Panamanian and American critics of the occupation later claimed that four thousand to six thousand civilians were killed in the fighting at El Chorrillo and other places and that their bodies were secretly buried in mass graves under the supervision of the U.S. military.[4]

These figures seem unlikely. The U.S. military's casualty figures reported 32 U.S. dead, 50 enemy dead, and 314 civilians dead. A Human Rights Watch report immediately after the war questioned the military's estimates but discounted the possibility of thousands of secretly buried bodies. It nevertheless blamed the "inordinate number of civilian victims" on the "tactics and weapons" used during the invasion and suggested that "the devastation created in the neighborhood of El Chorrillo" was possibly caused by American shelling and tracer bullets. The authors also questioned the decision to attack the PDF headquarters in the first place as a violation of "the rule of proportionality, which mandates that the risk of harm to impermissible targets be weighed against the military necessity of the objective pursued."[5]

Some of these "impermissible targets" were among the bodies lined up in the morgue in Panama City, which Juantxu Rodríguez, the *El País* reporter and colleague of Maruja Torres, photographed shortly before he was shot dead by U.S. soldiers in a crossfire. But these less-than-glorious dimensions of the war were swiftly forgotten, along with El Chorrillo's thousands of homeless refugees, as television cameras captured Noriega's opponents thanking "God—and the U.S. military" and as Noriega surrendered to U.S. troops in January after briefly taking refuge at the papal nuncio's residence in Panama City. In March 1990, President George H.W. Bush hailed "the roll call of glory, the roster of great American campaigns, Yorktown, Gettysburg, Normandy, and now Panama." The defeat of a few thousand soldiers and paramilitaries by the most powerful military force in human history was not the most obvious cause for such celebration. For the U.S. military, however, the invasion was a vindication of its new "surgical force engagement capabilities" and "a success, even a masterpiece of the operational art," which demonstrated that "U.S. forces could deploy on short notice into an environment that required a combination of both violent engagement and sensitive restraint." It heralded even bigger campaigns to come.[6]

The First Gulf War

Within a year, the military gave an even more convincing demonstration of the new American way of war against a far more powerful enemy. On August 2, 1990, the world was plunged into the most serious international crisis since the Soviet invasion of

Afghanistan when Iraq invaded and annexed Kuwait. Though Saddam Hussein believed that he had implicit U.S. approval from the American ambassador to Iraq April Glaspie to carry out the invasion, the Bush administration ordered Iraq to withdraw from Kuwait without preconditions or face military action. These demands were supported by the United Nations and most of Iraq's neighbors. As a result, the United States assumed leadership of an international military coalition charged with enforcing the UN Security Council's Resolution 678 of November 29, 1990, which established a deadline of January 15, 1991, for Iraqi withdrawal from Kuwait and authorized member states to use "all necessary means" if the deadline was not acknowledged.

Though the United States officially fought as part of a coalition, the war was always an American-dominated and American-dependent enterprise. Of the 956,600 troops deployed in Saudi Arabia and other countries at the war's peak, some 697,000 were American, and the U.S. military took care of the logistics and supplied most of the planes, missiles, and other weaponry for the ground and air campaigns. These forces faced some 545,000 Iraqi troops in forty-two or forty-three divisions, including elite Republican Guard units, equipped with some 4,200 tanks and 3,000 heavy artillery pieces, in Kuwait and along the southern Iraqi border. Expectations of potential heavy casualties shaped a coalition campaign strategy that was very different from Operation Just Cause.

The coalition commander, General H. Norman Schwarzkopf, planned to use airpower to cut Iraq's lines of communication with Kuwait. Having cut off the Iraqi army, the coalition would proceed to "kill it," as chairman of the Joint Chiefs of Staff Colin Powell put it, with a ground offensive that drew heavily on Liddell Hart's indirect strategy.[7] Rejecting proposals from the U.S. Marine Corps for an amphibious assault on Kuwait City, Schwarzkopf proposed to combine a two-corps assault on Kuwait from Saudi Arabia and western Iraq with a drive along the Kuwait coastline by marines of the First Expeditionary Force and Arab coalition forces. This would be followed by a "Hail Mary punch," in which a combined force of 250,000 American and French troops would enter Iraq 480 miles to the west of Kuwait from Saudi Arabia and swing back to enter Kuwait.

On January 16, 1991, Allied planes initiated Operation Desert Storm with multiple air strikes in Iraq and Kuwait. Over the next forty-two days, coalition planes dropped 88,000 tons of bombs in the most sustained and relentless bombing campaign in military history. More than two hundred Tomahawk cruise missiles fired from ships and carriers in the Persian Gulf added to the devastating technological assault. On February 24, the Eighteenth Airborne Corps, supported by the French Sixth Airborne Division and the 101st U.S. Airborne Division, entered Iraq from Saudi Arabia, having successfully reached their starting positions without detection.

By the end of the day, the Eighteenth Corps had advanced 170 miles toward the Euphrates River and the main highway connecting Iraq to Kuwait, completely circumventing Iraqi defensive positions farther south, before swinging back into Kuwait, where the 150,000-strong Seventh Corps had also made a decisive breakthrough. Battered by more than a month of air strikes, the much-vaunted Iraqi army quickly crumbled, and the "mother of all battles" never materialized, as hundreds of thousands of Iraqi soldiers surrendered in Kuwait and Iraq, while others attempted a chaotic retreat. On the night of February 26–27, more than a thousand vehicles, many of them carrying loot from Kuwait, were bombed and strafed by Allied planes along the Mutla Ridge on the road to Basra in what one U.S. pilot described as a "turkey shoot." Macabre photographs of wrecked vehicles and burned corpses along this "Highway of Death" became iconic images of the disparity between the contending forces.

On February 28, Iraq agreed to a cease-fire, which was formalized on March 3. In all, coalition forces suffered fewer than two hundred casualties. Estimates of Iraqi military casualties initially ranged from 100,000 to 200,000 in the immediate aftermath of the war, but subsequent research put the number from the low thousands to 20,000–22,000 combat deaths cited in a 1993 survey by the U.S Air Force.[8] The stunning rapidity of the ground campaign was partly a tribute to coalition tactics and strategies and partly a consequence of the unimaginative and often nonexistent leadership of the Iraqi components, but it was also made possible by a new kind of bombing strategy that seemed, at first sight, to bear out the new narratives of humanitarian war.

Dismantling Iraq

In the course of the war, coalition planes attacked more than three hundred targets in Iraq and Kuwait, many on multiple occasions. This campaign was intended to weaken and "degrade" Saddam Hussein's military machine and destroy his arsenal of chemical and biological weapons, but many of the bombs were dropped on "dual use" targets and inevitably killed civilians. Coalition spokesmen insisted that laser- and satellite-guided missiles and smart bombs made these raids less destructive to ordinary people than their predecessors. "For the first time we had a capability to focus on military targets and avoid civilian areas, "Schwarzkopf later declared, "so there was a degree of discrimination within the execution of the plan that made it much more palatable than it would have been . . . like the firebombing of Tokyo or something like that, that was just an indiscriminate destruction of the entire city."[9]

The destruction was not always so "palatable." There is no doubt that the bombing campaign was different from many of its predecessors. Residential areas were not systematically razed, and targeting systems made it possible to pick out individual targets with greater precision than in any previous war, while reducing the damage to the surrounding area. Nevertheless, the war was punctuated by incidents in which such discrimination was absent, such as the bombing of the Yarmuk Hotel in Diwaninieh, in which eleven civilians were killed, destruction of the Amiriyah Public Shelter No. 25 with a bunker-busting bomb that killed more than four hundred civilians, and the bombing of a plant that produced powdered milk for baby formulas. Most of these episodes were the result of poor intelligence rather than deliberate attacks, but after the war it was revealed that only 7 percent of the bombs dropped were guided (smart) and that even these didn't always hit their targets; the conventional bombs were much less precise.

The rhetoric of "surgical" targeting also obscured the new forms of destruction resulting from a bombing campaign that targeted the "joints" of a modern industrial society, as opposed to indiscriminate carpet or area bombing. In addition to Baath Party headquarters and military bases, the United States blew up telephone and radio transmission towers and lines, food processing, storage, and distribution facilities, animal vaccination facilities, power stations, water treatment plants, irrigation water pumping stations, railroads, bus depots, oil wells and pumps, pipelines, refineries, and storage tanks to paralyze Iraq "strategically, operationally, and tactically," as U.S. Air Force secretary Donald Rice described it.

In these attacks, as a Department of Defense interim report prepared for Congress noted after the war, "It was impossible . . . to destroy the electrical power supply for Iraqi command and control facilities or chemical weapons factories, yet leave untouched that portion of the electricity supplied to the general populace." Yet the scope of the bombing campaign clearly went beyond "unavoidable hardships" and combined psychological, economic, and military objectives in a very Shermanlike attempt to target the enemy's will to resist—a goal made explicit by one air force officer who told a reporter, "Big picture, we wanted to let people know, 'Get rid of this guy and we'll be more than happy to assist in rebuilding. We're not going to tolerate Saddam Hussein or his regime. Fix that, and we'll fix your electricity.'"[10]

In 1991 the Commission of Inquiry for the International War Crimes Tribunal headed by former U.S. attorney general Ramsey Clark determined that "civilian vehicles including public buses, taxicabs and passenger cars were bombed and strafed at random to frighten civilians from flight, from seeking food or medical care, finding relatives or other uses of highways. The effect was summary execution and corporal punishment indiscriminately of men, women and children, young and old, rich and poor."[11] Human Rights Watch also reported eyewitness accounts of attacks on civilian vehicles, schools, mosques, wedding parties, and gas stations.[12]

The civilian death toll was initially calculated by Iraqi and other observers at more than 100,000, but later estimates revised it to as low as 2,500–3,000.[13] Considering the intensity of the bombing, these figures were relatively low and appeared once again to vindicate coalition claims of surgically applied destruction and smart technologies. But these statistics did not fully encapsulate the impact of the war on Iraqi society. In March 1991, a UN report on the humanitarian situation in Kuwait and Iraq found that the conflict had "wrought near-apocalyptic results upon the economic structure of what had been, until January 1991, a rather highly urbanized and mechanized society. Now, most means of modern life support have been destroyed or rendered tenuous. Iraq has, for some time to come, been relegated to a pre-industrial age, but with all the disabilities of post-industrial dependency on an intensive use of energy and technology."[14] The report described a paralyzed and dismembered society in which "all previously viable sources of fuel and power . . . and modern means of communication are now, essentially, defunct." Untreated sewage was being dumped directly into rivers from bombed water-treatment plants, the electricity grid had virtually ceased to operate, and Iraqis were able to communicate only by person-to-person contact as a result of the collapse of the telephone and postal systems.

Within a few months, most essential services in Iraq had been restored, much of its electricity grid was functioning again, and rationing was abolished. But the casualties of the bombing campaign were not limited to immediate wartime destruction. A 1993 study carried out by Beth Daponte and funded by Greenpeace claimed that 111,000 civilians, including 70,000 children and adolescents under the age of fifteen, had died from "war-induced adverse health effects" due to the disruption of food production and damage to water-treatment and sanitation facilities and the electricity grid.[15]

Though caused by the bombing, these deaths were seldom attributed to it, making it easier to sustain the notion of a "clean" conflict with minimal destruction. But as another Greenpeace report, on the environmental consequences of the war, pointed out, the "efficient destruction" of "crucial life support functions of the civilian population" was a new form of war, in which the "old fashioned definition of collateral damage . . . that shrapnel has to scar civilians, or rubble has to fall on them" had been replaced by a "new definition . . . that water, electricity, and fuel are taken away from civil society. People who live in cities, in modern societies, are dependent for their lives, not just their comfort, on such support systems. Thus their destruction is as much de facto terror bombing, as destruction of oil wells is environmental terrorism."[16]

The "Most Perfect Instrument"

The unraveling of Iraqi society was not due only to the bombs and missiles. In his authoritative study of the impact of war on civilians, the Oxford humanitarian ethics scholar Hugo Slim has written, "The two main ways of using food and starvation as weapons of war are through policies of blockade or scorched earth—the former often being a more subtle and more easily disguised form of the latter."[17] Economic blockades have a long pedigree in American military history; they were used in the Civil War and in World War I, and also against Cuba, Vietnam, and Nicaragua during the Cold War. During World War I, Woodrow Wilson approvingly described the blockade against Germany and the Central Powers as "this economic, peaceful, silent deadly remedy." In the 1990s the United States began to reemploy this "remedy" against a range of countries that included Haiti, Iran, and Serbia. In the aftermath of the Gulf War, the United Nations Security Council extended the embargoes against Iraq, introduced after the invasion of Kuwait, into one of the most comprehensive and stringent sanctions packages in history.

Ostensibly intended to "contain" Saddam Hussein's regime and neutralize Iraq's ability to reconstitute its chemical and biological weapons programs, sanctions also had a wider purpose. In March 1991, the *New York Times* reported that "the United States has argued against any premature relaxation in the belief that by making life uncomfortable for the Iraqi people it will eventually encourage them to remove President Saddam Hussein from power." The U.S. deputy national security adviser Robert Gates also proclaimed, "Saddam is discredited and cannot be redeemed. Iraqis will pay the price while he remains in power. All possible sanctions will be maintained until he is gone."[18]

Despite supposed exemptions for humanitarian and medical purposes, the UN sanctions prohibited key Iraqi exports and an extensive range of "dual use" imports that included syringes, medicines, and medical equipment and chlorine, spare parts, and new pumps for water-treatment plants, as well as fertilizer and farm equipment. Coming so soon after the bombings, these restrictions compounded the impact of the war on Iraqi society, creating what the journalist Andrew Cockburn has called an "immense slow-motion disaster," in which the population was reduced to a "lower-tier Third World standard of living" where pharmacies were empty but hospital wards were filled with "sickly, wasted infants."[19]

By the middle of the decade, 567,000 Iraqi children were reported to have died as a consequence of malnutrition, inadequate health care, and cholera, gastroenteritis, and dysentery caused by drinking contaminated water, according to an epidemiological survey by the British medical journal *The Lancet*. In 1995, the sanctions were slightly eased by the UN's "oil for food" program, but many restrictions remained in place. In 1998 Denis J. Halliday, the UN humanitarian coordinator in Iraq, resigned, declaring, "We are in the process of destroying an entire society. It is as simple and terrifying as that." Two years later, his successor, Hans von Sponeck, followed suit, asking, "For how long should the civilian population, which is totally innocent on [*sic*] all this, be exposed to such punishment for something they have never done?"

In a 1999 article in the journal *Foreign Policy*, John Mueller and Karl Mueller compared the impact of the sanctions to the atomic bombing of Hiroshima and Nagasaki and argued that "a so far futile effort to remove Saddam from power and a somewhat more successful effort to constrain him militarily" may have constituted "a necessary cause of the deaths of more people in Iraq than have been slain by all so-called weapons of mass destruction throughout history."[20] The United States and its allies have downplayed this impact or blamed it on the allocation of resources by Saddam Hussein's regime. In a television interview in 1996, however, Secretary of State Madeleine Albright famously replied that the price was "worth it" when asked if the deaths of half a million children were necessary to contain Saddam.

Other U.S. officials also argued that sanctions were essential to "keep Saddam in his box." In an interview with the *New York Times* in 2003, James Rubin, chief spokesman for the State Department during the Clinton years, reiterated that sanctions had been necessary and predicted that such methods might be a preferable alternative to war in the future, when the United States would increasingly rely on such methods "in self-defense or with U.N. Security Council authorization . . . as the ultimate method of coercion in international relations."[21] Robert McBrien, the director of global targeting at the Office of Foreign Assets, which oversees U.S. sanctions programs, described sanctions to Andrew Cockburn as "the soft edge of hard power. They make people suffer. They hurt. They can destroy."

Cockburn described the political advantages of "conduct-based targeting," which enables the United States government to wage a form of "modern economic warfare" that "bends the global financial system to its ends and can blight entire societies, operates well below the radar, frequently justified as a benign alternative to military action." In terms of their impact on the targeted society and their broader coercive intentions, sanctions can also constitute a "Sherman's march" without armies or soldiers. And in the case of Iraq, their full impact would not become clear until U.S. troops entered Iraq a second time, thirteen years after Schwarzkopf's troops hurtled through the Iraqi desert.

Hyperwar

Even more than Panama, the Gulf War was a watershed in American warfare; it confirmed and demonstrated to the world the technological and organizational supremacy of the U.S. military. In a 1993 article in the military journal *Parameters*, Major Wayne K. Maynard compared the war to nineteenth-century colonial wars that "pitted small numbers of disciplined, well-trained Western troops with rifles against hordes of tribal warriors armed with only shields and spears."[22] In the aftermath of the war, the Pentagon's prime futurist thinker, Andrew Marshall, argued that the United States was in the throes of a "revolution in military affairs" (RMA), because of which it had outstripped any potential rival. Though Marshall and some proponents of the RMA worried that this supremacy might be only temporary, others emanated a sense of triumphalism and omnipotence and heralded the advent of a new form of American warfare, in which victories could be obtained by surgically dismembering armies and their command-and-control structures rather than destroying them, warfare in which computers and satellites would become as significant as soldiers.[23]

Some called this transformation postmodern war.[24] Others saw the Gulf War as an example of hyperwar, whose essential components, according to the Federation of American Scientists, were "surprise, intensity, lethality, decapitation, scope, and mass" in operations directed at the enemy's leadership, resources, infrastructure, armed forces, and population.[25] In 1995 Colonel John Warden, one of the architects of the Gulf War bombing campaign, outlined a new strategy of "applying pressure against the enemy's innermost strategic ring—its command structure. . . . It is pointless to deal with enemy forces if they can be bypassed, by strategy or technology, either in the defense or offense."[26] In Warden's opinion, America's domination of the battle space now makes it possible to carry out multiple simultaneous attacks in order to inflict "strategic paralysis" on the enemy "system" while avoiding "imprecision" that would be "too expensive physically and politically to condone."

Other analysts made similar arguments. Some air force strategists saw the Gulf War as a paradigm of "effects-based operations" (EBOs), in which conventional military power and nonmilitary capabilities have broad "effects" on the enemy, without inflicting mass casualties, through simultaneous attacks on multiple targets that isolate and neutralize enemy armed forces without actually destroying them. The Department of Defense articulated a vision of "network-centric warfare" (NCW), in which a fully digitized U.S. Army would be able to "see" all dimensions of the battle space and achieve "unequivocal military decision with minimum cost to both sides."

Technological omnipotence has not always been seen as a justification for restraint, however. In a report to the United States National Defense University in 1996, the naval officers Harlan K. Ullman and James P. Wade elaborated a strategic doctrine called shock and awe. They proposed that space-based observation systems, sensors, computers, and robotics now made it possible to inflict "instant, nearly incomprehensible levels of massive destruction" on people and their resources so as to nullify "the will, understanding, and perception of an adversary" through "the non-nuclear equivalent of the impact that the atomic weapons dropped on Hiroshima and Nagasaki had on the Japanese."[27] According to the authors, "The Japanese simply could not comprehend the destructive power carried by a single airplane. This incomprehension produced a state of awe. One recalls from old photographs and movie or television screens, the comatose and glazed expressions of survivors of the great bombardments of World War I and the attendant horrors and death of trench warfare. These images and expressions of shock transcend race, culture, and history." America's future wars, Ullman and Wade recommended, could similarly develop the ability to "frighten, scare, intimidate and disarm" the enemy and induce a state of shock and awe. Though "humanitarian considerations . . . cannot or should not be ignored" in such campaigns, Ullman and Wade rejected "the attempt to keep war 'immaculate,' at least in limiting collateral damage" and reminded their readers that "one point should not be forgotten. Above all, war is a nasty business or, as Sherman put it, 'war is hell.'"

The willingness to "frighten, scare, intimidate and disarm" was an essential component of Sherman's low-tech campaign of destruction, and it is possible to trace other continuities in the visions of perfect technological warfare that percolated through the U.S. military in the last decade of the century. In a 1989 article in the *Marine Corps Gazette*, the conservative military pundit William S. Lind argued that the U.S. military had entered a new era of "fourth-generation warfare" (4GW) that differed radically from a first-generation war like the Civil War. On the fourth-generation battlefield of the future, Lind argued, "the distinction between war and peace will be blurred to the vanishing point. . . . The distinction between 'civilian' and 'military' may disappear," and attacks on traditional military targets, such as airfields, communications facilities, power plants, and infrastructure would "become rarities because of their vulnerability," while psychological operations would become "the dominant operational and strategic weapon in the form of media/information intervention," to the point that "television news may become a more powerful operational weapon than armored divisions."[28]

In 1995 Colonel Richard Szafranski, the chair of national military strategy at the Air War College, proposed an even more comprehensive model of information warfare, in which military force could be directed against the enemy's "knowledge or beliefs" and "epistemology" in order to "influence adversary choices, and hence adversary behavior, without the adversary's awareness that choices and behavior are being influenced." This outcome could be achieved by "deception and disinformation, radioelectronic combat, propaganda, and the whole gamut of 'psychological warfare' or command and control warfare attacks against enemy combatants at the *operational* level," which would make it possible to "subdue without fighting or to reduce the amount of violence required."[29]

Sherman also referred to war as an "epistemology," and his campaigns in the South had likewise been intended to change the "knowledge or beliefs" of the Confederacy by providing civilians new "information" to counter what it received through the Southern press. The Pentagon's attempts at media management in the last decade of the twentieth century were motivated by a similar determination to ensure that coverage of its wars didn't affect their outcome, at a time when war was subject to unprecedented international media scrutiny. Thus the military stage-managed press conferences, disseminated information only through specially selected reporters under the pool system, and placed promilitary pundits on chat shows and news programs.

From the military's perspective, the need for such management was underlined by the collapse of the U.S. military mission in Somalia when the deaths of eighteen U.S. soldiers and more than five hundred Somalis in the botched arrest in Mogadishu that Somalis now call Ranger Day led to a domestic outcry that forced the Clinton administration to withdraw. Restricted, false, or demoralizing information may be a weapon of modern war, but it's available to all, and weaker opponents can use it to compensate for lack of military strength, as the Pentagon discovered during America's last war of the century.

Kosovo

In its objectives and in the way it was fought, NATO's seventy-eight-day aerial campaign to force Serbia to withdraw from Kosovo in 1999 exemplified the new paradigm of "humanitarian war" and the emerging doctrine of responsibility to protect (R2P). Whereas Operation Desert Storm had been dictated by clear geostrategic considerations regarding the threat posed by Saddam Hussein to the world's key oil reserves, the NATO intervention in Kosovo was presented as an attempt to prevent "genocide"—the brutal repression of the Kosovar Albanians by the remnant of Yugoslavia (Serbia and Montenegro) in its counterinsurgency operations against the Kosovo Liberation Army (KLA).

On March 18, 1999, members of the NATO Contact Group presented the Federal Republic of Yugoslavia (FRY) with an ultimatum at the Château de Rambouillet in France, which called on Slobodan Milošević's regime to withdraw Serbian security forces from Kosovo and replace them with a NATO peacekeeping force. Milošević refused to accept, and each side blamed the other for the collapse of negotiations. On March 24, the ultimatum expired, and NATO warplanes began bombing targets in Kosovo, Serbia, and Montenegro as part of Operation Allied Force. As in the Gulf War, the U.S. military played the leading role in a nineteen-member coalition commanded General Wesley Clark, the supreme allied commander Europe (SACEUR). Unlike the war against Iraq, however, many members of the coalition had strong reservations about the use of force in Kosovo, and political considerations resulted in a very different campaign. Initially the coalition believed that Serbia would come to terms quickly through a limited and tightly regulated bombing campaign against "enabling" military targets, such as air-defense systems, army barracks, and antiaircraft installations, just as the Bosnian Serbs had done during NATO's Operation Deliberate Force in the autumn of 1995.

The ambivalence of some members of the coalition obliged a reluctant Clark to adopt a gradualist bombing strategy that harked back to the Vietnam War, a strategy that the U.S. military continued to regard as one of the reasons for losing the war. In order to keep collateral damage to a minimum, all bombing targets had to be approved by teams of lawyers, and particularly sensitive targets had to be personally approved by President Bill Clinton, Prime Minister Tony Blair, and President Jacques Chirac in order to reduce the possibility of "unintended consequences." These constraints resulted in a bombing campaign of remarkable precision. On April 3, the Serbian dissident journalist Jasmina Tešanović watched NATO planes bomb the Ministry of the Interior and other targets within twenty yards of the largest maternity hospital in the Balkans without damaging it, and she marveled at the skill of the NATO pilots "responsible for hitting military targets without harming a single new-born baby."[30]

Such precision was not always present, and the war was punctuated by incidents in which civilians were killed and wounded in attacks on targets in residential neighborhoods, and refugees became casualties during attacks on public transport. On April 13, a mistimed missile attack on a railway bridge hit the Belgrade–Salonika train near Leskovac, south of Belgrade, killing 10 passengers. On May 13, NATO planes killed up to 100 civilians in an attack on Serb positions in the village of Korisa in southern Kosovo. In the course of the war, between 90 and 150 civilians were killed by cluster bombs, each of which deploys 150 to 200 bomblets in patterns designed to destroy as much property and kill as many people as possible in the affected area.

The worst incident took place on May 16, when a cluster-bomb attack on an airfield in the city of Niš killed sixteen people and wounded sixty more. As in the Gulf War, these incidents were mostly due to operational and intelligence errors, but such mistakes became more likely as the list of targets widened. Despite the Bosnian Serbs' murderous ethnic-cleansing operations under Milošević a few years earlier, NATO was unprepared for Serbia's defiance and caught completely off balance by its ruthless expulsion of more than 90 percent of the Kosovar population into neighboring countries, which provoked an even worse humanitarian crisis than the one the bombing was intended to address.

By week three of the war, the absence of tangible gains prompted even the establishment journal *The Economist* to question the U.S.

Defense Department's "post-Gulf-war prestige" and "the doctrines of high-tech dominance that the Gulf war encouraged
people to believe." Faced with continued Serbian resilience and unwilling to mount a ground offensive, NATO intensified its effort
with a bombing campaign based on the "four Ds"—"demonstrate,
deter, damage, degrade." At the beginning of the war, the NATO
"Master Target File" identified 169 targets. By its end, 976 targets
had been hit, including oil refineries, petroleum depots, road and
rail bridges, factories, the electricity grid, and "crony" targets—
businesses and resources closely related to the regime. In theory,
bombing was intended to prevent the Serbian security forces from
carrying out military operations in Kosovo and force its government to submit to the terms imposed at Rambouillet. However,
because many NATO members were reluctant or unwilling to un-
dertake a ground invasion, airpower increasingly became a weapon
of intimidation directed against civilians.

Though air strikes did not target civilians directly and NATO
pilots went to considerable lengths to avoid civilian casualties, the
coercion of the Serbian government was increasingly dependent
on the use of force to make ordinary Serbs feel the impact of the
war. In her wartime diaries, Jasmina Tešanović vividly describes
the terror of her children, friends, and neighbors during the
NATO bombings of Belgrade as they faced blackouts, water and
food shortages, and the constant threat of death experienced by
all civilians in such circumstances. Within four weeks, fifty-nine
bridges, nine major airports, and 80 percent of Serbia's oil production facilities had been destroyed, in addition to 70 percent of
its electricity grid.

On April 21, NATO attacked a new "military" target, using
three cruise missiles to destroy the Belgrade headquarters of Radio Television of Serbia (RTS), run by Milošević's wife, Mirjana
Marković, killing sixteen journalists and technicians. The attack
on Serbia's television network reflected the coalition's frustration

at the Milošević regime's careful control of the foreign media inside Yugoslavia and the media's role in mobilizing Serbian and international opinion. In a subsequent examination of NATO's failure to achieve "information dominance" in the war, U.S. Air Force Major Wayne A. Larsen argued that the Serbian television and radio network prolonged domestic resistance through its patriotic appeals to Serbian nationalism and its exploitation of "collateral damage incidents" for propaganda purposes.[31]

In Larsen's estimation, these "defensive" information operations made the Serbian media network a legitimate object of "offensive" military force. The designation of a television and radio station as a military target of "fundamental military importance" received widespread international criticism, however, and was rejected by Human Rights Watch, which concluded that "the purpose of the attack . . . seems to have been more psychological harassment of the civilian population than to obtain direct military effect."[32] Such harassment was always an implicit objective of the air campaign. By the time the war ended, more than a hundred thousand Serbs were out of work as a result of the bombing of factories, infrastructure, and transportation links, and Belgrade and many other cities were without water and electricity. Had the war continued, the destruction would have been escalated and widened still further, and so would its impact on the civilian population. On June 10, however, Serbia capitulated and accepted most of the conditions in the Rambouillet ultimatum, including the deployment of an international peacekeeping force in Kosovo.

The extent to which Serbia's acquiescence was due to the fear of a ground invasion and pressure from its ally Russia are questions that have never been resolved. But NATO had achieved its objectives with no combat casualties on its own side and the loss of only two U.S. soldiers in a helicopter accident. Serbian military casualties have been estimated at between 5,000 and 10,000, while some 500 civilians were killed and 6,000 wounded. In Kosovo,

4,300 bodies of Kosovar civilians were exhumed by 2001, most of whom had been killed during the expulsions that followed the outbreak of war. In its after-action report, NATO hailed this outcome as a triumphant vindication of "the most precise and lowest-collateral-damage air campaign in history."[33] Some military experts, like the British historian John Keegan, heralded the advent of a new era of warfare in which wars could be won entirely from the air. Subsequent estimations have questioned such triumphalism. In his own account of the war, Wesley Clark described Operation Allied Force as a very different campaign from the Napoleonic "nation-state against nation-state" wars and the targeting of civilians in World War II.[34] Because it was successfully conducted in the glare of the Internet, faxes, and satellite television, Clark asserted that Kosovo epitomized a new form of "modern war" that was "limited, carefully constrained in geography, scope, weaponry, and effects."

A former critic of the Rolling Thunder bombing campaign, Clark argued that the road to "compellence" in war lay through the use of "decisive force" rather than "failed gradualism." He described Operation Allied Force as a form of "coercive diplomacy" that violated all the "principles of war" imbibed in American military academies. It was characterized by "extraordinary concern for military losses, on all sides. Even accidental damage to civilian property was carefully considered." These claims have not been universally accepted. In 2000 a *Newsweek* investigation accused the Pentagon of deliberately exaggerating the number of Serbian military targets during the war and discounting the impact of bombing on the civilian population. In *Newsweek*'s estimation, "Air power was effective in the Kosovo war not against military targets but against civilian ones. Military planners do not like to talk frankly about terror-bombing civilians ('strategic targeting' is the preferred euphemism), but what got Milošević's attention was turning out the lights in downtown Belgrade."[35]

Despite the relatively low casualty numbers and the humanitarian pretensions, therefore, NATO's "fight for justice over genocide," as Secretary of State William Cohen described it, once again devolved into a war that was waged not just against the Serbian government and armed forces but against the population that supported or tolerated it. In this war, as in so many of its predecessors, these "psychological" objectives relied on the threat of continual escalation. And from NATO's point of view, it was fortunate that Milošević capitulated when he did—otherwise the seductive fiction that a war could be fought for humanitarian reasons and with humanitarian methods would have been even more difficult to sustain than it actually was.

9

Wars Without War

"In such dangerous things as war, the errors which proceed from a spirit of benevolence are the worst," observed the Prussian strategist Carl von Clausewitz.[1] For Clausewitz, war is "an act of violence pushed to its utmost bounds, as one side dictates the law to the other," thereby creating a "reciprocal action" in which attempt at moderation or restraint by one side can only be counterproductive, since "he who uses force unsparingly, without reference to the bloodshed involved, must obtain a superiority if his adversary uses less vigour in its application." From the Civil War onward, most American wars have been fought in accordance with these precepts. As George S. Patton once put it, "There is only one tactical principle which is never subject to change. It is to use the means at hand to inflict the maximum amount of wound, death, and destruction on the enemy in the minimum amount of time."

America's dazzling high-tech wars of the last decade of the twentieth century seemed to herald another possibility, in which wars could be fought and won with minimal levels of "wound, death, and destruction" for civilians and soldiers alike. These expectations were partly a consequence of America's technological, tactical, and organizational superiority against enemies who could not even begin to retaliate in kind—an imbalance that naturally reduced the "reciprocal dynamic" Clausewitz described. In a 2000 treatise on urban warfare written for the U.S. Army's Command and General Staff College at Fort Leavenworth, the military historian Anthony Spiller predicted, "The era of the iron force is over. The nation that will lead the military world this next century already produces and employs its coercive power differently from any army in history. Finesse is replacing weight as the basis of American military power."[2]

To some American foreign-policy hawks and military strategists, this awesome technological power suggested that wars could be less "hellish" than those of Sherman and his successors—and also more palatable to the public as an instrument of policy. In Panama, Iraq, and Kosovo, such "coercive power" was directed toward the achievement of very specific political and strategic objectives, and American technological supremacy—coupled with the weakness of its opponents—made it possible to achieve them at very little cost while still maintaining the illusion of "surgical" and "humanitarian" war. At the beginning of the twenty-first century, however, the United States entered an era of permanent global war, which demonstrated once again the supremacy of its military machine, but which also revealed its limitations in a series of murky and often chaotic confrontations in which finesse was conspicuously absent.

The War on Terror

The catalyst for this transformation took place on September 11, 2001, when nineteen hijackers enacted a spectacle of destruction and mass killing that had not been seen on American soil since the Civil War. The attacks on New York and Washington were frequently compared to the Japanese attack on Pearl Harbor, and were immediately declared by the Bush administration to be acts of war, even though they were carried out by an amorphous nonstate terrorist organization that offered no commensurate military target. On September 20, 2001, George W. Bush promised the American people that the United States would respond to these attacks with a global "war on terror" that "begins with al Qaeda, but it does not end there. It will not end until every terrorist group of global reach has been found, stopped and defeated."

In this war, Bush warned, "Americans should not expect one battle, but a lengthy campaign, unlike any we have ever seen. It may include dramatic strikes, visible on TV, and covert operations, secret even in success." The most obvious object for a military response consisted of the "al Qaeda bases" in Afghanistan, but Bush also issued a wider warning that "every nation, in every region, now has a decision to make. Either you are with us, or you are with the terrorists."

Even at this stage, the CIA had already identified a "worldwide attack matrix" of targets for covert and overt military operations in more than eighty countries. In his January 2002 State of the Union address, Bush identified Iran, North Korea, and Iraq as members of an "axis of evil" whose development of weapons of mass destruction posed an ongoing security threat to the United States. Other countries were listed by the administration and its supporters as "outposts of tyranny" that also constituted potential enemies of the United States. From the outset, therefore, the "global war on terror" (GWOT) became a recipe for a rolling series of wars, military interventions, and covert operations directed not only against al-Qaeda, but against an array of "terrorist" organizations considered by the United States to be in some kind of alliance with Osama bin Laden's network and also against the states that were deemed to be their supporters.

This framework transformed the world into a global battle space for the limitless projection of U.S. military power. Bush administration officials and intelligence officers repeatedly warned that such a war would not be subject to moral or legal restraints, and these claims were reflected in the introduction of new measures and procedures that included torture, or "enhanced interrogations," Special Forces assassination teams, trials of terrorist suspects by military courts, indefinite detention of "enemy combatants," and kidnapping, or "rendition," of suspects across international boundaries to secret prisons in countries with weak or nonexistent legal protections.

As in previous American wars, the determination to "take the gloves off" was justified on the basis that the United States faced an existential threat to its "way of life" comparable to Nazism or Communism from an enemy that did not fight by the same "rules." The persistent references by the Bush administration to the "evil" of al-Qaeda and the "axis of evil" that was somehow connected to it echoed the crusading zeal that was also intrinsic to American warfare. During the 2004 presidential election campaign, Vice President Dick Cheney mocked Democratic nominee John Kerry's proposal to wage a "more sensitive" war on terror, saying, "President Lincoln and General Grant did not wage sensitive warfare— nor did President Roosevelt, nor Generals Eisenhower and MacArthur." A "sensitive war," Cheney argued, would not "destroy the evil men who killed 3,000 Americans and who seek the chemical, nuclear, and biological weapons to kill hundreds of thousands more."[3]

These comparisons were not entirely outlandish. The Lincoln administration also adopted an "iron fist" war policy that was regarded as a departure from conventional warfare, and it suspended certain civil liberties in order to pursue the war more effectively. But Cheney's suggestion that al-Qaeda represented a threat to the national existence of the United States comparable to the Confederacy was more propaganda than history, and his invocation of Lincoln ignored the fact that the Union from the very beginning of the war had a very clear strategic goal—the surrender of the Confederacy and its reincorporation into the Union—that was realistic and achievable, even if it took some time to achieve it. By contrast, the Bush administration's proposals to eliminate "every terrorist group of global reach" and "rid the world of evil" established a benchmark that was difficult if not impossible to achieve and defied long-established military principles, such as economy of force and the accurate assessment of the enemy's strengths and vulnerabilities.

"No one starts a war—or rather, no one in his senses ought to do so," declared Clausewitz, "without first being clear in his mind what he intends to achieve by that war and how he intended to conduct it." This principle was entirely absent from the GWOT from its inception. In 2005 the U.S. Army's *National Military Strategic Plan* analyzed the first four years of the GWOT and offered strategic guidance for its future conduct. On the one hand, its authors defined al-Qaeda as a "movement" and identified its primary "center of gravity" as its "extremist ideology," which "motivates anger and resentment and justifies, in the extremists' eyes, the use of violence to achieve strategic goals and objectives."[4]

From a military point of view, the question of whether al-Qaeda was a "movement," an "ideology," or—as the Bush administration often insisted—a hierarchical military organization with a chain of command and control was important because very different uses of force might be required, depending on the answer, and the *Strategic Plan*'s authors didn't seem sure themselves about who or what should be targeted and how this might be done. In order to bring military power effectively to bear against al-Qaeda's "center of gravity," the authors made the obvious suggestion that "knowledge of indigenous population's cultural and religious sensitivities and understanding of how the enemy uses the U.S. military's actions against us should inform the way the U.S. military operates.

Where U.S. military involvement is necessary, military planners should build efforts into the operation to reduce potential negative effects."

These recommendations suggested a calibrated and careful use of military force coupled with a global ideological attempt to win over al-Qaeda's potential constituency, but these guidelines were not always observed in the chaotic, incoherent swathe of global violence that ensued. Two full-scale wars and occupations, proxy wars like the Ethiopian invasion and occupation of Somalia, "targeted assassinations" by drones (unmanned aerial vehicles, or UAVs), and the global deployment of Special Forces death squads have generated "negative effects" that undermined the ideological justifications of the Bush administration's antiterror crusade. In Somalia, the United States gave diplomatic and military support in 2006 to Ethiopia's toppling of the Islamic Courts Union (ICU), a broad coalition of Islamist groups that opposed the corrupt and warlord-dominated Transitional Federal Government (TFG).

Regarded by the Bush administration as an affiliate of al-Qaeda, the ICU was followed by the far more radical al-Shabaab movement, which fought the Ethiopian army and the TFG in one of the bloodiest periods in Somalia's recent history. In 2007 some two hundred thousand people were driven from Somalia as a result of the fighting between the Ethiopian army/TFG forces and al-Shabaab. Though al-Shabaab's harsh version of Islam is now well known, its Islamist nationalist insurgency was fueled by the brutality of the Ethiopian security forces, which burned villages and shot, raped, and tortured Somali civilians with impunity.[5]

Somalia was not the only country where the war on terror generated more violence than it was supposedly intended to eliminate. And nowhere was this discrepancy between expectations and outcomes more glaring than in Iraq, where the U.S. military fought a war and occupation that many analysts have considered to be one of the worst disasters in American military history.[6]

Iraq Redux

On March 19, 2003, the U.S.-led coalition planes and missiles struck at targets throughout Iraq in the opening salvo of a war that, according to George W. Bush, was intended "to disarm Iraq, to free its people and to defend the world from grave danger." The following day, the U.S. Third Infantry Division and First Marine Expeditionary Force crossed the Kuwait border and raced into the Iraqi hinterland in a rapid two-pronged advance, while their British allies concentrated on Basra and the south. In seventy-two hours, U.S. forces covered 240 miles in a classic example of "indirect," fast-moving, deep territorial penetration in the tradition of Sherman's and Patton's armies.

In general, cities and urban areas were bypassed where possible; support troops were left to pin down their defenders and mop up, while most of the army drove north toward Baghdad. Despite occasionally stiff resistance and sporadic ambushes from the Iraqi army and the paramilitary Saddam Fedayeen, American firepower crushed the poorly armed and often badly led defenders. Despite a sandstorm on March 26, which restricted visibility, the first U.S. units reached the outskirts of Baghdad on April 4, three hundred miles from their starting point, and began conducting armored "thunder raids" into the heart of the city.

On April 10, Baghdad fell to coalition forces, and the Iraqi leadership went into hiding. The quick victory was a triumph for Bush and a vindication of his secretary of defense Donald Rumsfeld's doctrine of a nimble, high-tech army that was able to achieve rapid results through a combination of airpower and minimal ground forces. Whereas the Union had once taken four years to conquer 6 million Southerners with more than a million soldiers, in Iraq fewer than 160,000 troops had conquered a country of 30 million in what Bush described as "one of the swiftest and most humane military campaigns in history." Despite the frequent media references to the shock and awe that preceded the war, the bombing of Iraq owed more to Kosovo than to the first Gulf War. According to the U.S. Army's official history of the invasion, its planners were "haunted" by "images of Berlin, Hue, and Grozny" and determined to avoid "wanton physical destruction, rampant human misery, and post-fighting devastation" whose "human, political, and financial cost . . . would be unacceptable in a campaign of liberation."[7]

As on previous occasions, these aspirations were not always realized in practice. An estimated 3,750 Iraqi civilians were killed and injured by cluster munitions air-launched or ground-launched against Iraqi cities, in addition to some 9,200 combatant casualties. But the most violent phase of the war began after the iconic toppling of Saddam Hussein's statue on April 9. Baghdad was subjected to a different form of "wanton physical destruction" as a result of the security vacuum created by the collapse of the Iraqi state. On April 10, crowds of looters robbed, stripped, and sometimes burned offices, shops, former Baathist headquarters, and cultural, medical, and educational institutions, destroying or robbing nearly 60 percent of the content of both the National Museum and the National Library and Archive, a massive loss of irreplaceable books, sculptures, pottery, and documents, including cuneiform tablets dating back to Sumerian times.

The unwillingness of the occupying forces to provide the necessary security and protection mandated by international law was an alarming indication of the lack of planning for postinvasion chaos, a lack that was even more mystifying given the U.S. Army's extensive experience with postcombat occupations. It is difficult to imagine that Sherman, with his very pragmatic attitude toward postwar stabilization and reconstruction in the South, would have approved of the catastrophic decision by the Coalition Provisional Authority to dissolve the Iraqi army, police, and bureaucracy overnight, and the disastrous consequences of this decision soon became even more glaringly apparent.

On May 1, George Bush announced from the deck of the carrier USS *Abraham Lincoln* that all major combat operations in Iraq were over. As the summer wore on, however, coalition troops found themselves subjected to daily attacks from an ad hoc array of demobilized soldiers and domestic and foreign organizations, using car bombs, suicide bombers, snipers, and the ubiquitous improvised explosive devices (IEDs), whose nineteenth-century precursors had so infuriated Sherman and his officers in Georgia. Some of the methods adopted to deal with this situation, such as the "porno interrogations" at Abu Ghraib and other detention centers, were historical novelties based on a catastrophically wrongheaded and often profoundly racist American understanding of Arab cultural norms, but others would have been entirely familiar to U.S. soldiers in the Philippines and Vietnam. First Lieutenant Paul Rieckhoff, a platoon leader in the First Brigade, Third Infantry Division, described the reaction of a Baghdad family to a no-knock raid on their home in search of weapons and insurgents. "They screamed and yelled in Arabic. We screamed and yelled in English—sweat pouring, babies wailing, muzzles swinging and hearts pounding. We huddled them into the far corner so we could cuff them, control them, and search the house. The women cried uncontrollably, the men were angry and proud—always glaring. . . . We occupied their home, invaded their personal space. . . . We stormed into their house like the Gestapo."[8]

These "cordon-and-search" operations were a major factor in spreading the insurgency and were eventually replaced in many areas by milder knock-and-search variants or handed over to Iraqis. But many army commanders adopted a hard-line policy of collective punishment of Iraqi civilians to try to isolate the insurgents or simply get information, using well-established techniques of terror and coercion. "Hostile" villages and towns were cordoned off with barbed wire and dirt walls; the only entrances were controlled by soldiers; and electricity, food, and water were cut off for days in order to turn the people against the fighters in their midst.

In a press conference in March 2005, Jean Ziegler, the UN special rapporteur on the right to food, accused the coalition of "using hunger and deprivation of water as a weapon of war against the civilian population" in what he called a "flagrant violation of international humanitarian law." In some cases, most of the people were forced to leave, while military-age men were ordered to remain in quarantined towns or neighborhoods designated as weapons-free zones that could be fired upon with impunity by U.S. troops. As in the Vietnam War, houses used by rebels were blown up, and crops and orchards were also destroyed as a punishment for "allowing" insurgents to use their property to fire on U.S. troops.

Despite strict rules of engagement designed to prevent indiscriminate retaliation, U.S. troops frequently responded to attacks by firing into densely packed neighborhoods. On March 31, 2004, insurgents at the resistance stronghold of Fallujah ambushed and mutilated four private military contractors. The killings provoked a wave of revulsion in the United States, and politicians and media commentators urged the military to "raze" a "sick" and "diseased" city and subject Fallujah to a Carthaginian punishment.[9]

On April 4, American units headed by the First Marine Expeditionary Force subjected the city to an aerial and ground assault involving seven hundred air strikes, attacks from AC-130 Specter gunships equipped with Gatling guns firing 1,800 rounds per minute, and the prolific use of snipers. In addition to known or suspected insurgent houses and bases, U.S. forces fired on ambulances, hospitals, and civilians fleeing their homes, in some cases even while the victims were waving white flags, killing an estimated six hundred civilians before the operation was called off without bringing Fallujah under American control.

Following George Bush's reelection in November, the administration resolved to bring Fallujah, which it regarded as a symbol of the insurgency, back under control of the Iraqi Interim Government. To prepare, U.S. troops surrounded Fallujah and ordered civilians to leave. Some 350,000 people obeyed these orders, leaving an estimated 30,000–50,000 noncombatants and 4,500 insurgents in the city. On November 8, U.S. forces subjected Fallujah to a massive aerial and ground bombardment, followed by a ground assault by U.S. Marines, with British and Iraqi forces in support, in which insurgent fighters were shot or blown up in houses, mosques, and on the street, and burned to death with white phosphorus in "shake and bake" bombings.

As in the first siege, there were reports of civilians shot in their homes, in the streets, and in hospitals, in some cases while waving white flags. After three weeks, the military announced that the city had been brought under control. By this time, much of it had been reduced to what a Reuters correspondent called a "sea of rubble and death." In a visit to Fallujah in December, the *New York Times* reporter Erik Eckholm found "a desolate world of skeletal buildings, tank-blasted homes, weeping power lines, and several palm trees."[10] In the aftermath of the battle, military planners talked of transforming the ruined city from a "bastion of militant anti-Americanism" into what one army officer described as "a benevolent and functional metropolis."[11]

These predictions did not come true. By March 2006, less than 20 percent of Fallujah's destroyed or damaged houses had been repaired, and only twenty-four out of eighty-one reconstruction projects in the city had been completed. Today, nearly ten years after the two sieges, doctors in the city continue to report a disturbing rise in the number of malformed children born to mothers in the city, which some attribute to the use of depleted-uranium antitank shells and other poisonous munitions by U.S. forces.

The "pacification" of Fallujah had no impact on the insurgency, but other cities were subjected to similar operations. In 2004 the epidemiologist Les Roberts watched "the shredding of entire blocks" by U.S. gunships in Sadr City in Baghdad, the base of support for Shiite leader Muqtadā al-Ṣadr's Mahdi Army. During the siege of Ramadi in June 2006, some 70 percent of the population fled the cordoned-off city before U.S. forces carried out air strikes and a ground assault in which eight blocks of the city were systematically demolished and U.S. snipers on rooftops fired down at pedestrians. "They bombed the power stations, water treatment facilities, and water pipes," a local sheikh told the Inter Press Service reporter Brian Conley. "This house is destroyed, that house is destroyed. You will see poverty everywhere. The things that the simplest human in the world must have, you won't have it here."[12]

In other cities, civilians were killed and wounded during close air-support missions or shot dead by snipers while buying food during curfews. Despite the rules of engagement, civilians were regularly shot at random "flash" checkpoints or "tactical control points" that were set up without warning on roads and highways, either because they failed to understand orders to stop or because panicky American soldiers shot at them in anticipation of suicide bomb attacks.

Insurgent car bombs and suicide bombings wreaked havoc among Iraqi civilians and security forces alike, and civilian "soft targets" were attacked with merciless ferocity. American occupation officials frequently emphasized the military's restraint and humanity in comparison with their "terrorist" opponents, but numerous testimonies from American soldiers, Iraqi civilians, and foreign journalists tell a story that recalls the Philippines and Vietnam, of an army permeated with contempt for Iraqi "hajis" and "camel jockeys" and terrified soldiers brutalized by a shockingly violent and unpredictable guerrilla war. In August 2006, a military court investigating the killing of three Iraqi prisoners at Samarra by soldiers from the 101st Airborne Division's Third Brigade heard testimony from a member of the unit who described "a culture of racism and unrestrained violence" encouraged by its commanding officer, Colonel Michael Steele, who reportedly gave knives to his troops as rewards for their kills in an attempt to foster a competitive body count of insurgents.

In 2008, Iraq Veterans Against the War conducted Winter Soldier hearings in Washington that recalled the 1971 Winter Soldier hearings held in Detroit by Vietnam Veterans Against the War. More than two hundred veterans described a war that bore little relation to its altruistic intentions. Two soldiers from the First Cavalry Regiment told the audience of a "weapons-free" assault on the Abu Ghraib neighborhood in April 2004 in which their unit bulldozed dozens of buildings, crushed vehicles, and left the streets "littered" with seven or eight hundred corpses of humans and animals. Various soldiers claimed that they were encouraged by their officers to take shovels or "drop weapons" with them on patrol that would be left on the bodies of civilians they shot to make it look as if they'd been attacking.[13]

Many U.S. soldiers respected Iraqis, and believed in their mission, and conducted themselves in accordance with the U.S. military's best traditions, but as in Vietnam the army's willingness to use force to coerce civilians made for an atrocity-producing environment in which killing and destruction were always likely. In April 2004, a senior British army officer echoed Reginald Thompson's criticisms in Korea when he anonymously condemned the American tendency to use overwhelming firepower in densely populated residential areas, on the grounds that "the Americans' use of violence is not proportionate and is over-responsive to the threat they are facing. They don't see the Iraqi people the way we see them. They view them as *untermenschen*."[14]

Whether such bigotry was rare or rampant, destruction also had a strategic purpose. During the second assault on Fallujah, an anonymous Pentagon official told the *New York Times* reporters Thom Shanker and Eric Schmidt, "If there are civilians dying in connection with these attacks, and with the destruction, the locals at some point have to make a decision. Do they want to harbor the insurgents and suffer the consequences that come with that, or do they want to get rid of the insurgents and have the benefits of not having them there?"[15]

Generals James Franklin Bell and William Westmoreland had offered Filipinos and Vietnamese a similar choice in their respective wars. In 2003 Lieutenant Colonel Nathan Sassaman, commander of the Fourth Infantry's 1-8 Battalion, ordered his troops to cordon off the village of Abu Hishma with barbed wire after a soldier was shot. Interviewed by *New York Times* reporter Dexter Filkins, the former star quarterback memorably predicted, "With a heavy dose of fear and violence, and a lot of money for projects, I think we can convince these people that we are here to help them."[16]

In 2004 Sassaman was relieved of his command after two of his soldiers drowned a detainee. He subsequently criticized his superior officers for losing "sight of our primary purpose—to destroy the enemy with overwhelming force at every opportunity" and described the confusing "duality" of a war in which "there were many nights spent hunting, fighting, and killing fanatical insurgents, followed by a swift transition into daytime reconstruction efforts with peaceful Arab citizens."[17] This "duality" was a persistent feature of the Iraq War from the earliest days of the occupation, as military engineers built or repaired schools, soccer fields, mosques, and other public buildings, and civil affairs teams were sent out to reestablish local administrations and neighborhood councils and provide Iraqis with information about the democratic process in "governance operations."

But reconstruction was patchy and often nonexistent; war, neglect, monumental levels of corruption, and inappropriate development strategies designed to favor well-connected American companies compounded the decay of Iraq's infrastructure and its education and hospital systems. Unlike Germany or Japan, military-driven reconstruction never became a catalyst for a wider economic and social transformation, and its intended impact on the Iraqi population was negated by a war that allowed increasingly little space for the "humanitarian" components of "full-spectrum operations."

The Carrot and Stick

In January 2005, an article in *Newsweek* claimed that Pentagon officials were preparing a new policy in Iraq called the Salvador Option, modeled on the "so-called death squads" that had hunted down and killed "rebel leaders and sympathizers" in El Salvador during the 1980s. The article quoted one official who justified such actions by saying, "The Sunni population is paying no price for the support it is giving to the terrorists. . . . From their point of view, it is cost-free. We have to change that equation."[18]

Over the next few months, newspapers began reporting the kidnapping and murder of Iraqis by Shiite paramilitary groups, who dumped the bodies, bearing obvious marks of torture, as warnings in public places—the same methods used in the U.S.-backed war in El Salvador. Most of the victims were Sunni Muslims, and the militias were well armed and well equipped, with close connections to the Shia-dominated Ministry of the Interior in the Iraqi Interim Government. Their activities reached a peak of ferocity following the bomb attack on the Shia Golden Dome Mosque in Samarra in February 2006, when scores of Sunni civilians and insurgents were murdered by an array of "pop-up" militias.

As in El Salvador, American involvement in these operations is murky, but some paramilitary units, such as the Special Police Commandos, received training from U.S. military advisers, including Colonel James Steele, the former head of the U.S. military mission in El Salvador. The campaign of what can be described only as state terror carried out by the Shiite "pop-up" militias coincided with the escalation of raids carried out by Joint Special Operations Command (JSOC) hunter-killer teams and the British Special Air Service between 2006 and 2008, in which thousands of "terrorists" were captured or killed. Though lawyers were supposedly present during the target selection process, it has never been explained who these targets were or what determined the decision to capture or kill them. Whether these operations merely coincided with the sectarian violence directed by the Ministry of the Interior or were designed to complement it, the state-directed campaign of terror ended the last prospect of a national resistance to the occupation unified across sectarian lines, and it drove the Sunni population to regard the U.S. Army as the lesser of two evils, at least temporarily, to the point where its leaders were increasingly willing to turn to their former enemy for protection.

A 1994 counterinsurgency manual, *Foreign Internal Defense Forces: Techniques for Special Forces*, which was used by U.S. forces in Iraq, emphasized the importance of "national programs to win insurgents over to the government side with offers of amnesty and rewards" in addition to the "persuasive power" that "pressure from the security forces" was able to provide.[19] From 2005 onward, an influential group of military intellectuals centered around Major General David Petraeus, commander of the 101st Airborne Division in Mosul, argued that the army had concentrated too much on "enemy-centric" counterinsurgency and "kinetic operations" that emphasized killing insurgents rather than winning over the Iraqi population.

To the advocates of COIN, as this approach to counterinsurgency became known, the army had dangerously isolated itself from ordinary Iraqis by sealing itself up in fortified compounds and conducting large-scale operations with armored columns. Borrowing from a strategy developed by the French army in Algeria known as clear-hold-build, the "COINistas" advocated a return to small-unit operations in which U.S. soldiers would drive insurgents from a particular locality and "live amongst the people" in smaller forward operating bases in order to protect and gain the trust of the local population and bring them under the control of the Iraqi government.

COIN was given official status in the U.S. Army/Marine Corps Field Manual 3-24 (FM 3-24), which was presented to military officers and selected journalists with great fanfare in February 2005. Hundreds of delegates listened to Petraeus and the manual's authors expound the principles of population protection, nation building, cultural sensitivity, and "measured" force. These ideas were not entirely revelatory, and some commanders in Iraq already practiced them of their own volition. Nevertheless, some delegates were puzzled about how to fulfill FM 3-24's requirements to "apply force without killing or crippling the enemy" and about maxims like "The best weapons for counterinsurgency do not fire bullets" and "Mounting an operation that kills 5 insurgents is futile if collateral damage leads to the recruitment of 50 more." The former marine and military writer Francis West questioned the relevance of such methods in Iraq and exclaimed, "An insurgency—it's war! The weapons we have, the reason people want us there, is *we kill people!*"[20]

That same year, Petraeus was appointed to command the Multi-National Force—Iraq (MNF-I), which was bolstered by twenty thousand extra troops in the Bush administration's "surge." Over the next two years, "population-centric" counterinsurgency appeared to achieve some success, as the overall level of violence declined by more than 90 percent and Sunni sheikhs and tribal leaders in the war-torn Anbar Province entered into negotiated agreements with U.S. forces and the Iraqi government. For Petraeus and his many admirers, the reduction in violence and the relative stabilization that followed was a triumph of COIN's "non-kinetic" methodology.[21]

The idea that the Sunni population was won over by a gentler and more culturally attuned U.S. Army tended to overlook a number of contributing factors, however, such as the effective bribing of Sunni insurgents that accompanied the "Sunni Awakening," the disenchantment of Sunni tribal sheikhs with the more extremist al-Qaeda-linked jihadist insurgents, the ethnic division of Baghdad and much of Iraq into Sunni and Shiite ghettoes that made further violence unnecessary, and the continued reliance on hard military power that also accompanied the advent of COIN. By the time the United States withdrew its forces from Iraq in 2011, the war and occupation had claimed the lives of 4,475 U.S. soldiers and wounded 32,220 more. The civilian death toll has been variously calculated from the hundreds of thousands to a million. Such an outcome might not seem the most obvious cause for celebration. After years of barely credible blunders that had brought the most powerful military in the world to the brink of strategic defeat, the surge success story was welcomed by the Bush administration and the American public, and COIN was regarded as the magic key that had unlocked the Iraq War, and could unlock other wars as well.

Afghanistan

In 2009, the incoming Obama administration announced plans for a troop surge in Afghanistan in an attempt to defeat the long-running insurgency that followed the toppling of the Taliban government in 2001–2. In June 2009, General Stanley McChrystal, the head of the Joint Special Operations Command in Iraq, was appointed head of the International Security Assistance Force (ISAF) and U.S. Forces Afghanistan (USFOR-A) in preparation for the Afghan surge. The former director of JSOC hunter-killer teams in Iraq seemed an unlikely practitioner of nonkinetic warfare. Nevertheless, McChrystal issued a tactical directive to American and ISAF military units shortly after his arrival, urging his commanders to adopt the COIN approach and "avoid the trap of winning tactical victories—but suffering strategic defeats—by causing civilian casualties or excessive damage and thus alienating the people."[22] Many U.S. officers conducted their operations in accordance with these principles. "I very deliberately told the Marines to focus on the population first and the enemy second. I will maintain that the firefight is a distraction that must be worked through in order to maintain contact with the population," reported Third Reconnaissance Battalion commander Lieutenant Colonel Travis Homiak on marine operations in the Upper Sangin Valley.[23]

Social scientists, ethnologists, and anthropologists were also dispatched to Afghanistan as a part of the Pentagon's human terrain system (HTS), to assist the army with information on the cultural norms, conditions, and attitudes that would enable more appropriate operational decisions in dealing with the local population. These developments were not met with universal enthusiasm. In a widely circulated letter written to the secretary of the army in August 2010, Colonel Harry Tunnell, commander of the Fifth Stryker Combat Brigade of the Second Infantry Division, accused "COIN dogma" of having "degraded our willingness to properly, effectively, and realistically train for combat" and claimed that "population-centric approaches to war have resulted in senior officers that are almost pacifistic in their approach to war."[24] These criticisms came from an infantry commander with a reputation for aggressive search-and-destroy tactics. In April 2011, a *Rolling Stone* investigation revealed that members of Tunnell's brigade ran a secret "kill team" that murdered Afghan civilians and took mutilated body parts as souvenirs.[25] Tunnell was not found to be responsible for these events, but he was relieved of his command after an internal army investigation concluded that he had fostered a culture of violence that might have affected his soldiers.

To officers like Tunnell, killing was the essential task of the infantry. In an article in *Joint Forces Quarterly* in 2009, Colonel Gian Gentile, a serving officer in Iraq and one of Petraeus's most articulate critics, also claimed that the army's "operational capability to conduct high-intensity fighting operations other than counterinsurgency has atrophied over the past 6 years" and called for a new balance between counterinsurgency and "operations at the higher end of the conflict spectrum."[26] In another critique of COIN, in *Harper's* magazine in 2007, the political scientist Edward Luttwak denounced the "crippling ambivalence of occupiers who refuse to govern" and exhorted the U.S. military in Iraq to "out-terrorize the insurgents, the necessary and sufficient condition of a tranquil occupation." An admirer of the scorched-earth "counterterror" policies of the Guatemalan army in the 1980s, Luttwak praised the reprisals and massacres carried out by Nazi armies in the World War II as "very effective . . . in containing resistance with very few troops."[27]

These criticisms ignored the fact that COIN was not quite the radical departure from American military practice that its opponents or its supporters claimed. In Afghanistan, as in Iraq, the concern with "protecting the population" and "living amongst the people" in towns and cities was accompanied by significant degrees of "kinetic" force, including an escalation in rural night raids conducted by Special Forces and Afghan troops, in which real or suspected Taliban were often killed on the spot. Supposedly aimed at "high-value" and "mid-level" Taliban, the raiders often failed to distinguish among militants, sympathizers, and civilians. Non-combatants were often selected on the basis of their mobile phone numbers and shot simply because they happened to be in the wrong place at the wrong time. On February 12, 2010, a Special Forces unit raided a house in the village of Khataba in Paktia Province in the belief that a Taliban gathering was under way. Without warning, snipers opened fire and killed five guests and family members, including two pregnant women and a teenage girl; other troops beat up and arrested a number of male guests. The party was actually to celebrate the naming of a newborn baby.

Similar incidents took place in other areas. In 2009 Matthew Hoh, a senior U.S. diplomat in Kabul and former marine, resigned in protest at what he called a "Special Operations form of attrition warfare" that had increased popular support for the Taliban. In April 2010, McChrystal admitted to his own officers, "We've shot an amazing number of people and killed a number and, to my knowledge, none has proven to have been a real threat to the force." Since his arrival, the number of IED attacks had soared from 250 per month to more than 900. In July that year, McChrystal was replaced by Petraeus, who continued to combine nonkinetic and population-centric counterinsurgency with an intensification of air strikes and special-forces raids. In August 2011, Petraeus left Afghanistan and the army to become director of the CIA. At his retirement ceremony, Admiral Michael Mullen, chairman of the Joint Chiefs of Staff, described him as one of the "great battle captains of American history," alongside Grant, Marshall, and Eisenhower, and claimed that "Afghanistan is now a more secure and hopeful place than a year ago" as a result of his efforts.

These claims did not go unchallenged. In a book-length critique of COIN, Gian Gentile accused Petraeus and his colleagues of misapplying an already flawed and overrated strategy in Afghanistan and promoting a seductive but delusional form of sanitized warfare designed to conceal the unavoidable reality of "death, destruction, and human suffering."[28] In a speech in 2013 to the Association of the United States Army, George Bush's former defense secretary Robert Gates made a more oblique reference to COIN when he quoted Sherman's famous observation that "every attempt to make war easy and safe can only end in humiliation and disaster" and rejected "idealized, triumphalist, or ethnocentric notions of future conflict that aspire to upend the immutable principles of war: where the enemy is killed, but our troops and innocent civilians are spared."[29]

Long-Distance War

Such criticisms tended to ignore the fact that the "immutable principles" that Gates outlined were not necessarily appropriate to wars that U.S. armies were now fighting. With its scaled-down professional army and a public with a limited appetite for foreign military adventures, the minimization of American casualties was even more of a priority than usual for U.S. military planners, and reducing the extent—or at least the visibility—of wartime destruction was an essential strategic component of "information operations." These considerations have influenced the deployment of unmanned combat aerial vehicles (UCAVs) as an essential weapon of twenty-first-century American warfare. Initially used for surveillance during the Afghan War in 2001–2, these drones were subsequently fitted with missiles and have been used to kill hundreds of alleged terrorists and militants in various countries, including Iraq, Afghanistan, Somalia, Yemen, and Pakistan.

For the first time in military history, "pilots" thousands of miles away from the battle zone could observe, select, and kill specific persons in their cars, their homes, or public places, in town or countryside, in undeclared wars. From the perspective of the U.S. military and intelligence services, drones were the ideal weapon for media-managed warfare against a stateless enemy. They could simply kill people instead of trying to capture and arrest them, thereby eliminating the negative domestic political repercussions of taking casualties and the legal complications of due process and detention of "enemy combatants."

Reaper and Predator drones are often presented to the public as the ideal instrument of "humane" and "surgical" warfare, minimizing physical destruction and making it possible to selectively eliminate "high-value" targets rather than civilians. In 2012 President Obama stated that "drones have not caused a huge number of civilian casualties" but are a "targeted, focused effort at people who are on a list of active terrorists trying to go in and harm Americans" and were used only when there was a "near certainty" that civilian casualties could be avoided.[30]

Such claims are difficult to confirm, given the absence of information about a target-selection process based on signature strikes. Any male of military age behaving "suspiciously" in a certain area acquires "signatures" that qualify him for killing as a member of the Afghan or Pakistani Taliban or an al-Qaeda affiliate. In May 2012, the *New York Times* reported that President Obama personally signed off on targets from a kill list drawn up by agents of the CIA and other spy agencies, who gathered "every week or so, by secure video teleconference, to pore over terrorist suspects' biographies and recommend to the president who should be the next to die."[31]

The primary battleground in the U.S. drone wars has been the Federally Administered Territorial Area (FATA) in northern Pakistan. Between 2004 and 2013, from 330 to 374 drone strikes were carried out in Waziristan, killing 2,000 to 4,700 people, including 400 to 900 civilians. Investigations carried out by Amnesty International and other NGOs in Waziristan have listed attacks on mosques, bakeries, weddings, funerals, houses, bus depots, and public places in which men, women, and children have been killed and wounded.[32] On March 17, 2011, more than forty people were killed when two missiles were fired on a *jirga*, or tribal council, in the town of Datta Khel, North Waziristan. In October 2012, the son of sixty-seven-year-old midwife Momina Bibi told five members of the U.S. Congress how his mother was blown to pieces by a drone-fired missile in front of her grandchildren while picking vegetables in her garden the previous year.[33]

Some civilians have been killed by drones as a result of faulty intelligence information or as an accidental consequence of strikes not specifically aimed at them. Others were killed as a result of a "double tap" policy, in which drone-fired missiles are directed at first responders coming to help victims of the initial strike. In 2010, the Department of Defense began posting videos on YouTube of drone missions, showing anonymous "militants" and "armed criminals" being blown up in Iraq and Afghanistan. This video-game footage of bad guys vanishing in puffs of smoke does not include the images of blasted homes, rubble, and civilian mourners taken by Pakistani photographer and antidrone campaigner Noor Behram, who has described the typical aftermath of a drone strike thus: "There are just pieces of flesh lying around. . . . You can't find bodies. So the locals pick up the flesh and curse America. They say that America is killing us inside our own country, inside our own homes, and only because we are Muslims."[34]

The Obama administration has paid scant attention to criticisms from the Pakistan government that these weapons may be creating more enemies than they kill, and it has rejected suggestions from lawyers and human-rights activists that drone killings may breach international laws of armed conflict and humanitarian war. A 2012 report by Stanford University researchers on the drone war on Waziristan describes a traumatized and exhausted population living in constant fear of the drones cruising out of sight and hearing above their heads, children who do not dare to go to school, and adults who avoid going to the mosque or any public gathering, who even avoid inviting guests to their own homes for fear of being targeted as hosts of Taliban conclaves. "We are always thinking that it is either going to attack our homes or whatever we do," one survivor of a drone strike on his taxi told the Stanford University researchers. "It's going to strike us; it's going to attack us. . . . No matter what we are doing, that fear is always inculcated in us."[35]

The drone war has also damaged Pashtun society politically and economically, through the killing of influential tribal elders and family breadwinners and the destruction or disruption of businesses and transportation. Given the facts, it's hard to avoid the conclusion that the remote-control war in Waziristan is aimed not

Future war? Simulated drone strike from video installation, "5000 Feet Is the Best." Courtesy of Omer Fast.

simply at militants but at all of the people, no matter how many support or merely tolerate the Taliban presence and regardless of whether they have any choice in the matter.

It's symptomatic of the strategic incoherence at the heart of this "long war" that the United States has tried to fight terrorism by terrorizing other societies thousands of miles away on the basis of nebulous assumptions about their cultural behavior, such as carrying guns or gathering in groups, while anthropologists gather information on rural Afghans in an attempt to win their hearts and minds. In effect, technology appears to have defied Sherman's dictum and proved that it is possible to make war "easy and safe"—for one side at least. In doing so, it has paved the way for a world in which fully autonomous drones may soon hover permanently over the world's "lawless" spaces and select their own targets on the basis of computerized data without any human input.

Future War

The U.S. military's embrace of drone warfare doesn't mean it has relinquished the search for destructive supremacy that has always been intrinsic to America's military objectives. In 2000, the Department of Defense published a remarkable document, *Joint Vision 2020*, which outlined its new grand strategy for future warfare. Elaborating on a strategic concept first mooted in a 1998 U.S. Space Command document, *Vision for 2020*, the DoD looked forward to the creation of "a force that is dominant in the full spectrum of military operations—persuasive in peace, decisive in war, preeminent in any form of conflict" that would make it possible for U.S. forces, "operating unilaterally or in combination with multinational and interagency partners, to defeat any adversary and control any situation across the full range of military operations" on land and sea, in the air, and in space.[36]

As a result of the "war on terror," the United States has extended its visible military presence into Central Asia, Africa, and South America and made numerous less visible deployments of special operations forces and military advisers in countries throughout the world. These forces include what retired lieutenant colonel and leading COINista John Nagl has called an "industrial strength counterterrorism killing machine" run by the Joint Special Operations Command.[37] In pursuit of this megalomaniacal vision of "full-spectrum dominance," the Pentagon has used the soaring budgets of the past decade to expand its destructive arsenal with autonomous robots, laser weapons, thermobaric fuel bombs, bunker-busting mini-nukes, and new generations of UAVs, including small hand-launched models and the giant Gorgon Stare drone. In 2002 the DoD's *Quadrennial Defense Review* outlined its intention to acquire "non-nuclear forces that can strike with precision at fixed and mobile targets throughout the depth of an adversary's territory; active and passive defenses; and rapidly deployable and sustainable forces that can decisively defeat any adversary."

For the past decade the military has been developing a "prompt global strike" system to make it possible for submarine-based missiles to "strike virtually anywhere on the face of the Earth within 60 minutes." In the same period, the military's cutting-edge Defense Advanced Research Projects Agency (DARPA) and a host of universities and military research institutes have continued to seek new technologies to extend the RMA into the indefinite future. Future developments include autonomous self-sustaining robo-soldiers, laser-guided bullets, cyborg "insects" that can spy or kill, and a semimythical weapon known as the rod of God or finger of God, which could destroy any target with a space-based laser.[38]

Where Sherman's ragged and often barefoot armies tramped through mountains and swamps, the twenty-first-century U.S.

Army envisages future generations of war fighters equipped with smart bulletproof nano-uniforms that could heal wounds, enable the wearers to scale walls and buildings, and incorporate load-bearing exoskeletons for super strength. Other research projects include development of super-speed drugs to enable soldiers to go days without sleeping and post-combat pills to eliminate PTSD. At the same time, the military is also carrying out research into nonlethal technologies to disable rather than kill, such as incapacitating foams, flight-inducing sounds or smells, shotgun Taser rounds, and pulsed-energy projectiles (PEPs) that use microwave beams to project exploding plasma at targets, causing temporary paralysis. At mock Middle Eastern cities in California and the Midwest, U.S. soldiers rehearse "military operations in urban terrain" (MOUT) to emulate "global slums" and "feral cities" in anticipation of future military operations against a constantly widening range of enemies that include terrorists, insurgents, drug cartels, and rogue states.

Whereas Sherman once feared that the United States might become "like Mexico" as a result of the Civil War, the projection of U.S. military power in the early twenty-first century is often presented as an essential bulwark against global chaos and implosion of the international order. In *The Pentagon's New Map* (2004), the military geostrategist Thomas P.M. Barnett compared the U.S. military to a "SWAT team within any metropolitan police force" that would "enter and exit crime scenes according to circumstances" against an array of rogue states, terrorists, and drug lords that belonged to what he called the "non-integrating gap." Barnett lauded the U.S. military's unique ability to kill and destroy "bad actors while leaving behind societies otherwise unimpaired; it will surgically remove unwanted tissue, not riddle the body politic with smoking holes." These "surgical" interventions, Barnett argued, would facilitate postconflict integration of targeted countries into the international economic order and enable the United

States to direct military force against "bad guys, using weapons with a real moral dimension, such as smart bombs and new non-lethal forms of warfare that target enemy systems without harming people."[39]

Others have questioned whether war can—or should—be fought "without harming people." Some have argued that the wars of the past decade have not been destructive *enough* and have undermined the military's core task of destroying the enemy regardless of the consequences. In a discussion paper for the National Intelligence Council (NIC) 2020 project written in May 2004, the former U.S. intelligence officer and military pundit Ralph Peters argued that these wars proved that "there is no substitute for shedding the enemy's blood in adequate quantities; that an enemy must be convinced practically and graphically that he is defeated." For Peters, such "virtuous destruction" might include attacks against property and infrastructure, and also against "hostile populations," who "must be broken down to an almost childlike state . . . before being built up again."[40]

In May 2012, *Wired* magazine published a July 2011 Power-Point presentation by a West Point instructor, Lieutenant Colonel Matthew Dooley, for a course on Islam at the Defense Department's Joint Forces Staff College in Norfolk, Virginia. Dooley considered the possibility that the United States might wage "near total war" against the world's Muslim population in order to defeat terrorism. In such a war, Dooley suggested, the 1949 Geneva Convention might no longer be applicable, and the military might be obliged to emulate "the historical precedents of Dresden, Tokyo, Hiroshima, Nagasaki" and ensure that "Saudi Arabia [was] threatened with starvation, Mecca and Medina destroyed, Islam reduced to cult status."[41]

This course was discontinued and denounced by the chairman of the Joint Chiefs of Staff General Martin Dempsey as "counter to our values of appreciation for religious freedom and cultural awareness." But the precedents that Dooley referred to were also part of an American tradition that remains pertinent to the era of information warfare and knowledge-based war. In a 2007 study by Dr. Dan Plesch and Martin Butcher for the School of Oriental and African Studies on the potential consequences of a U.S. war on Iran, the authors claimed that the military was poised to hit over ten thousand targets in Iran with smart conventional weapons and that "hundreds of thousands" of Iranians would be killed due to the targets' location in cities and other populated areas.[42]

The recent rapprochement between Iran and the United States suggests that this possibility may be averted, but the ability to inflict large-scale destruction both in the battle space and beyond it remains fundamental to America's military preparedness. It's no surprise that such threats may not be restricted to "feral cities" and "rogue states." A 2008 study by the Center for Strategic and Budgetary Assessment suggested that U.S. Special Forces might be required to conduct "large-scale, overt unconventional warfare operations" against China in order to defend U.S. interests in the "global commons" of space, cyberspace, land, and sea.[43] In recent years, Southeast Asia and the Pacific region have been progressively remilitarized in an ongoing attempt to encircle and "deter" China as part of the Obama administration's "Pacific pivot."

For all the U.S. military's concern with counterinsurgency, hyperwar, and high-tech wars based on limited, surgical destruction, these preparations suggest that major conventional wars remain as much a part of its contingency planning for the future as its rehearsals for policing operations in the "feral cities" of the Third World and the global "littoral." Whether these conflicts are fought by human beings, robots, or remote-control machines and cyborg insects, they will inevitably be waged among and often against civilians, as well as soldiers, and fought in accordance with the central aim of war that Sherman once defined to his wife after the battle of Shiloh: "to produce results by death and slaughter."[44] For all the alluring rhetoric of humanitarian warfare, kinetic operations, and nonlethal force, the ability to inflict decisive destruction is likely to remain a central component of the American way of war, and Sherman's name will continue to provide inspiration to those who wish to intensify these capabilities and escalate our wars.

Epilogue

It is 150 years since Sherman marched his army out of Atlanta and set out to "make Georgia howl." At that time, the destructive consequences of war between industrialized states and societies were still a historical novelty whose strategic implications were only just becoming visible to nineteenth-century armies. Today, at the beginning of the twenty-first century, such confrontations have become something of a rarity. Sir Rupert Smith, the former British commander of UN forces in Bosnia and Wesley Clark's deputy in Kosovo, has argued that "war as battle in a field between men and machinery, war as a massive deciding event in a dispute in international affairs, such war no longer exists." For Smith, Sherman's "strategic decision to destroy the material base of the South . . . signalled the future direction of industrial warfare, both in the targeting of the enemy's industrial and economic infrastructure, and in the development of an industrial base at home."[1]

Such warfare, Smith asserts, has been replaced by "wars among the people" that are fought within states rather than between them, wars in which "the people in the streets and houses and fields—all the people, anywhere—are the battlefield" and the "destructive function" of military force is only one of an array of strategic options. Other analysts have made similar claims. "In the future, wars perpetrated by states will no longer include a Sherman's march to the sea or the firebombing of Tokyo. Civilians and their property are now, to a large degree, off limits," writes the former U.S. Special Forces officer–turned–counterterrorism adviser John Robb in his analysis of twenty-first-century warfare *Brave New War* (2007). In Robb's estimation, the absence of "life-and-death stakes" in the more limited wars of the twenty-first century fought in the glare of an omnipresent "global media" makes it more difficult to "transcend moral boundaries" in the conduct of war and imposes moral constraints that "radically limit military options" for Western armies.[2]

Such claims are not without foundation. The last major interstate war fought between "men and machinery" with battles, trenches, mass infantry assaults, bayonet charges, and fixed front lines was the eight-year Iran-Iraq War. Though the First Gulf War threatened to become a similar confrontation, it was ultimately decided by a massive aerial bombing campaign that caused surprisingly few casualties. Recently airpower has not been used to inflict the mass civilian casualties that characterized the total wars of the twentieth century. Technological innovations in weaponry have resulted in more precise and selective forms of destruction by militarily advanced states, and computerization offers new possibilities of cyber war that can target the enemy society and economy. An increasingly demilitarized and unmilitaristic public is—at least for now—unwilling to tolerate wars based on the mass slaughter of combatants or civilians. The guerrilla wars and insurgencies that now dominate twenty-first-century warfare have blurred the boundaries between combatants and civilians, and experience has shown time and again that such conflicts are not generally decided by battlefield confrontations, let alone by rampaging armies engaged in campaigns of strategic devastation against civilians.

Nevertheless, the notion of a general moral transformation in the conduct of war is exaggerated and likely premature. Many nineteenth-century governments and armies believed that the conduct of war had reached a new level of moral advancement, only to dispense with such assumptions in order to win the new wars they found themselves fighting. Today, many of the Union practices that so appalled Southerners during the Civil War are prohibited by a corpus of international humanitarian law and the accumulated laws of war that have developed since the Hague Conventions. Article 54 of Additional Protocol I of the 1977 Geneva Convention states:

> It is prohibited to attack, destroy, remove, or render useless objects indispensable to the survival of the civilian population, such as foodstuffs, agricultural areas for the production of foodstuffs, crops, livestock, drinking water installations and supplies, and irrigation works, for the specific purpose of denying them for their sustenance value to the civilian population or to the adverse Party, whatever the motive, whether in order to starve out civilians, to cause them to move away, or for any other motive.

These prohibitions are still subject to exceptions and reinterpretations based on specific and contingent notions of military necessity, just as they were in Sherman's time, and the ability to enforce them or punish those who break them still depends largely on who wins. Today many of the strategies and tactics that Sherman and his fellow commanders once applied remain intrinsic to war—forced removal of civilians, reprisals against noncombatants, starvation, devastation of infrastructure and industries, bombardment of towns and cities. The bloody denouement of the Sri Lankan Civil War in 2009, in which some forty thousand Tamil civilians were killed during the Sri Lankan army's bombardment of the "safe zone" adjoining the Indian Ocean; the destruction of some 2,800 Darfuri villages by Sudanese government forces and Arab Janjaweed militias; the scorched-earth campaigns waged by various warlords, armies, and rebel groups in the civil wars in the Democratic Republic of Congo; the siege and bombardment of Sarajevo by the Bosnian Serb army; the destruction of Grozny by Russian forces in the Second Chechen War; the bombardment of civilian areas by the Syrian army in the ongoing civil war—all these episodes demonstrate the continued prevalence of what Hugo Slim calls "anti-civilian thinking and practices" in modern war.

In some cases, civilians may become indirect victims of military operations directed against armed opponents, but the proliferation of "wars among the people" means that civilians are likely to be deliberate objects of terror and intimidation. In 2006 Israel responded to a cross-border raid by Hezbollah fighters from Lebanon with a ground offensive in south Lebanon and aerial attacks throughout the whole country that were specifically intended to turn the Lebanese civilian population against Hezbollah. Airports, bridges, electrical facilities, ports, supermarkets, water-treatment plants, gas stations, and residential areas were targeted in seven thousand air strikes that reduced many neighborhoods to rubble, including the Hezbollah stronghold Dahiya in Beirut. The strategy of bombing civilians in response to armed attacks has a long-established tradition in Israeli military thinking, based on the belief that popular anger at the resulting destruction will be turned against Israel's enemies rather than Israel itself.

These aspirations have never been realized, either in Lebanon or anywhere else, but Israel has never abandoned them. In 2008 Major General Gadi Eizenkot outlined a strategy known as the Dahiya doctrine. He promised, "What happened in the Dahiya Quarter of Beirut in 2006, will happen in every village from which shots are fired on Israel. We will use disproportionate force against it and we will cause immense damage and destruction. From our point of view these are not civilian villages but military bases."[3]

In an article for Tel Aviv University's Institute for National Security Studies that same year, Dr. Gabriel Siboni, a colonel in the Israel Defense Forces Reserves, made the objectives of this strategy more explicit, declaring,

> With an outbreak of hostilities, the IDF will need to act immediately, decisively, and with force that is disproportionate to the

enemy's actions and the threat it poses. Such a response aims at inflicting damage and meting out punishment to an extent that will demand long and expensive reconstruction processes.... Punishment must be aimed at decision makers and the power elite ... attacks should both aim at Hezbollah's military capabilities and should target economic interests and the centers of civilian power that support the organization.[4]

These principles also shaped Israel's three assaults on the Gaza Strip, in 2008–9, 2011, and 2014. The idea that civilian populations bear responsibility for the armed groups in their midst and for the decisions of their governments was one of the essential assumptions of the hard-war policies of Sherman, Sheridan, and other Union generals and also of the strategic bombing of German and Japanese cities during World War II. In justifying the 9/11 attacks, Osama bin Laden made the same argument:

The American people are the ones who pay the taxes which fund the planes that bomb us in Afghanistan, the tanks that strike and destroy our homes in Palestine, the armies which occupy our lands in the Arabian Gulf, and the fleets which ensure the blockade of Iraq.... Also the American army is part of the American people.... The American people are the ones who employ both their men and their women in the American Forces which attack us.[5]

The continued acceptance of this principle of collective responsibility by both state armies and "non-state actors" suggests that war has not changed as much as it might seem. If anything, the displacement or irrelevance of battle and combat as the defining components of war foretells amorphous conflicts in which civilians are likely to be the primary targets, whether by killing or simply intimidating them, or by destroying the economic and infrastructural basis of civilian society. Such conflicts may not be decided by a Shermanesque march, but Sherman's willingness to wage war against civilians as well as armies continues to form an essential component of twenty-first-century warfare.

The world's only superpower is no exception. Despite all the "humanitarian" considerations in the new American way of war, civilians have been the primary victims in all the wars that the U.S. military has fought since World War II. Even in the new era of "surgical" warfare, civilian casualties have outnumbered combatant deaths, whether as an immediate consequence of military operations or from longer-term effects on food production, access to health care, and damage to essential services and infrastructure. After watching the Grand Review of the Civil War Armies on May 24, 1865, the *New York Herald*'s editors looked forward to a new era of American military power, in which the U.S. military would establish republics everywhere and go on "till the soldiers of Grant, Sherman and Sheridan have saved the world as they saved the Union."

Today the United States remains a global military colossus with a defense budget in 2013 of $716 billion, more than the next ten countries combined. Though proponents of American exceptionalism still regard America's armed forces as an essential instrument for the world's salvation, the country's appetite for military intervention since World War II has left a trail of death, destruction, and chaos and produced very few positive results, either for the countries it set out to save or for the United States itself. Since the Bush administration launched its open-ended "war on terror" in 2001, American military power has been checked or neutralized by far less powerful opponents and has produced outcomes that are unlikely to produce the triumphal victory parades that once greeted Grant's and Sherman's armies.

This disjunction between stated aims and actual outcome raises questions about the legitimacy of these wars, the strategies that have been adopted to win them, and whether they were ever winnable in the first place. In theory, the U.S. military's primary mission remains the defense of the nation, just as it was in Sherman's time, but the wars of the twenty-first century have been "defensive" only by an extremely elastic and tortuous definition of *defense*, which in the case of Iraq was based entirely on false and essentially fabricated premises. Stripped of its "preemptive" and "preventive" rationalizations, Iraq was a war of choice and another product of a culture of militarism that has become deeply rooted in the American elite since World War II, one that sees enemies and threats everywhere and uses these perceptions to justify the endless projection of U.S. military power in pursuit of geopolitical advantage and ultimately unrealizable fantasies of absolute military supremacy.

Enraged by the humiliation of 9/11, the United States has embarked on a succession of ill-conceived wars in the new century that have contributed little to its national interest but have enriched the weapons manufacturers, defense contractors, private military companies, and logistics and military-services companies that have profited from them. At a time when the U.S. economy has yet to emerge from its worst financial crisis since the 1930s, when its infrastructure and cities are crumbling, when the wars in Afghanistan and Iraq have drained the U.S. treasury of trillions of dollars, Dwight Eisenhower's warning of the dangers to the American republic of a preponderant military-industrial complex appears particularly prescient.

Like the Civil War, the war on terror was seen by some of its more fervent supporters as a moral crusade that would regenerate a supposedly decadent and materialistic American society with a new sense of purpose and "moral clarity." Since then these expectations have been eclipsed by Abu Ghraib, Haditha, the Stryker Brigade "kill teams," and the killing spree of Sergeant Robert Bates. "Clarity" has been conspicuously absent from a sordid trail of violence that has produced thousands of dead and wounded noncombatants and record numbers of military and veteran suicides.

In 2013, a war-weary Congress and American public forced the Obama administration to back away from another potential Middle Eastern war, in Syria. This reticence may be the beginning of a new preference for diplomacy rather than war, or it may be just a fad. The retired colonel and Vietnam veteran Andrew Bacevich has written that Americans are "seduced" by war. Today that attraction may be wearing off. Bacevich has warned that America must wean itself from its "addiction" to militarism and its "outsize martial pretensions" or face ruin.[6]

The memory of William Tecumseh Sherman can contribute to such rehabilitation. Sherman has often been cited as the great military realist. His most famous observation, "War is hell," has become an endlessly repeated justification for those who want to wage war more hellishly. But Sherman was not a militarist and did not take war lightly. Though he once described war as "part of the grand machinery by which this world is governed," he dreaded the Civil War and did not welcome it when it came. Today when so many Americans who've never been near a battlefield advocate new wars and pursue dreams of military omnipotence based on fantasies of immaculate destruction, Sherman's actual attitude to war is more relevant than ever. In the Civil War's aftermath, he described its glory as "moonshine" and denounced "those who have never heard a shot, never heard the shriek and groans of the wounded and lacerated . . . [but] cry aloud for more blood, more vengeance, more desolation." That sentiment, too, is part of Sherman's legacy.

Notes

INTRODUCTION

1. Charles Royster, *The Destructive War: William Tecumseh Sherman, Stonewall Jackson, and the Americans* (New York: Vintage, 1993), 356.

2. J.F.C. Fuller, *The Conduct of War, 1789–1961: A Study of the Impact of the French, Industrial, and Russian Revolutions on War and Its Conduct* (New York: Da Capo Press, 1992), 107.

3. Paddy Griffiths, *Battle Tactics of the American Civil War* (Ramsbury, UK: Crowood Press, 2001), 9.

4. Russell F. Weigley, *The American Way of War: A History of United States Military Strategy and Policy* (Bloomington: Indiana University Press, 1973), 151.

5. Russell F. Weigley, "The Necessity of Force: The Civil War, World War II, and the American Way of War," in *War Comes Again: Comparative Vistas on the Civil War and World War II*, ed. Gabor Boritt (New York: Oxford University Press, 1995), 232.

6. James Reston Jr., *Sherman's March and Vietnam* (New York: Macmillan, 1984), 6.

7. Victor Davis Hanson, "Sherman's War," *American Heritage*, November 9, 1999, victorhanson.com/wordpress/?p=5133http://victorhanson.com/wordpress/?p=5133.

8. White House, *2010 National Security Strategy of the United States*, www.whitehouse.gov/sites/default/files/rss_viewer/national_security_strategy.pdf.

1. THE IRON HAND OF WAR

1. Alfred Stillé, *War as an Instrument of Civilization: An Address Before the Society of the Alumni of the University of Pennsylvania* (Philadelphia: Collins, 1862).

2. Andrew S. Coopersmith, *Fighting Words: An Illustrated History of Newspaper Accounts of the Civil War* (New York: The New Press, 2004), 14.

3. Archer Jones, *Civil War Command and Strategy: The Process of Victory and Defeat* (New York: The Free Press, 1992), 23.

4. Baron Antoine Henri de Jomini, *The Art of War*, trans. G.H. Mendell and W.P. Craighill (West Point, NY: U.S. Military Academy, 1862; Radford, VA: Wilder Publications, 2008), 89.

5. Karen Stokes, *South Carolina Civilians in Sherman's Path* (Charleston, SC: The History Press, 2003).

6. On the guerrilla war in Missouri, see Michael Fellman, *Inside War: The Guerrilla Conflict in Missouri During the American Civil War* (New York: Oxford University Press, 1989).

7. On the environmental impact of the war on the South, see Lisa M. Brady, *War upon the Land: Military Strategy and the Transformation of Southern Landscapes During the American Civil War* (Athens: University of Georgia Press, 2012); see also Megan Kate Hudson, *Ruin Nation: Destruction and the American Civil War* (Athens: University of Georgia Press, 2012).

8. Fellman, *Inside War*, 101.

9. The Civil War was not the first war in which railroads had been used to transport supplies and soldiers. Railways played an important role in the Crimean War (1853–56) and particularly in the 1859 Franco-Austrian War, in which both sides made tactical use of the railway network to deploy their troops, particularly the French. But these precedents were small in scale compared to the more comprehensive militarization of the railway network by both sides in the Civil War. See Christian Wolmar, *Engines of War: How Wars Were Won and Lost on the Railways* (London: Atlantic Books, 2010).

10. John J. Tierney Jr., *Chasing Ghosts: Unconventional Warfare in American History* (Dulles, VA: Potomac Books, 2006), 37.

11. Charles W. Wills, *Army Life of an Illinois Soldier, Including a Day by Day Record of Sherman's March to the Sea* (Washington, DC: Globe Printing Co., 1906), 121.

12. Jomini, *Art of War*, 34–35.

13. Fellman, *Inside War*, 163.

14. Lloyd Lewis, *Sherman: Fighting Prophet* (New York: Konecky & Konecky, 1932), 295.

15. For a study of the Union shift toward "hard war," see Mark Grimsley, *The Hard Hand of War: Union Policy Toward Southern Civilians, 1861–1865* (New York: Cambridge University Press, 1995). Grimsley distinguishes the "marked severities" that he regarded as the essence of the Union's hard-war policy from subsequent manifestations of "total war." On the impact of Southern guerrilla warfare on this transformation, see Clay Mountcastle, *Punitive War: Confederate Guerrillas and Union Reprisals* (Lawrence: University Press of Kansas, 2009).

16. Grimsley, *Hard Hand of War*, 152.

17. Lieut. Col. Freemantle, *Three Months in the Southern States: April–June, 1863* (New York: John Bradburn, 1864), 110–11.

18. Edmund Wilson, *Patriotic Gore: Studies in the Literature of the American Civil War* (New York: W.W. Norton, 1994), 313.

19. Philip Sheridan, *Personal Memoirs of P. H. Sheridan*, 2 vols. (New York: Charles L. Webster, 1888), 487–88.

2. UNCLE BILLY'S WAR

1. To Ellen Ewing, September 7, 1841, in *Home Letters of General Sherman*, ed. Mark Antony De Wolfe Howe (New York: Charles Scribner's Sons, 1909), 14.

2. Lloyd Lewis, *Sherman: Fighting Prophet* (New York: Konecky & Konecky, 1932), 137–38.

3. To Ellen Sherman, April 11, 1862, in Howe, *Home Letters*, 222.

4. Basil Henry Liddell Hart, *Sherman: Soldier, Realist, American* (New York: Da Capo Press, 1993), 205.

5. Charles Edmund Vetter, *Sherman: Merchant of Terror, Advocate of Peace* (Gretna, LA: Pelican, 1992), 132.

6. Ibid., 169.

7. Lewis, *Sherman: Fighting Prophet*, 329.

8. To Major R.M. Sawyer, January 31, 1864, in *The Sherman Letters: Correspondence Between General and Senator Sherman from 1837 to 1891*, ed. Rachel Sherman Thorndike (New York: Charles Scribner's Sons, 1894), 232.

9. To Ellen Sherman, August 3, 1861, in Howe, *Home Letters*, 214.

10. Lewis, *Sherman: Fighting Prophet*, 239.

11. Ibid., 269.

12. James M. Merrill, *William Tecumseh Sherman* (Chicago: Rand McNally, 1971), 231.

13. Bruce Catton, *Never Call Retreat* (London: Phoenix Press, 2001), 303.

14. Vetter, *Sherman: Merchant of Terror, Advocate of Peace*, 183.

15. Lewis, *Sherman: Fighting Prophet*, 352.

16. Ibid., 398.

17. Ibid., 353.

18. To Ellen Sherman, June 26, 1864, in Howe, *Home Letters*, 298.

19. Marc Wortman, *The Bonfire: The Siege and Burning of Atlanta* (New York: PublicAffairs, 2009), 269.

20. James Marten, *The Children's Civil War* (Chapel Hill: University of North Carolina Press, 1998), 110.

21. Edward Caudill and Paul Ashdown, *Sherman's March in Myth and Memory* (Lanham, MD: Rowman & Littlefield, 2008), 21.

22. For the full exchange between Hood and Sherman, see William Tecumseh Sherman, *Memoirs of General William T. Sherman*, 2d ed., 2 vols. (New York: D. Appleton, 1889). For Hood's perspective, see John Bell Hood, *Advance and Retreat: Personal Experiences in the United States and Confederate Armies* (New Orleans: G.T. Beauregard, 1880).

23. See General Orders No. 100: Instructions for the Government of Armies of the United States in the Field, avalon.law.yale.edu/19th_century/lieber.asp.

24. Sherman, *Memoirs*, 128–29.

25. Ibid., 124–27.

26. Lance Janda, "Shutting the Gates of Mercy: The American Origins of Total War, 1860–1880," *Journal of Military History* 59, no. 1 (January 1995): 7–26.

27. Sherman, *Memoirs*, 164–70.

28. Russell Weigley, "American Strategy from Its Beginnings Through the First World War," in *Makers of Modern Strategy from Machiavelli to the Nuclear Age*, ed. Peter Paret, Gordon A. Craig, and Felix Gilbert (Princeton, NJ: Princeton University Press, 1986), 408–43, 415.

3. THE DESTRUCTION MACHINE

1. William of Malmesbury, *A History of the Norman Kings, 1066–1125*, trans. Joseph Stephenson (Burnham-on-Sea, UK: Llanerch Press, 1989), 25.

2. Sean McGlynn, *By Sword and Fire: Cruelty and Atrocity in Medieval Warfare* (London: Phoenix Press, 2009), 200.

3. John Hale, *The Civilization of Europe in the Renaissance* (New York: HarperPerennial, 2005), 185.

4. John A. Lynn, *The Wars of Louis XIV: 1667–1714* (Abingdon, UK: Routledge, 1999), 181.

5. Ibid., 196.

6. Alexis de Tocqueville, *Writings on Empire and Slavery*, trans. Jennifer Pitts (Baltimore: Johns Hopkins University Press, 2003), 70.

7. E.L. Doctorow, *The March* (London: Abacus, 2006), 62–63.

8. To Ellen Sherman, December 31, 1864, in *Home Letters of General Sherman*, ed. Mark Antony De Wolfe Howe (New York: Charles Scribner's Sons, 1909), 321.

9. Burke Davis, *Sherman's March: The First Full-Length Narrative of General William T. Sherman's Devastating March Through Georgia and the Carolinas* (New York: Vintage, 1988), 29.

10. Lee Kennett, *Marching Through Georgia: The Story of Civilians and Soldiers During Sherman's Campaign* (New York: HarperPerennial, 1995), 310–11.

11. Andrew J. Boies, *Record of the Thirty-Third Volunteer Massachusetts Infantry from Aug. 1862 to Aug. 1865* (Fitchburg, MA: Sentinel Printing Co., 1880), 162.

12. David P. Conyngham, *Sherman's March Through the South* (New York: Sheldon & Co., 1865), 247.

13. George W. Pepper, *Personal Recollections of Sherman's Campaigns in Georgia and the Carolinas* (Zanesville, OH: Hugh Dunne, 1866), 275.

14. Conyngham, *Sherman's March*, 237.

15. Ibid., 268.

16. Pepper, *Personal Recollections*, 279.

17. Lloyd Lewis, *Sherman: Fighting Prophet* (New York: Konecky & Konecky, 1932), 465.

18. William Tecumseh Sherman, *Memoirs of General William T. Sherman*, 2d ed., 2 vols. (New York: D. Appleton, 1889), 2:249.

19. Ibid., 2:226–28.

20. Henry Hitchcock, *Marching with Sherman* (Lincoln: University of Nebraska Press, 1995), 125.

21. Pepper, *Personal Recollections*, 277.

22. This figure of three hundred thousand was arrived at through Sherman's sociological analysis of Southern society, and the particular classes that he held most responsible for causing the war.

23. Sherman, *Memoirs*, 2:213.

24. Ibid., 2:227–28.

25. George Ward Nichols, *The Story of the Great March* (New York: Harper & Bros., 1865), 279.

26. Sherman, *Memoirs*, 2:223.

27. Conyngham, *Sherman's March*, 323.

28. Charles Wright Wills, *Army Life of an Illinois Soldier* (Washington, DC: Globe Printing Co., 1906), 342.

29. Richard Harwell and Philip N. Racine, eds., *The Fiery Trail: A Union Officer's Account of Sherman's Last Campaigns* (Knoxville: University of Tennessee Press, 1986), 153.

30. Pepper, *Personal Recollections*, 337.

31. Richard Taylor, *Destruction and Reconstruction: Personal Experiences in the Late War in the United States* (London: William Blackwood & Sons, 1879), 325.

32. William Gilmore Simms, *A City Laid Waste: The Capture, Sack, and Destruction of the City of Columbia* (Columbia: University of South Carolina Press, 2005), 73. A well-known novelist before the war, Simms was known to Sherman's soldiers as a pro-secession propagandist, and his Woodlands plantation was singled out for similar treatment. Not only did soldiers refuse his requests to protect his property, but they went on to loot his library, carrying away books as mementos.

33. Boies, *Record of the Thirty-Third*, 118.

34. Joseph T. Glatthaar, *The March to the Sea and Beyond: Sherman's Troops in the Savannah and Carolinas Campaigns* (Baton Rouge: Louisiana State University Press, 1985), 136.

35. Charles Edmund Vetter, *Sherman: Merchant of Terror, Advocate of Peace* (Gretna, LA: Pelican, 1992), 219.

36. Marc Wortman, *The Bonfire: The Siege and Burning of Atlanta* (New York: PublicAffairs, 2009), 338.

37. Raymond Hyser and J. Chris Arndt, *Voices of the American Past*, 2 vols. (Belmont, CA: Thompson Wadsworth, 2008), 1:274.

38. Karen Stokes, *South Carolina Civilians in Sherman's Path* (Charleston, SC: The History Press, 2003), 60.

39. Conyngham, *Sherman's March*, 334.

40. Simms, *City Laid Waste*, 113.

41. Richard Wheeler, *Sherman's March: An Eyewitness History of the Cruel Campaign That Helped End a Crueler War* (New York: HarperPerennial, 1978), 208; Conyngham, *Sherman's March*, 346.

42. Daniel Heyward Trezevant, *The Burning of Columbia, S.C.: A Review of Northern Assertions and Southern Facts* (Columbia: South Carolinian Power Press, 1866), genealogytrails.com/scar/richland/burning_columbia.htm.

43. Hitchcock, *Marching with Sherman*, 92.

44. Karma Nabulsi, *Traditions of War: Occupation, Resistance and the Law* (New York: Oxford University Press, 1999), 30. Nabulsi's book is a lucid and brilliant analysis of the philosophical, legal, and political dimensions of nineteenth-century precursors to "total war."

45. A punishment that subsequently turned out to be unwarranted, when it was revealed that the quartermaster in question had not been murdered by guerrillas but had been captured by Confederate soldiers and shot while trying to escape. See Harry S. Stout, *Upon the Altar of the Nation: A Moral History of the Civil War* (New York: Penguin, 2006), 380.

46. Mark Coburn, *Terrible Innocence: General Sherman at War* (New York: Hippocrene Books, 1993), 86.

47. Sherman, *Memoirs*, 2:194.

48. For an account of Wilson's raid, see James Pickett Jones, *Yankee Blitzkrieg: Wilson's Raid Through Alabama and Georgia* (Athens: University of Georgia Press, 1976).

49. To Ellen Sherman, April 9, 1865, in Howe, *Home Letters*, 342.

50. To Ellen Sherman, April 5, 1865, in Howe, *Home Letters*, 340.

4. CIVILIANS AND SOLDIERS

1. Larry Zuckerman, *The Rape of Belgium: The Untold Story of World War I* (New York: New York University Press, 2004), 28.

2. Mark Mazower, *Inside Hitler's Greece: The Experience of Occupation, 1941–44* (New Haven, CT: Yale University Press, 1995), 3.

3. Marcus Cunliffe, *Soldiers and Civilians: The Martial Spirit in America 1775–1865* (London: Eyre & Spottiswoode, 1993), 344.

4. Marli F. Weiner, ed., *A Heritage of Woe: The Civil War Diary of Grace Elmore, 1861–1868* (Athens: University of Georgia Press, 1997), 103.

5. Felton made this much-quoted observation in an address to the Daughters of the Confederacy in Augusta, Georgia, in 1900. For an account of her

own experiences in Georgia during the Civil War, see Rebecca Latimer Felton, *Country Life in Georgia in the Days of My Youth* (Atlanta: Index Printing Co., 1919).

6. Dolly Lunt Burge, *A Woman's Wartime Journal: An Account of the Passage over Georgia's Plantation of Sherman's Army on the March to the Sea, as Recorded in the Diary of Dolly Sumner Lunt (Mrs. Thomas Burge)* (New York: Century, 1918).

7. William Tecumseh Sherman, *Memoirs of General William T. Sherman*, 2d ed., 2 vols. (New York: D. Appleton, 1889), 2:254.

8. Karen Stokes, *South Carolina Civilians in Sherman's Path* (Charleston, SC: The History Press, 2003), 98.

9. Michael Golay, *A Ruined Land: The End of the Civil War* (New York: John Wiley & Sons, 1999), 59.

10. Marc Wortman, *The Bonfire: The Siege and Burning of Atlanta* (New York: PublicAffairs, 2009), 326.

11. Stokes, *South Carolina Civilians*, 27.

12. To Ellen Sherman, June 27, 1863, in *Home Letters of General Sherman*, ed. Mark Antony De Wolfe Howe (New York: Charles Scribner's Sons, 1909), 268.

13. Larry M. Logue, *To Appomattox and Beyond: The Civil War Soldier in War and Peace* (Chicago: Ivan R. Dee, 1996), 24.

14. Charles Royster, *The Destructive War: William Tecumseh Sherman, Stonewall Jackson, and the Americans* (New York: Vintage, 1993), 87.

15. See Mary Boykin Chestnut, *Mary Chestnut's Diary* (New York: Penguin, 2011).

16. Noah Andre Trudeau, *Southern Storm: Sherman's March to the Sea* (New York: Harper Perennial, 2008), 313.

17. Vasily Grossman, *A Writer at War: A Soviet Journalist with the Red Army, 1941–1945* (New York: Vintage, 2007).

18. Andrew S. Coopersmith, *Fighting Words: An Illustrated History of Newspaper Accounts of the Civil War* (New York: The New Press, 2004), 216–17.

19. Stokes, *South Carolina Civilians*, 47.

20. Ibid., 46

21. William Gilmore Simms, *A City Laid Waste: The Capture, Sack, and Destruction of the City of Columbia* (Columbia: University of South Carolina Press, 2005), 90.

22. Weiner, *Heritage of Woe*, 84.

23. Philip Dray, *At the Hands of Persons Unknown: The Lynching of Black America* (New York: Modern Library, 2003), 125.

24. Trudeau, *Southern Storm*, 155.

25. Henry Hitchcock, *Marching with Sherman* (Lincoln: University of Nebraska Press, 1995), 70–71.

26. William Dusinberre, *Them Dark Days: Slavery in the American Rice Swamps* (New York: Oxford University Press, 1996), 210.

27. To Ellen Sherman, July 10, 1860, in Howe, *Home Letters*, 178.

28. David P. Conyngham, *Sherman's March Through the South* (New York: Sheldon & Co., 1865), 277.

29. For a detailed account of this grim episode, see Trudeau, *Southern Storm*, 380–84. Davis was not censured by Sherman for his actions, but they were widely criticized in Washington when they became known and may have contributed to the subsequent decision by Congress not to confirm his promotion. Davis's behavior at Ebenezer Creek was also criticized by some of his own soldiers, one of whom was moved to observe, "Where can you find in all the annals of plantation cruelty anything more completely inhuman and fiendish than this?" See Joseph T. Glatthaar, *The March to the Sea and Beyond: Sherman's Troops in the Savannah and Carolinas Campaigns* (Baton Rouge: Louisiana State University Press, 1985), 64.

30. Michael Fellman, "Lincoln and Sherman," in *Lincoln's Generals*, ed. Gabor S. Boritt (New York: Oxford University Press, 1994), 150.

31. W.E.B Du Bois, *The Souls of Black Folk* (State College: Pennsylvania State University, 2006), 18.

32. Stokes, *South Carolina Civilians*, 77.

33. Ibid., 112–15.

34. Emmerich de Vattel, *The Law of Nations; or, The Principles of Natural Law* (1758), www.lonang.com/exlibris/vattel, bk. 3, chap. 8.

35. Edmund Wilson, *Patriotic Gore: Studies in the Literature of the Civil War* (New York: W.W. Norton, 1994), 312–13.

36. Ibid., 154–55.

37. Glatthaar, *March to the Sea*, 37.

38. Mark Grimsley, *The Hard Hand of War: Union Policy Toward Southern Civilians, 1861–1865* (New York: Cambridge University Press, 1995), 169.

39. Burke Davis, *Sherman's March: The First Full-Length Narrative of General William T. Sherman's Devastating March Through Georgia and the Carolinas* (New York: Vintage, 1988), 41.

40. Stokes, *South Carolina Civilians*, 58.

41. John McElroy, *Andersonville: A Story of Rebel Military Prisons* (Toledo: D.R. Locke, 1879), 393.

42. George W. Pepper, *Personal Recollections of Sherman's Campaigns in Georgia and the Carolinas* (Zanesville, OH: Hugh Dunne, 1866), 311.

43. George Ward Nichols, *The Story of the Great March* (New York: Harper & Bros., 1865), 153.

44. Richard Harwell and Philip N. Racine, eds., *The Fiery Trail: A Union Officer's Account of Sherman's Last Campaigns* (Knoxville: University of Tennessee Press, 1986), 132.

45. Trudeau, *Southern Storm*, 213.

46. S.A. McNeil, *Personal Recollections of Service in the Army of the Cumberland and Sherman's Army* (Richwood, OH: 1910), 69–70.

47. Hitchcock, *Marching with Sherman*, 77.

48. Ibid., 125.

5. "MORE PERFECT PEACE"

1. Noah Andre Trudeau, *Southern Storm: Sherman's March to the Sea* (New York: HarperPerennial, 2008), 547–48.

2. William T. Sherman, *From Atlanta to the Sea*, ed. B.H. Liddell Hart (London: Folio Society, 1961), 9.

3. Trudeau, *Southern Storm*, 526.

4. Alfred Castel, *Articles of War: Winners, Losers, and Some Who Were Both in the Civil War* (Mechanicsburg, PA: Stackpole Books, 2001), 230. Castel also gives a much more detailed critique of Sherman's performance during the Atlanta campaign in *Decision in the West: The Atlanta Campaign of 1864* (Lawrence: University Press of Kansas, 1995).

5. Wesley Moody, *Demon of the Lost Cause: Sherman and Civil War History* (Columbia: University of Missouri Press, 2011), 118.

6. Mark Antony De Wolfe Howe, ed., *Home Letters of General Sherman* (New York: Charles Scribner's Sons, 1909), 337.

7. Lloyd Lewis, *Sherman: Fighting Prophet* (New York: Konecky & Konecky, 1932), 499.

8. Archer Jones, *Civil War Command and Strategy: The Process of Victory and Defeat* (New York: The Free Press, 1992), 216.

9. Charles Royster, *The Destructive War: William Tecumseh Sherman, Stonewall Jackson, and the Americans* (New York: Vintage, 1993), 369.

10. William Tecumseh Sherman, *Memoirs of General William T. Sherman*, 2d ed., 2 vols. (New York: D. Appleton, 1889), 1:293.

11. Frank Moore, ed., *Rebellion Record: A Diary of American Events: Documents and Narratives*, vol. 9 in *Sabin Americana, 1500–1926* (Independence, KY: Gale Digital Collections, 2012), 203.

12. To Ellen Sherman, April 28, 1865, in Howe, *Home Letters*, 349.

13. Sherman, *From Atlanta to the Sea*, 402.

14. John H. Kennaway, *On Sherman's Track; or, The South after the War* (London: Seeley, Jackson & Halliday, 1867), 106.

15. Karen Stokes, *South Carolina Civilians in Sherman's Path* (Charleston, SC: The History Press, 2003), 100.

16. See, for example, Alan Conway, *The Reconstruction of Georgia* (Minneapolis: University of Minnesota Press, 1966). According to Conway, the damage inflicted by Sherman's army was limited to "little more than a fortieth of the state's acreage, albeit of its richest areas, and the major part of Georgia remained untouched by actual warfare" (p. 20).

17. Stokes, *South Carolina Civilians*, 68.

18. Marli F. Weiner, ed., *A Heritage of Woe: The Civil War Diary of Grace Elmore, 1861–1868* (Athens: University of Georgia Press, 1997), 125.

19. "Reconstruction in South Carolina," *New York Times*, September 13, 1865.

20. Baron Antoine-Henri de Jomini, *The Art of War*, trans. G.H. Mendell and W.P. Craighill (West Point, NY: U.S. Military Academy, 1862; Radford, VA: Wilder Publications, 2008), 33.

21. On Reconstruction and the general postwar situation in the South, see Eric Foner's magisterial *Reconstruction: America's Unfinished Revolution* (New York: Harper & Row, 1988).

22. Carl Schurz, *Condition of the South*, 1865, 39th Congress, Senate, executive document, 1st session, no. 2, wwnorton.com/college/history/america9/full/docs/CSchurz-South_Report-1865.pdf.

23. Stephen Graham, *Children of the Slaves* (London: Macmillan, 1920), 158.

24. Russell F. Weigley, *The American Way of War: A History of United States Military Strategy and Policy* (Bloomington: Indiana University Press, 1973), 160.

25. Sherman to U.S. Grant, December 28, 1866, quoted in Lance Janda, "Shutting the Gates of Mercy: The American Origins of Total War, 1860–1880," *Journal of Military History* 59, no. 1 (January 1995): 7–26.

26. For accounts of the Washita battle, see George Bird Grinnell, *The Fighting Cheyennes* (New York: Charles Scribner's Sons, 1915). Also see Stephen E. Ambrose, *Crazy Horse and Custer: The Parallel Lives of Two American Warriors* (London: Macdonald and Jane's, 1976).

27. Janda, "Shutting the Gates of Mercy," 21.

28. Ibid.

29. To Ellen Sherman, September 16, 1883, in Howe, *Home Letters*, 391.

30. Eugene C. Tidball, *"No Disgrace to My Country": The Life of John C. Tidball* (Kent, OH: Kent State University Press, 2002).

31. Royster, *Destructive War*, 392.

32. Edward Caudill and Paul Ashdown, *Sherman's March in Myth and Memory* (Lanham, MD: Rowman & Littlefield, 2008), 143.

6. SOLDIERS

1. Steven E. Woodworth, *Sherman: Lessons in Leadership* (Basingstoke, UK: Palgrave Macmillan, 2009), xi.

2. Michael Pearlman, *Warmaking and American Democracy* (Lawrence: University Press of Kansas, 1999), 215.

3. Ibid., 211.

4. On the evolution of the U.S. Army in this period, see Carol Reardon, *Soldiers and Scholars: The U.S. Army and the Uses of Military History, 1865–1920* (Lawrence: University Press of Kansas, 1990); also see Timothy K. Nenninger, *The Leavenworth Schools and the Old Army: Education, Professionalism, and the Officer Corps of the United States Army, 1881–1918* (Westport, CT: Greenwoood Press, 1978).

5. Reardon, *Soldiers and Scholars*, 97–98.

6. John Codman Ropes, *Papers of the Military Historical Society of Massachusetts* 10 (1895): 148–51, quoted in J.F.C. Fuller, *The Conduct of War, 1789–1961: A Study of the Impact of the French, Industrial, and Russian Revolutions on War and Its Conduct* (New York: Da Capo Press, 1992), 110–11.

7. Brian McAllister Linn, *The Philippines War: 1899–1902* (Lawrence: University Press of Kansas, 2000), 95.

8. Ibid., 60.

9. Louise Barnett, *Atrocity and American Justice in Southeast Asia* (Abingdon, UK: Routledge, 2010), 81.

10. For Bell's circulars, see Robert D. Ramsey III, *A Masterpiece of Counterguerrilla Warfare: BG [Brigadier General] J. Franklin Bell in the Philippines,*

1901–1902, Long War Series Occasional Paper 25 (Fort Leavenworth, KS: Combat Studies Institute Press, 2012).

11. Glenn Anthony May, *Battle for Batangas: A Philippine Province at War* (New Haven, CT: Yale University Press, 1991), 264. May attributes much of the death toll caused by Bell's operations to an increase in malaria, partly because so much livestock had been slaughtered that mosquitoes were more likely to feed off humans.

12. Michael Fellman, *In the Name of God and Country: Reconsidering Terrorism in American History* (New Haven, CT: Yale University Press, 2010), 230.

13. T.R. Brereton, *Educating the U.S. Army: Arthur L. Wagner and Reform, 1875–1905* (Lincoln: University of Nebraska Press, 2000), p. 91.

14. Colin Powell with Joseph E. Persico, *A Soldier's Way: An Autobiography* (London: Arrow Books, 2001), 87.

15. Bernd Greiner, *War Without Fronts: The USA in Vietnam* (New York: Vintage, 2010), 251.

16. Kendrick Oliver, *The My Lai Massacre in American History and Memory* (Manchester: Manchester University Press, 2006), 160–61.

17. Charles Royster, *The Destructive War: William Tecumseh Sherman, Stonewall Jackson, and the Americans* (New York: Vintage, 1993), 358.

18. Oliver, *My Lai Massacre*, 161.

19. On search-and-destroy operations and U.S. war atrocities, see Greiner, *War Without Fronts*.

20. Julian J. Ewell and Ira A. Hunt Jr., *Sharpening the Combat Edge: The Use of Analysis to Reinforce Military Judgment* (Washington, DC: Department of the Army, 1995).

21. Jonathan Schell, *The Real War* (New York: Random House, 1988), 244.

22. James William Gibson, *The Perfect War: Technowar in Vietnam* (New York: Atlantic Monthly Press, 2000), 234–37.

23. Ibid., 234.

24. Russell F. Weigley, *The American Way of War: A History of United States Military Strategy and Policy* (Bloomington: Indiana University Press, 1973), 204–5.

25. Basil Henry Liddell Hart, *Strategy*, 2d ed. (New York: Meridian Books, 1967), 212.

26. Fuller, *Conduct of War*, 243.

27. For an analysis of Chaffee's career and U.S. mechanized warfare before World War II, see George F. Hoffman, *Through Mobility We Conquer:*

The Mechanization of U.S. Cavalry (Lexington: University Press of Kentucky, 2006).

28. Ladislas Farago, *Patton: Ordeal and Triumph* (Yardley, PA: Westholme Publishing, 2005), 283–84.

29. Basil Henry Liddell Hart, *The Memoirs of Captain Liddell Hart*, vol. 1 (London: Cassell, 1965), 170.

30. Dwight Eisenhower, *D Day to VE Day 1944–45: General Eisenhower's Report on the Invasion of Europe*, ed. Tim Coates (London: Stationery Office, 2001), 155. On the Third Army's campaigns in Normandy, see Martin Blumenson, *D-Day and the Battle for Normandy: Breakout and Pursuit*, U.S. Army Green Book (Washington, DC: U.S. Army Center of Military History, 1993).

31. Farago, *Patton*, 492.

32. General staff of Douglas MacArthur, *Reports of General MacArthur: The Campaigns of MacArthur in the Pacific*, vol. 1 (Washington, DC: U.S. Army Center of Military History, 1994), 100.

33. After-action report on Manila quote from Thomas M. Huber, "The Battle of Manila: Tactical Lessons Relevant to Current Military Operations" (Fort Leavenworth, KS: Combat Studies Institute, U.S. Army Command and General Staff College, n.d.), battleofmanila.org/pages/01_huber.htm.

34. Charles B. MacDonald, *The Last Offensive: U.S. Army in World War II—The European Theater of Operations* (Atlanta: Whitman Publishing, 2012), 262.

35. The leftist historian and activist Howard Zinn also participated in this raid as a pilot and later wrote a powerful account of it in tracing his subsequent evolution toward pacifism. See Howard Zinn, *The Bomb* (San Francisco: City Lights Books, 2010).

36. James Reston Jr., *Sherman's March and Vietnam* (New York: Macmillan, 1984), 16.

37. John T. Smith, *The Linebacker Raids: The Bombing of North Vietnam, 1972* (London: Arms & Armour Press, 1998), 11.

38. Fuller, *Conduct of War*, 241.

39. William C. Sherman, *Air Warfare* (repr., Maxwell Air Force Base, AL: Air University Press, 2002), 6.

40. For an account of these debates, see Michael Sherry, *The Rise of American Air Power: The Creation of Armageddon* (New Haven, CT: Yale University Press, 1987).

41. Ibid., 135.

42. Adrian R. Lewis, *The American Culture of War*, 2d ed. (Abingdon, UK: Routledge, 2011), 40.

43. Conrad C. Crane, *Bombs, Cities, and Civilians: American Airpower Strategy in World War II* (Lawrence: University Press of Kansas, 1993), 33.

44. U.S. Strategic Bombing Survey, Franklin D'Olier, chair, Morale Division, *The United States Strategic Bombing Survey: The Effects of Strategic Bombing on German Morale*, vol. 1 (Washington, DC: Strategic Bombing Survey, 1947), babel.hathitrust.org/cgi/pt?id=mdp.39015008510300;view=2up; seq=4; and *United States Strategic Bombing Survey Summary Report (European War)* (Washington, DC: Strategic Bombing Survey, 1945), www.anesi.com /ussbs02.htm.

45. Robert F. Dorr, *Mission to Berlin: The Men Who Took the War to the Heart of Hitler's Reich* (Osceola, WI: Zenith Press, 2011), 184.

46. John Dower, *War Without Mercy: Race and Power in the Pacific War* (New York: Pantheon, 1986), 41.

47. Sherry, *Rise of American Air Power*, 315.

48. Ibid., 282.

49. Ibid., 287–88.

50. Interestingly, in his co-written book *Wilson's Ghost*, McNamara cites Sherman's "War is cruelty" message again, in an argument about the conduct of war and a critique of the American self-image of always fighting on the side of good versus evil in war. See Robert McNamara and James G. Blight, *Wilson's Ghost: Reducing the Risk of Conflict, Killing, and Catastrophe in the 21st Century* (New York: PublicAffairs, 2003), 130. As the title suggests, the book is primarily concerned with preventing wars rather than escalating their destructiveness.

51. This was the central thesis of Gar Alperovitz's *Atomic Diplomacy: Hiroshima and Potsdam* (London: Pluto Press, 1994).

52. Reginald Thompson, *Cry Korea: The Korean War—a Reporter's Notebook* (London: MacDonald, 1951), 94.

53. Conrad C. Crane, *Airpower Strategy in Korea, 1950–1953* (Lawrence: University Press of Kansas, 2000), 47.

54. Bruce Cumings, *The Korean War: A History* (New York: Modern Library, 2011), Kindle loc. 2446.

55. Crane, *Airpower Strategy*, 116.

56. Gibson, *Perfect War*, 97.

57. Mike Gravel, ed., *The Pentagon Papers: The Defense Department History of United States Decisionmaking on Vietnam*, vol. 4 (Boston: Beacon Press, 1971), 224.

58. For an account of the raids and an analysis of the debates about their strategic impact, see Smith, *Linebacker Raids*. For a revisionist rebuttal of suggestions that such attacks constituted terror bombing, see Guenter Lewy, *America in Vietnam* (New York: Oxford University Press, 1978), 410–17.

7. CIVILIANS

1. John Bennett Walters, "General William T. Sherman and Total War," *Journal of Southern History* 14, no. 4 (November 1948): 447–80.

2. Charles Edmund Vetter, *Sherman: Merchant of Terror, Advocate of Peace* (Gretna, LA: Pelican, 1992), 299.

3. David Bell, *The First Total War: Napoleon's Europe and the Birth of Warfare as We Know It* (Boston: Mariner Books, 2008), 160.

4. See Detlef Bald, "Traditions in Military-Strategic Thought in Germany and the Problem of Deterrence," SOWI-Arbeitspapier, German Armed Forces Institute for Social Research, 1989.

5. For an analysis of Ludendorff's concept of total war, see Jan Willem Honig, "The Idea of Total War: From Clausewitz to Ludendorff," in *The Pacific War as Total War: Proceedings of the 2011 International Forum on War History* (Tokyo: National Institute for Defence Studies, 2012), www.nids.go .jp/english/event/forum/pdf/2011/08.pdf, 29–41.

6. George Ward Nichols, *The Story of the Great March* (New York: Harper & Bros., 1865), 277.

7. John Lawrence Tone, *War and Genocide in Cuba, 1895–1898* (Columbia: University of South Carolina Press, 2006), 210.

8. Ibid., 223.

9. Valeriano Weyler y Nicolau, *Mi Mando en Cuba: Historia Militar y Política de la Última Guerra Separatista, por el General Weyler* (Madrid: F. Gonzalez Rojas, 1910), 13–15.

10. Halik Kochanski, *Sir Garnet Wolseley: Victorian Hero* (London: Hambledon Press, 1999), 71.

11. G.F.R. Henderson, *The Civil War: A Soldier's View*, ed. Jay Luvaas (Chicago: University of Chicago Press, 1958), 211.

12. Tabitha Jackson, *The Boer War* (London: Channel 4 Books, 1999), 132.

13. Ibid., 133.

14. Ibid.

15. Ibid., 130.

16. Ibid., 145. Sheridan does not mention this episode in his own account of the war. See Philip H. Sheridan, "An American Account of the Franco-Prussian War: 'From Gravelotte to Sedan.'" *Scribner's Magazine* 4, no. 5 (November 1888): 514–35.

17. There is no evidence that the American Civil War had any particular impact on the Prussian army's decision to resort to harsh methods in the Franco-Prussian War, nor that Prussian harshness had any reciprocal effect on the U.S. Army. Sheridan's visit reflected American interest in Prussian mobilization methods and organization, particularly its staff college system, rather than any admiration or concern with irregular warfare. See Jay Luvaas, "The Influence of the German Wars of Unification on the United States," in Stig Forster and Jorg Nagler, eds., *On the Road to Total War: The American Civil War and the German Wars of Unification, 1861–1871* (Cambridge, UK: Cambridge University Press, 2002), 597–619.

18. See J.M. Spaight, *War Rights on Land* (London: Macmillan, 1911).

19. On both campaigns, see Thomas Pakenham, *The Scramble for Africa 1876–1912* (London: Abacus, 1991).

20. J.H. Morgan, *The German War Book: Being "The Usages of War on Land" Issued by the Great General Staff of the German Army* (London: John Murray, 1915), 55.

21. For a full account of the occupation, see Larry Zuckerman, *The Rape of Belgium: The Untold Story of World War I* (New York: New York University Press, 2004).

22. The complex and often fraught debates that accompanied the elaboration of these rules can be found in J.M. Scott, *The Proceedings of the Hague Peace Conferences, Translation of the Official Texts: The Conference of 1899* (Oxford, UK: Oxford University Press, 1920).

23. Henry Fawcett, *Manual of Political Economy*, 7th ed., 1888, quoted in Alan S. Milward, *War, Economy and Society 1939–1945* (London: Allen Lane, 1976), 294.

24. Daniel Rothbart et al., eds., *Civilians and Modern War: Armed Conflict and the Ideology of Violence* (Abingdon, UK: Routledge, 2012), 34.

25. Andrew Cockburn, "A Very Perfect Instrument," *Harper's*, February 9, 2014, harpers.org/archive/2013/09/a-very-perfect-instrument.

26. J.F.C. Fuller, *The Conduct of War, 1789–1961: A Study of the Impact of the French, Industrial, and Russian Revolutions on War and Its Conduct* (New York: Da Capo Press, 1992), 279.

27. Ibid., 281.

28. Mark Mazower, *Inside Hitler's Greece: The Experience of Occupation, 1941–44* (New Haven, CT: Yale University Press, 1995), 153.

29. On these operations and the overlapping of counterinsurgency with purges of "political and racial enemies," see Omer Bartov, *The Eastern Front 1941–45* (New York: Macmillan, 1985).

30. Ibid., 141.

31. Chalmers A. Johnson, *Peasant Nationalism and Communist Power: The Emergence of Revolutionary China, 1937–1945* (Palo Alto, CA: Stanford University Press, 1963), 56.

32. Lincoln Li, *The Japanese Army in North China 1937–1941: Problems of Political and Economic Control* (Oxford, UK: Oxford University Press, 1975), 209. See also Chong Sik Lee, *Counterinsurgency in Manchuria: The Japanese Experience, 1931–1940* (Santa Monica, CA: RAND Corporation, 1967), www.rand.org/pubs/research_memoranda/RM5012.html.

33. Major Sean Condron, ed., *Operational Law Handbook* (Charlottesville, VA: U.S. Army Judge Advocate General's Legal Center and School, 2011), 16, www.loc.gov/rr/frd/Military_Law/pdf/operational-law-hand book_2011.pdf.

34. Basil Henry Liddell Hart, *The Memoirs of Captain Liddell Hart*, vol. 1 (London: Cassell, 1965), 165.

35. Ibid., 170.

36. James S. Corum, *The Roots of Blitzkrieg: Hans Von Seeckt and German Military Reform* (Lawrence: University Press of Kansas, 1992), 141–42. Other critiques of Liddell Hart have made similar accusations. See John J. Meirsheimer, *Liddell Hart and the Weight of History* (Ithaca, NY: Cornell University Press, 1988). For a critique of Meirsheimer's critique, see Jay Luvaas, "Liddell Hart and the Meirsheimer Critique: A 'Pupil's' Retrospective," *Parameters* 20 (March 1990): 9–19, http://strategicstudiesinstitute.army.mil/pubs/parameters/articles/1990/1990%20luvaas.pdf.

37. Corum, *Roots of Blitzkrieg*, 30–31.

38. Guderian mentions Liddell Hart only in passing in his *Achtung-Panzer! The Development of Tank Warfare* (London: Cassell, 1999) and thus seems to bear out Corum's thesis that, whatever he said later, the Nazi gen-

eral was more interested in the practical and technical details of tank warfare proposed by Fuller than in Liddell Hart's "indirect" proposals.

39. On Nazi counterinsurgency operations in the Soviet Union and the treatment of "political and racial enemies," see Bartov, *Eastern Front*, and Robert Kershaw, *War Without Garlands: Operation Barbarossa 1941/42* (London: Ian Allan, 2000).

40. Daniel Marston, ed., *The Pacific War Companion: From Pearl Harbour to Hiroshima* (London: Osprey, 2005), 130–32.

41. Dr. Sam Sarkesian, "Low-Intensity Conflict, Concepts, Principles, and Policy Guidelines," *Air University Review* 36, no. 2 (January–February 1985): 4–24.

42. *The Dellums Committee Hearings on War Crimes in Vietnam: An Inquiry into Command Responsibility in Southeast Asia*, cited in Louise Barnett, *Atrocity and American Justice in Southeast Asia* (Abingdon, UK: Routledge, 2010), 174.

43. Edgar L. Jones, "One War Is Enough," *Atlantic Monthly*, February 1946, www.theatlantic.com/past/docs/unbound/bookauth/battle/jones.htm.

44. William I. Hitchcock., *The Bitter Road to Freedom: The Human Cost of Allied Victory in World War II Europe* (New York: The Free Press, 2008), 194. Such events never reached the scale of the vengeful mass rapes carried out by the Red Army, but they were frequent enough for the JAG to lament, "We were members of a conquering army, and we came as conquerors. The rate of reported rapes sprang skyward."

45. Earl F. Zeimke, *The U.S. Army in the Occupation of Germany, 1944–1946* (Washington, DC: Center of Military History, United States Army, 1975).

46. Reginald Thompson, *Cry Korea: The Korean War—a Reporter's Notebook* (London: MacDonald, 1951), 113–14.

47. Jonathan Schell, *The Real War* (New York: Random House, 1988), 240.

48. *United States Air Force Pamphlet 110-31, International Law–The Conduct of Armed Conflict and Air Operations* (Washington, DC: U.S. Department of the Air Force, 1976), 1–3.

49. Edmund Wilson, *Patriotic Gore: Studies in the Literature of the American Civil War* (New York: W.W. Norton, 1994), xxiii.

50. Smedley D. Butler, *War Is a Racket* (1935; repr., Port Townsend, WA: Feral House, 2003).

51. On the Veracruz occupation, see Jack Sweetman, *The Landing at Veracruz: 1914* (Annapolis, MD: U.S. Naval Institute, 1961).

52. U.S. Marine Corps, *Small Wars Manual*, 1940, 264, www.au.af.mil/au /awc/awcgate/swm/index.htm.

53. War Department, *Basic Field Manual* (Washington, DC: U.S. Government Printing Office, 1940), usacac.army.mil/cac2/cgsc/carl/docreposi tory/FM27_5_1940.pdf.

54. On the Haitian occupation, see Mary A. Renda, *Taking Haiti: Military Occupation and the Culture of U.S. Imperialism, 1915–1940* (Chapel Hill: University of North Carolina Press, 2001).

8. THE NEW AMERICAN WAY OF WAR

1. U.S. Joint Chiefs of Staff, *Joint Vision 2010* (Washington, DC: Defense Department, 1996), www.dtic.mil/jv2010/jv2010.pdf.

2. On Sherman's abrasive relationship with the press, see John F. Marszalek, *Sherman's Other War: The General and the Civil War Press* (Kent, OH: Kent State University Press, 1981).

3. Maruja Torres, "La última foto de Juantxu Rodríguez," *El País*, August 6, 2006, elpais.com/diario/2006/08/06/domingo/1154836356_850215. html.

4. Many of these claims are contained in a 1992 documentary, *The Panama Deception*, topdocumentaryfilms.com/the-panama-deception. See also Independent Commission of Inquiry on the U.S. Invasion of Panama, *The U.S. Invasion of Panama: The Truth Behind Operation Just Cause* (Boston: South End Press, 1991).

5. Kenneth Roth and Juan E. Méndez, *The Laws of War and the Conduct of the Panama Invasion* (New York: Human Rights Watch, 1990). See also Americas Watch, *Human Rights in Post-Invasion Panama: Justice Delayed Is Justice Denied* (New York: Human Rights Watch, 1991), www.hrw.org/re ports/1991/panama/#P94_36246. Both reports contain casualty statistics that more or less correspond with the military's low estimates.

6. Ronald H. Cole, *Operation Just Cause: The Planning and Execution of Joint Operations in Panama, February 1988–January 1990,* Joint History Office, Office of the Joint Chiefs of Staff, 1995, www.dtic.mil/doctrine/doc trine/history/justcaus.pdf. See also David B. Haight, *Operation JUST CAUSE: Foreshadowing Example of Joint Vision 2010 Concepts in Practice* (Newport, RI: Naval War College, 1998).

7. See Tan Suan Jow, "Gulf War: A Case Study of Indirect Strategy," *Journal of the Singapore Armed Forces* 21, no. 1 (January–March 1998), www

.mindef.gov.sg/safti/pointer/back/journals/1998/Vol24_1/6.htm. See also Alistair Finlan, *The Gulf War 1991* (London: Osprey Publishing, 2003).

8. Thomas A. Kearney and Eliot A. Cohen, *Gulf War Air Power Survey Summary Report* (Washington, DC: U.S. Government Printing Office, 1993), 249, www.afhso.af.mil/shared/media/document/AFD-100927-061.pdf.

9. Public Broadcasting Service, "The Gulf War: Oral History—Norman Schwarzkopf," *Frontline*, transcript, www.pbs.org/wgbh/pages/frontline/gulf/oral/schwarzkopf/1.html.

10. Barton Gelman, "Allied Air War Struck Broadly in Iraq: Officials Acknowledge Strategy Went Beyond Purely Military Targets," *Washington Post*, June 23, 1991.

11. Ramsey Clark et al., *War Crimes: A Report on United States War Crimes Against Iraq to the Commission of Inquiry for the International War Crimes Tribunal* (University Park, MD: Maisonneuve Press, 1992), deoxy.org/wc/wctoc.htm.

12. Human Rights Watch, *Needless Deaths in the Gulf War* (New York: Human Rights Watch, 1991), www.hrw.org/reports/1991/06/01/needless-deaths-gulf-war.

13. For a revisionist analysis of casualty statistics tending toward the lower estimates, see John Mueller, "The Perfect Enemy: Assessing the Gulf War," *Security Studies* 5, no. 1 (Autumn 1995): 77–117, politicalscience.osu.edu/faculty/jmueller/PERFECT.PDF.

14. Martti Ahtisaari, "Report to the Secretary General on Humanitarian Needs in Kuwait and Iraq in the Immediate Post-Crisis Environment," March 20, 1991, www.un.org/depts/oip/background/reports/s22366.pdf.

15. Beth Osborne Daponte, "A Case Study in Estimating Casualties from War and Its Aftermath: The 1991 Persian Gulf War," *PSR Quarterly* 3, no. 2 (1993): www.ippnw.org/pdf/mgs/psr-3-2-daponte.pdf.

16. William M. Arkin, Damian Durant, and Marianne Cherni, *On Impact: Modern Warfare and the Environment: A Case Study of the Gulf War*, www.greenpeace.org/international/Global/international/planet-2/report/1991/6/on-impact-modern-warfare-and.pdf.

17. See Hugo Slim, *Killing Civilians: Method, Madness, and Morality in War* (London: C. Hurst, 2008), Kindle loc. 493.

18. Andrew Cockburn, "A Very Perfect Instrument," *Harper's*, February 9, 2014, harpers.org/archive/2013/09/a-very-perfect-instrument.

19. Ibid.

20. John Mueller and Karl Mueller, "Sanctions of Mass Destruction," *Foreign Affairs*, May–June 1999, www.foreignaffairs.com/articles/55009 /john-mueller-and-karl-mueller/sanctions-of-mass-destruction.

21. David Rieff, "Were Sanctions Right?" *New York Times Magazine*, July 27, 2003, www.nytimes.com/2003/07/27/magazine/were-sanctions-right.html.

22. Wayne K. Maybard, "Spears vs Rifles: The New Equation of Military Power," *Parameters*, Spring 1993, 49–58.

23. The Pentagon's futurist in chief, Andrew Marshall, was often concerned with this possibility, as was the neoconservative think tank the Project for the New American Century (PNAC), with its September 2000 call for a huge rearmament program, *Rebuilding America's Defenses: Strategy, Forces, and Resources for a New Century*, www.informationclearinghouse.info/pdf /RebuildingAmericasDefenses.pdf.

24. Chris Hables Gray, *Postmodern War: The New Politics of Conflict* (Abingdon, UK: Routledge, 1991).

25. See Christopher Bolkcom and John Pike, "Hyperwar: The Legacy of Desert Storm," chap. 8 in *Aircraft Proliferation: Issues for Concern* (Washington, DC: Federation of American Scientists, 1993), www.fas.org/spp/aircraft /part08.htm.

26. John A. Warden III, "Air War for the Twenty-First Century," in *Battlefield of the Future: Twenty-First Century Warfare Issues*, ed. Barry R. Schneider and Lawrence E. Grinter (Maxwell Air Force Base, Montgomery, AL: Air War College, 1998).

27. Harlan Ullman and James Wade Jr., *Shock and Awe: Achieving Rapid Dominance* (Fort Leslie J. McNair, DC: National Defense University, Institute for National Strategic Studies, 1996), www.dodccrp.org/files/Ullman _Shock.pdf.

28. William S. Lind et al., "The Changing Face of War: Into the Fourth Generation," *Marine Corps Gazette* 73, no. 10 (October 1989).

29. Richard Szafranski, "Parallel War and Hyperwar: Is Every Want a Weakness?" in Schneider and Grinter, *Battlefield of the Future*.

30. Jasmina Tešanović, *The Diary of a Political Idiot* (Berkeley, CA: Midnight Editions, 2000).

31. Wayne A. Larsen, *Serbian Information Operations During Operation Allied Force* (Montgomery, AL: Air Command and Staff College, Air University, Maxwell Air Force Base, 2000), www.dtic.mil/dtic/tr/fulltext/u2 /a393976.pdf.

32. Human Rights Watch, *Civilian Deaths in the Kosovo Air Campaign*, February 2000, www.hrw.org/reports/2000/nato.

33. Statement of General (Ret.) Klaus Naumann, German Army, Former Chairman NATO, Senate Armed Services Committee Hearing on Kosovo After-Action Review, November 3, 1999, *Congressional Record*, November 5, 1999, 28704.

34. Wesley Clark, *Waging Modern War: Bosnia, Kosovo, and the Future of Combat* (New York: PublicAffairs, 2001).

35. John Barry and Evan Thomas, "The Kosovo Cover-Up," *Newsweek*, May 15, 2000.

9. WARS WITHOUT WAR

1. Carl von Clausewitz, *On War* (Ware, UK: Wordworth Editions, 1997), 6.

2. Roger J. Spiller, *Sharp Corners: Urban Operations at Century's End* (Fort Leavenworth, KS: U.S. Army Command and General Staff College Press, 2000), 125.

3. Dan Balz and Mark Leibovich, "Cheney Mocks Kerry's 'Sensitive' War on Terror," *Pittsburgh Post-Gazette*, August 13, 2004.

4. *National Military Strategic Plan for the War on Terrorism*, Department of Defense and the Chairman of the Joint Chiefs of Staff, 2005.

5. See Mary Harper, *Getting Somalia Wrong? Faith and War in a Shattered State* (London: Zed Books, 2012).

6. For example, General William Odon, former head of the National Security Agency, who in 2006 called Iraq "the greatest strategic failure in American history." Patrick Cockburn, *The Occupation: War and Resistance in Iraq* (London: Verso, 2007), 4.

7. Gregory Fonenant, E.J. Degen, and David Tohn, *On Point: The United States Army in Operation Iraqi Freedom Through 01 May, 2003* (self-published, 2012), 50.

8. Paul Rieckhoff, *Chasing Ghosts: A Soldier's Fight for America from Baghdad to Washington* (New York: New American Library Caliber, 2006), 169.

9. For an analysis of the "Carthaginian" media and political representations that preceded the two assaults on Fallujah, see Matt Carr, "The Barbarians of Fallujah," *Race and Class* 50, no. 1 (July 2008): 21–36.

10. Michael Schwartz, *War Without End: The Iraq War in Context* (Chicago: Haymarket Books, 2008), 112.

11. Ibid., 114.

12. Ibid., 127.

13. Aaron Glantz, *Winter Soldier: Iraq and Afghanistan—Eyewitness Accounts of the Occupations* (Chicago: Haymarket Books, 2008). See also Chris Hedges and Laila Al-Arian, "The Other War: Iraq Vets Bear Witness," July 9, 2007, *The Nation*, www.thenation.com/article/other-war-iraq-vets-bear-witness-0#.

14. Sean Rayment, "US Tactics Condemned by British Officers," *The Telegraph*, April 11, 2004, www.telegraph.co.uk/news/worldnews/middleeast/iraq/1459048/US-tactics-condemned-by-British-officers.html.

15. Michael Schwartz, "Falluja: City Without a Future?" in "Tomgram: Michael Schwartz, Desolate Falluja," TomDispatch, January 14, 2005, www.tomdispatch.com/post/2124.

16. Dexter Filkins, "The Fall of the Warrior-King," *New York Times*, October 23, 2005, www.nytimes.com/2005/10/23/magazine/23sassaman.html?pagewanted=all.

17. For Sassaman's critique of the war, see Nathan Sassaman, *Warrior King: The Triumph and Betrayal of an American Commander in Iraq* (New York: St. Martin's Press, 2008).

18. Michael Hirsch and John Barry, "'The Salvador Option': Pentagon Plans to Train Iraqi Death Squads," *Newsweek*, January 8, 2005.

19. Department of the Army, *Foreign Internal Defense Tactics, Techniques, and Procedures for Special Forces*, FM 31-20-3 (Fort Bragg, NC: U.S. Army John F. Kennedy Special Warfare Center and School, 1994).

20. Fred Kaplan, *The Insurgents: David Petraeus and the Plot to Change the American Way of War* (New York: Simon & Schuster, 2013), 161. For an overview of FM 3-24 within the broader historical context of U.S. war-fighting doctrine, see Walter E. Kretchik, *U.S. Army Doctrine: From the American Revolution to the War on Terror* (Lawrence: University Press of Kansas, 2011).

21. See, for example, Thomas Ricks, *The Gamble: General David Petraeus and the American Military Adventure in Iraq, 2006–2008*. For Ricks, Petraeus and his colleagues represented something of a Phoenix-like salvation of the war effort from the catastrophic failures that he described in his earlier book *Fiasco: The American Military Adventure in Iraq* (2006).

22. Kaplan, *Insurgents*, 325.

23. Jordan C.S. Stern, "Civil Military Operations & Military Information Support Operations Coordination: A Non-Kinetic Ballast for Disciplined

Counterinsurgency Operations," *Small Wars Journal*, November 1, 2011, smallwarsjournal.com/jrnl/art/civil-military-operations-military-informati on-support-operations-coordination.

24. Full text of Tunnell's letter: www.michaelyon-online.com/images/pdf /secarmy_redacted-redux.pdf.

25. Mark Boal, "The Kill Team: How U.S. Soldiers in Afghanistan Murdered Innocent Civilians," *Rolling Stone*, March 27, 2011, www.rollingstone .com/politics/news/the-kill-team-20110327.

26. Gian P. Gentile, "Let's Build an Army to Win *All* Wars," *Joint Forces Quarterly*, no. 52, 1st quarter 2009.

27. Edward Luttwak, "Dead End: Counterinsurgency Warfare as Military Malpractice," *Harper's*, February 2007.

28. Gian Gentile, *Wrong Turn: America's Deadly Embrace of Counterinsurgency* (New York: The New Press, 2013). There is no space here to do justice to Gentile's sophisticated and wide-ranging indictment of COIN and the misreading of history that he believed was primarily responsible for Petraeus's "wrong turn." Essentially, his critique is a rejection of "nation-building" wars and a call for more realistic strategic objectives, but Gentile also strongly rejects the new doctrinal preference for population protection rather than physical destruction, which he regards as a deviation from the U.S. military's core purpose.

29. Robert Gates, acceptance speech for Marshall Medal awarded by Association of the United States Army, Arlington, VA, October 2013, www .ausa.org/meetings/2013/AnnualMeeting/Pages/story49.aspx.

30. David Rohde, "The Obama Doctrine," *Foreign Policy*, February 27, 2012, www.foreignpolicy.com/articles/2012/02/27/the_obama_doctrine.

31. Jo Becker and Scott Shane, "Secret 'Kill List' Proves a Test of Obama's Principles and Will," *New York Times*, May 29, 2012, www.nytimes.com /2012/05/29/world/obamas-leadership-in-war-on-al-qaeda.html ?pagewanted=all.

32. *Will I Be Next? U.S. Drone Strikes in Pakistan* (London: Amnesty International, 2013).

33. These testimonies aroused little political or media interest. Only five members of Congress attended the briefing.

34. Medea Benjamin, *Drone Warfare: Killing By Remote Control* (London: Verso, 2013), 55.

35. International Human Rights and Conflict Resolution Clinic at Stanford Law School and Global Justice Clinic at NYU School of Law, *Living*

Under Drones: Death, Injury, and Trauma to Civilians from US Drone Practices in Pakistan, www.livingunderdrones.org/download-report.

36. U.S. Department of Defense, *Joint Vision 2020, America's Military: Preparing for Tomorrow*, www.fs.fed.us/fire/doctrine/genesis_and_evolution/source_materials/joint_vision_2020.pdf.

37. Nagl made this statement on the 2011 PBS *Frontline* program "Kill/Capture," by Stephen Grey and Dan Edge, www.pbs.org/wgbh/pages/frontline/afghanistan-pakistan/kill-capture/transcript.

38. For further discussion of futuristic American warfare, see Matt Carr, "Slouching Towards Dystopia: The New Military Futurism," *Race & Class* 51, no. 3 (January 2010): 13–32.

39. Thomas P.M. Barnett, *The Pentagon's New Map: War and Peace in the Twenty-First Century* (New York: Berkley Books, 2004), 323–25.

40. Ralph Peters, "Virtuous Destruction, Decisive Speed," discussion paper for NIC 2020 project, May 17, 2004, www.au.af.mil/au/awc/awcgate/cia/nic2020/destruction.pdf.

41. Noah Shachtman and Spencer Ackerman, "U.S. Military Taught Officers: Use 'Hiroshima' Tactics for 'Total War' on Islam," *Wired*, May 10, 2012, www.wired.com/dangerroom/2012/05/total-war-islam.

42. Dan Plesch and Martin Butcher, *Considering a War with Iran: A Discussion Paper on WMD in the Middle East*, School of Oriental and African Studies, Centre for International Studies and Diplomacy, University of London, 2007, www.cisd.soas.ac.uk/Files/docs/11202639-iran-study-07.07.pdf.

43. Robert Martinage, *Strategy for the Long Haul: Special Operations Forces: Future Challenges and Opportunities* (Washington, DC: Center for Strategic and Budgetary Assessment, 2008), viii.

44. Mark Antony De Wolfe Howe, ed., *Home Letters of General Sherman* (New York: Charles Scribner's Sons, 1909), 227.

EPILOGUE

1. Rupert Smith, *The Utility of Force: The Art of War in the Modern World* (New York: Penguin, 2006), 84.

2. John Robb, *Brave New War: The Next Stage of Terrorism and the End of Globalization* (Hoboken, NJ: John Wiley & Sons, 2007).

3. Graeme Goodman, Ishai Menuchin, and Assaf Oron, *No Second Thoughts: The Changes in Israeli Defense Forces' Doctrine in Light of Operation*

Cast Lead (Jerusalem: Public Committee Against Torture in Israel, 2009), www.stoptorture.org.il/files/no%20second%20thoughts_ENG_WEB.pdf.

4. Ibid.

5. Bruce Lawrence, ed., *Messages to the World: The Statements of Osama bin Laden* (London: Verso, 2005), 165.

6. Andrew J. Bacevich, *The New American Militarism: How Americans Are Seduced by War* (New York: Oxford University Press, 2013).

Index

About the Author

Matthew Carr is a writer, broadcaster, and journalist who has reported on a number of violent conflicts. He is the author of several works of nonfiction, including *Blood and Faith: The Purging of Muslim Spain*, *Fortress Europe: Dispatches from a Gated Continent*, and *The Infernal Machine: A History of Terrorism*, all published by The New Press, as well as the acclaimed memoir *My Father's House*. Carr lives in Derbyshire, England.

Publishing in the Public Interest

Thank you for reading this book published by The New Press. The New Press is a nonprofit, public interest publisher. New Press books and authors play a crucial role in sparking conversations about the key political and social issues of our day.

We hope you enjoyed this book and that you will stay in touch with The New Press. Here are a few ways to stay up to date with our books, events, and the issues we cover:

- Sign up at www.thenewpress.com/subscribe to receive updates on New Press authors and issues and to be notified about local events
- Like us on Facebook: www.facebook.com/newpressbooks
- Follow us on Twitter: www.twitter.com/thenewpress

Please consider buying New Press books for yourself; for friends and family; or to donate to schools, libraries, community centers, prison libraries, and other organizations involved with the issues our authors write about.

The New Press is a 501(c)(3) nonprofit organization. You can also support our work with a tax-deductible gift by visiting www.the newpress.com/donate.